EDWARD SAPIR — LIFE & WORK

Volume 36

Konrad Koerner (ed.)

Edward Sapir: Appraisals of his life and work

EDWARD SAPIR

APPRAISALS OF HIS LIFE AND WORK

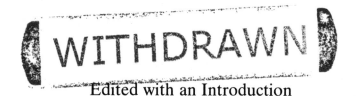

Edited with an Introduction

by

KONRAD KOERNER
University of Ottawa

JOHN BENJAMINS PUBLISHING COMPANY
AMSTERDAM/PHILADELPHIA

1984

Library of Congress Cataloging in Publication Data

Main entry under title:

Edward Sapir, appraisals of his life and work.

(Amsterdam studies in the theory and history of linguistic science. Series III, Studies in the history of the language science, ISSN 0304-0720; v. 36)
Bibliography
1. Sapir, Edward, 1884-1939 -- Addresses, essays, lectures. 2. Linguists -- United States -- Biography -- Addresses, essays, lectures. 3. Anthropologists -- United States -- Biography -- Addresses, essays, lectures. I. Koerner, E. F. K. II. Series.
P85.S14E4   1984   410'.92'4   [B]   84-24347
ISBN 90-272-4518-5 (hb.)
ISBN 90-272-4519-3 (pb.)

ACKNOWLEDGEMENTS

This volume is, like the special 1984 issue of *Historiographia Linguistica*, but a modest contribution leading to an important event honouring one of this century's modern masters in linguistic science, the Edward Sapir Centenary Conference, Victoria Memorial Museum, Ottawa, 1-3 October 1984. Unlike the special *HL* issue, the present venture is more clearly devoted to Edward Sapir, his career, his contribution to the study of language (with side-lights cast on anthropological subjects), and his personality.

This volume could not have materialized in its present form without the collaboration of a number of individuals. The regular copyright acknowledgements are made at the bottom of the first page of each item here reproduced from their early place of publication, and in the case of other items permission has been obtained for (re-)publication from their authors or copyright holders wherever this was possible to obtain. These acknowledgements need not be repeated here.

Expressions of thanks are due to the following individuals for useful comments on the original outline of this volume and/or advice at various stages of its development: William Cowan (Ottawa), Regna Darnell (Edmonton), Michael K. Foster (Ottawa), Victor Golla (Washington, D.C.), Tetsuro Hayashi (Fukuoka), Charles F. Hockett (Ithaca, N.Y.), Stephen O. Murray (San Francisco), Yoshio Nagashima (Tokyo), Richard J. Preston (Hamilton, Ont.), and Philip Sapir (Bethesda, Md.). In fact, no other person has taken a more active interest in this project (as well as others pertaining to his father) than Philip Sapir, Edward Sapir's second Ottawa-born son. Apart from offering a number of useful suggestions, Mr Sapir kindly sent me copies of various materials, including transcripts of personal letters from distinguished scholars addressed to Edward Sapir and photocopies of a number of reviews, several of which would otherwise have escaped my attention. Perhaps even more importantly, Mr Sapir has provided the organizers of the Sapir Conference and myself with negatives as well as prints of a variety of pictures of his father, the Sapir family, and others related to Edward Sapir's personal and scholarly life, several of which have been included here.

I also wish to record my thanks to the following for graciously waiving copyright fees: William Bright, Editor of *Language*, and Victoria A. Fromkin, former

Secretary-Treasurer of the Linguistic Society of America, for items previously published in *Language*; Edward J. Lehman, Executive Director of the American Anthropological Association, for reviews and notes which appeared in the *American Anthropologist*, and Alexander G. McKay, President of The Royal Society of Canada, for an obituary published in the Society's *Proceedings*.

I would like especially to mention the support received from Richard J. Preston, who sent copies of various papers and supplied the transcript of Kroeber's 1959 talk published here for the first time. I would also like to acknowledge the help obtained from various staff members of the Canadian National Museum, Ottawa, in particular Louise Dallaire of the Ethnological Division Archive, who patiently responded to various queries and provided useful information, including copies of unpublished papers.

Ottawa, July 1984   Konrad Koerner

CONTENTS

LOCATION OF PICTURES AND ILLUSTRATIONS

PUBLISHED ON THE OCCASION OF THE

EDWARD SAPIR CENTENARY CONFERENCE

VICTORIA MEMORIAL MUSEUM BUILDING
NATIONAL MUSEUM OF MAN
OTTAWA, CANADA

1-3 OCTOBER 1984

Edward Sapir

INTRODUCTION

0. *Aim and Scope*

This volume does not claim to be more than a collection for the most part of previously published material, ranging from 1919 to 1980; it is intended to offer a first acquaintance with Edward Sapir, the man and the scholar. Until now, those of Sapir's writings "which carry the gist of his thought" (Mandelbaum 1949:xi) have been available in the 600-page *Selected Writings of Edward Sapir in Language, Culture and Personality* (Sapir 1949), which has since been frequently reprinted; as well, eight papers from this volume have been accessible in a 1956 paperback edition, and Sapir's *Language*, first published in 1921, is still in print. (For details on these and other publications, see the Addenda to Sapir's bibliography at the end of this volume, pp.211ff.) By contrast, the papers appraising Sapir's life and work are scattered, and it seemed desirable to assemble them under single covers.

1. *Obituaries and Biographical Sketches, 1939-1952*

The present volume includes the majority of obituaries of Edward Sapir appearing during 1939-41; they are presented here in a chronological order, both with regard of the age of their respective authors and the date of their first publication. While the latter aspect is more accidental in nature, the former is not: it appears natural that the obituary by Sapir's former teacher at Columbia, Franz Boas, should take pride of place. Professionally, Sapir owned him a great deal, not only for having "roused him from dogmatic slumbers" in matters of language, as Lowie (this volume, p.124) put it some thirty years ago. This is followed by the necrology of his colleague at Yale, the Indo-Europeanist Franklin Edgerton, and the notice by his successor to the post of Chief of the Anthropological Division at the Canadian National Museum in Ottawa, Diamond Jenness. Given his close contacts during the last years of his life with Harry Stack Sullivan of the William Alanson White Psychiatric Foundation in New York, I have reproduced Sullivan's brief memorial of Sapir. Sapir's relationship with Ruth Benedict was still another one, and as her obituary reveals, she had a cordial relationship with the Sapir family as a whole and a friendship with Edward Sapir based on a number of common interests, including the writing of poetry. Thus, while there is a certain amount of repetition in these obituaries, especially with regard to the external dates of Sapir's career, each of them reveals a different perspective on him, as a scholar and as a person.

Leslie Spier, a one-time collaborator (e.g., Sapir & Spier 1930), was almost ten years younger than Sapir; from one of his two death notices of the same year I have excerpted observations not found in the other obituaries (Spier 1939a). The next two stem from former students of his, from Morris Swadesh, who followed Sapir from Chicago to Yale and with whom Sapir collaborated on a variety of projects for the remainder of his life (e.g., Sapir & Swadesh 1932, 1939, and 1946), and from David Mandelbaum, who did not take up a linguistics career but continued to work in anthropology.

As is to be expected, there is a certain amount of overlap in these accounts, but I felt I should not condense any of them to a mere list of excerpts, as they represent individual testimonies about Sapir.[1] Comparing Boas' obituary (which is characterized by its assessment of Sapir as an anthropologist rather than a linguist), for instance, with other statements included here, a composite picture of Sapir emerges, casting light on him as a human being, a teacher, a field worker, a colleague, and a writer with artistic leanings and wide cultural and scientific interests. It has been thought useful to conclude the first part with an appraisal written by Charles Voegel in more than a dozen years after Sapir's untimely death. Voegelin, unlike Benedict, Spier, Swadesh and Mandelbaum, was neither a student of Sapir's, nor a student of Boas. He thus was able to write with a certain detachment. However, as one of the few students that Kroeber trained (in addition to James Alden Mason [1885-1967], Jaime de Angulo y Mayo [1888-1950] and his wife L.S. ("Nancy") Freeland [1890-1972]), he was much in tune with the 'Boas tradition' – note that Kroeber was one of Boas' first Columbia Ph.D.s – he was, by extension, well acquainted with Sapir's work.

Mention should be made of two obituaries not included here, namely, Louis Hjelmslev's (1899-1965) notice of 1939, one of the few necrologies coming from outside North America, and the account in 1940 by the physical anthropologist Earnest Albert Hooton (1887-1954). Hooton's obituary may be of interest, as it makes mention of Sapir's involvement in the reorganization of Harvard's Anthropology Department, following the death of Roland Burrage Dixon (1875-1934) there. Hooton also mentions Sapir as "the cornerstone upon which that masterly organizer and teacher, Fay-Cooper Cole [(1881-1961)], rebuilt the department of anthropology in Chicago". (Regarding this reorganization Cole's own account of 1952 [p. 167] may also be consulted.) However, Hooton's (1940:158) admission that he "is incompetent to give any original and authoritative appraisal of Sapir's scientific contributions to anthropology [let alone linguistics]", and that he "was not privileged to know [him] intimately" beyond 'occasional contacts' (p.159), motivated me to exclude his obituary from the present collection. (For a summary of Edward Sapir's career, the reader is referred to Mandelbaum's well-known account of 1949.)

2. *Comments on Sapir's Work, 1919-1953*

Most of the items reprinted in this section were written a decade or more after Sapir's death, all by scholars who knew Sapir well, with the exception of Joseph Greenberg who, contrary what his anthologist asserts to (Greenberg 1971:xi), did not take a course from Sapir, though he studied for a year at Yale under Bloomfield and Bernard Bloch (1907-1965).

Lowie, a student of Boas like Sapir, published his review of *Time Perspective* fairly late, probably because of his personal ties with Sapir and the fact that he was assistant editor of the *American Anthropologist* at the time. (Cf. Sapir's inquiry of 10 July 1917 about the review in his letter to Lowie [1965:25].) I do not know of other contemporary reviews of Sapir's 1916 monograph, but the study is still frequently cited (cf. Kroeber's comments in this volume, pp. 132-33). By contrast, Sapir's book *Language*, published in fall 1921 in the United States and in spring 1922 in Britain, has had numerous reviews.[2] No doubt, many review copies were sent out to editors and publishers of periodicals, including those for 'educated laymen', and indeed newspapers with regional or national readerships. Both Harcourt and Sapir were interested in publicity and sales. From what we know of Sapir's biography, it is fair to assume that he was looking for international recognition and a regular academic position,[3] and that a number of colleagues and personal friends were eager to help him in attaining this goal.[4]

Out of the great number of reviews of *Language* (cf. note 2 and the references below), I have chosen what I believe to be the most significant ones, namely those by Lowie and Bloomfield, together with an excerpt of Kroeber's more popular account. A few others should at least be mentioned here.

Some of those not included in this volume are by such distinguished (frequently European) scholars as James Wilson Bright (1852-1926), the English philologist and editor-in-chief of *Modern Language Notes*, who is perhaps best known for his *Anglo-Saxon Reader*, first published in 1891, still in press in the 1950s, and revised and updated much more recently (cf. Bright-Cassidy-Ringler 1971); the most distinguished French comparative linguist Antoine Meillet (1866-1936); the Austrian-born Indo-Europeanist then teaching at Bryn Mawr College before his move to Yale, Eduard Prokosch (1876-1938) – who, in 1906, impressed Bloomfield so much that he decided to enter upon a career in linguistics, and Henry Bradley (1845-1923), the English philologist and joint editor of the *OED*, to mention just a few. Interestingly enough, most of these reviews compared Sapir's *Language* with Otto Jespersen's (1860-1943) much larger book by the same title as well as with Joseph Vendryes' (1875-1960) 439-page *Le Langage* of 1921 (Bradley 1923; Meillet 1922; cf. also Warnotte 1922), or with Joseph Schrijnen's (1969-1938) Introduction to Indo-European Philology of the same year (Prokosch 1922). These reviews certainly merit mention, as does the one by the British Germanicist at the University of Liverpool, William Edward Collinson (1889-c.1969), who, like Bloomfield, compared Sapir's book with Saussure's *Cours*, which had just appeared in a second edition (Collinson 1924).

As is well known, Bloomfield regarded both the *Cours* and Sapir's *Language* as belonging to 'the newer trend of linguistic study' (cf. the present volume, pp.47 and 48). Indeed, no reviewer of distinction failed to note the exquisite-ness of Sapir's style and the intellectual freshness of his approach. It is no wonder that Sapir's book is still recommended reading for linguistics students two generations after its first publication, a recommendation based on far more than the 'mentalism' some have claimed Sapir shares with Chomsky (cf. McCawley's remarks [1967:106, this volume p.153], with regard to phonologi-cal theory). Kroeber had stated in 1922 (see this volume, p.51) that Sapir's *Language* "is unique in its field, and is likely to become and long remain stan-dard."

I have given more space to reviews of Sapir's *Selected Writings*, for several reasons. To begin with, this volume is much broader in scope than Sapir's study of 1916 and the 1921 book; until we see the project of Sapir's Collected Writings materialize, the Mandelbaum volume will continue to be regarded as Sapir's 'summa'. The reviews reprinted here are, with the exception of the brief one by George Trager (b.1906), a pupil of Bloomfield, all those published in North American linguistics journals. Typically, while Newman (1951:185; this volume, p.64) was concerned that the (anti-)mentalism debate launched by Bloomfield might "have obscured Sapir's position on the relation of linguistics to the other sciences of human behavior", Trager was relieved to note that despite "the possible 'mentalistic' implications of some of the phrasing, [. . .] on closer inspection [. . . there] is very little that is not highly objective scientific statement" (1951:18; cf. also Harris, this volume, p.99).[5]

While both Harry Hoijer and Stanley Newman did their doctorates under Sapir (at Chicago and Yale, respectively), Zellig Harris followed in the main the descriptive and 'mechanist' approach associated with Bloomfield. But this difference in background and outlook alone does not make Harris' review article an important statement (though it is interesting to note that Harris is reported never to have completed one field report on an Amerindian language, and that he, like his student Chomsky, has been more interested in working out theoretical constructs, steps removed from the living language). By early 1947, Harris had completed his work on his influential *Methods in Structural Linguistics (Chicago, 1951)*, and he evidently took out much time to read and reread Sapir's *Selected Writings*. Although his preference was for Sapir's linguistic work — the analytic technique and the theoretical flights — Harris devoted considerable space to Sapir's cultural, social, and psychological interests, much of which went beyond language description. Indeed, Harris' 45-page review constitutes a valuable document of the linguistic paradigm of the period and its surrounding *Zeitgeist* (cf. the references to Marx and Freud on pages 78 and 91 in the present volume), while at the same time revealing, more than any other publication, the author's scientific credo. Thus we find explicit references to Saussure's synchronic theory of language (e.g., 1951:289; this volume, p.69), an argument in favour of a 'process model' (291 = 71), which was further developed by Hockett (1954) and subsequently exploited by the transformationalists, and a clear awareness of the importance of Bloomfield's use of 'base forms' in morphophonemics (ibid., note 7), which no doubt is the source of Chomsky's 'generative' approach in his 1951 M.A. thesis, to mention just a few points of interest to the historian of modern linguistic science. To this we could add Harris' frequent references to mathematical procedure in linguistics; note his affirmation (p.301 = 74): "The formal analysis of language is an empirical discovery of the same kinds of relations and combinations which are devised in logic and mathematics", an affirmation which foreshadows much of what is commonly (and misleadingly) associated with the 'Chomskyan revolution'.

An evaluation of Sapir's work, however, would be incomplete if no mention was made of his work as a teacher and field researcher. As regards the first point, references to Sapir's success as a lecturer and teacher can be found in various obituaries reprinted in Part One of the present volume, to which may be added Kenneth Pike's recent statement (Pike 1984). Mary Haas' comment on "Sapir and the Training of Anthropological Linguists" (reprinted here pp.115-118) at least offers us an inkling of Sapir's general approach. Sapir's celebrated article of 1933, "La réalité psychologique des phonèmes" (which I still require my third-year linguistics students to study carefully), offers a good idea of both his method and analytical talent.

3. *Appraisals of Sapir's Life and Work, 1956-1980*

Those scholars in North America who never regarded linguistics as an autonomous discipline, divorced from social context and cultural patterns, have continued to work in a broadly Sapirian framework. However, already during the 1950s these anthropologically oriented scholars represented more an undercurrent (albeit an important one) in linguistics, with the post-Bloomfieldians and their successors, the Chomskyites, representing the positivistic tradition (which has its origin in the Neogrammarians and Saussure) and forming much of 'mainstream' linguistics. Part of this development is reflected in the paucity of papers *on* Sapir during the later 1950s and 1960s. The fact that Lowie's edition of Sapir's letters to him, though ready to go to press by 1956, did not see publication (ans then only in typescript form) before 1965, may just be an indication of the lack of interest in Sapir at the time. Similarly, papers given by Alfred Kroeber and Yakov Malkiel in May 1959 on the same campus where Lowie had been anthropology professor for many years, remained unpublished to the present day, though tape recordings had been available to interested parties. While Kroeber's retrospective on Sapir's career appears here in only slightly amended form − his talk having not been intended for publication, Malkiel's paper has benefitted from its author's revisions (see Malkiel 1984). Papers of a comparable nature also did not see the light of day before 1976, until Regna Darnell published her paper, included here in somewhat revised form, unless we are to refer to a string of articles by Dell Hymes, who has written extensively on the Sapirian tradition (as he sees it) from about 1960 onwards, and who has no doubt instilled in Darnell the interest in the history of anthropology and in Sapir so clearly manifested in her work since the mid-1960s. (For references to Sapir in Hymes' writings, see his recent collection of papers [Hymes 1983].[6])

Actually, following Sapir's death in 1939, only a small group of scholars in North America and elsewhere wrote about Sapir, if we leave out the writings of Sapir's students and associates, in particular the obtuaries of 1939-41, a few incidental notes (e.g., Voegelin 1942), and the memorial volume (Spier et al. 1941; cf. the discussion in Hymes 1983:161-63). The 1950s saw reviews of *Selected Writings*. To those mentioned in the previous section, we may add the accounts of Sommerfelt (1952) and Gregores (1953), Mikuš's (1953) discussion of Sapir's syntagmatics, and Guxman's (1954) of his ethnolinguistic views. Otherwise the harvest was rather meagre. The 1960s saw a few papers, notably by Hymes and by anthropologists (e.g., Preston 1966; Mandelbaum 1968) and linguists (see Swadesh 1961 and McCawley, both reprinted here), but also, and more importantly, several translations of Sapir's *Language* into German, Italian, and French.[7] The 1970s witnessed a few more studies, but all written by anthropologists, not linguists (e.g., Ferry, Woolfson, Allen 1970 and 1974, Darnell 1976), apparently with few exceptions (e.g., Haas 1976). This trend continued into the 1980s (see Preston 1980, Cain 1980, and Murray 1981a,b). Part III of the present volume reflects this distribution: in addition to the evaluations of Sapir's *œuvre* and personality by Lowie and Kroeber, it contains two papers by linguists (Swadesh, McCawley) and two by still other anthropologists (Darnell, Preston).

Since the emphasis in this volume is on linguistic, rather than anthropological aspects of Sapir's legacy, a few remarks on the reception of his ideas in the study of language are called for. Generally speaking, there are several areas in which Sapir's work has received, at times considerable, attention. One concerns language classification, a subject which follows the Humboldtian tradition (cf. Koerner 1977) and which has been frequently discussed in the literature, among many others by his former student and successor at Chicago, Harry Hoijer (1904-1976), in a variety of papers (e.g., Hoijer 1941, 1946), and of course by Morris Swadesh (1909-1967), who followed Sapir from Chicaco to Yale and who published more studies in collaboration with him than anyone else (cf. also the posthumous publications of 1953, 1955, and 1960 listed in the Addenda to Sapir's bibliography in this volume, pp.211ff.), having received many of Sapir's unpublished manuscripts either directly or indirectly through the offices of Franz Boas. Swadesh's (1961) paper, here reprinted, is just one example of the debate that Sapir aroused following the publication of *Language* in 1921 with its chapter six, "Types of Linguistic Structure", and the note on the grouping of American Indian languages north of Mexico published in the same year (cf. the reproduction on p.140 of the present volume).

McCawley's (1967) paper included here, though written by a pupil of Noam Chomsky and a linguist with a background in mathematics and not languages, addresses another subject in which Sapir inspired much fruitful debate: phonology. As Hayashi's (1984) listing of Japanese translations of Sapir's writings informs us, there have been a number of translations into that language of "Sound Patterns of Language" (Sapir 1925) in 1940, 1957, 1958, and of "The Psychological Reality of Phonemes" (Sapir 1933) in 1958 in 1983. In North America itself, these two papers have been reprinted not only in Mandelbaum's 1949 volume, but also in an anthology on Descriptive Linguistics in America (1957, [4]1966)[8] and in another one on the history and current practice of phonology (1972, [2]1977). The French version of the 1931 paper, "La réalité psychologique des phonèmes", which preceded the publication of the original English version by 18 years, was retranslated on the basis of the English text in 1968, followed by a reprinting of the 1931 version, and excerpts of it appeared in another anthology (Léon et al. 1977:179-82), largely based on a mistaken interpretation of Sapir as a precursor of generative phonology, a view already criticized by McCawley in 1967.

Another subject which received widespread attention was Sapir's concept of 'drift', elaborated on in chapter seven of *Language*, "Language as an Historical Product", though first adumbrated in his 1916 monograph on *Time Perspective in Aboriginal American Culture* (cf. the observations made by Kroeber in 1959 = this volume, pp.134-35). This fascination with Sapir's concept of drift is also evidenced in references made by many other scholars, e.g. Spier (1939a; this volume p.13), Lowie (1923 = p.44), Harris (1951 = p.89), and Preston (1980 = p.193). More recently, linguists of the transformational school have offered us their interpretations of Sapir's suggestions (e.g., Lakoff 1972, Vennemann 1975) concerning the complex question of language change. (For a more sophisticated account, see Malkiel 1981.)

It seems impossible to speak of Edward Sapir without mentioning the so-called 'linguistic relativity principle' or the 'Sapir-Whorf hypothesis', with which his name is frequently associated, though perhaps not justly, as Kroeber pointed out in 1959 (cf. this volume, pp.135-36). Interestingly the Dutch Anglicist Etsko Kruisinga (1875-1944), in his 1925 review of *Language*, noted, with disappointment, that Sapir did not support the *Weltanschauungstheorie* he subscribed to himself, citing two statements from Sapir to the contrary: "It is impossible to show that the form of a language has the slightest connection with national temperament" (Sapir 1921:232), and, on the next page, "Nor can I believe that culture and language are in any true sense causally related" (cf. Kruisinga 1925: 79). Indeed, as early as 1912, Sapir had affirmed that "apart from the reflection of environment in the vocabulary of a language, there is *nothing* in the language itself that can be shown to be directly associated with [the physical] environment" (Sapir 1949:100; emphasis added: KK).

It is true that we find in Sapir's 1929 paper, "The Status of Linguistics as a Science", remarks that sound 'Whorfian', especially when read out of context:

> Human beings do not live in the objective world alone, nor alone in the world of social activity as ordinarily understood, but are very much at the mercy of the particular language which has become the medium of expression of their society. It is quite an illusion to·imagine that one adjusts to reality essentially without the use

of language and that language is merely an incidental means of solving specific problems of communication or reflection. The fact of the matter is that the 'real world' is to a large extent unconsciously built up on the language habits of the group. [. . .] We see and hear and otherwise experience very largely as we do because of the language habits of our community predispose certain choices. (Sapir 1921: 209-210 = 1949:162)

In this quotation we may see a source for Benjamin Lee Whorf's (1897-1941) much more radical views on the subject of the interrelationship between language and world view. But as early as 1951, Zellig Harris, quoting another statement further down in the same paragraph from which this quotation was taken, noted:

There is no contradiction here [and Sapir's statement of 1912, from which Harris quotes to support his claim], since the 'environing world' is the physical world, whereas the 'real world', in quotes, is also called 'social reality' ([Sapir 1949.]162) and constitutes the physical world as socially perceived: 'Even the simplest environmental influence is either supported or transformed by social forces' ([Sapir 1949.] 89); 'The physical environment is reflected in language insofar as it has been influenced by social forces' (90). (Harris 1951:305n.22 = this volume, p.85)

Despite Harris' observation, a close follower of Sapir's as Harry Hoijer did continue to speak, as most others, of the 'Sapir-Whorf Hypothesis' (e.g., Hoijer 1954), though we may notice that more recent scholarship (e.g., Davis 1976, Jessel 1978) is more careful by connecting the much debated 'theory' with Whorf alone. A full account of Sapir's views on the matter, at different stages of his career, however, still needs to be written. (For further references see this volume, p.139, n.8, and the exchange between Dürbeck 1975 and Gipper 1976.)

4. *Bibliography of Edward Sapir's Publications*

The bibliography of Sapir's writings 1906-1944, which constitutes the bulk of this section, is a reprint of the one published by David Mandelbaum in *Selected Writings* (Sapir 1949.601-613), with a few minor corrections. The original heading 'Scientific Papers and Prose Writings' has been maintained because the bibliography includes a number of publications, especially reviews, which appeared in *The Dial, Queen's Quarterly, Poetry, The Freeman*, and other literary or other than strictly professional periodicals. However, the list of Sapir's poetry, based on the author's own account and handed over to Mandelbaum by Sapir's son Philip (hence the ascription to the latter in Mandelbaum's Introduction, p.xi), has not been included in the present volume, as no attempt was made to consider Sapir's poetic output in scholarly terms.[9]

The "Addenda to Edward Sapir's Scientific Bibliography, 1916-1984" (pp. 211-17) contain a number of items not included in the main list, including references to translations of *Language* into Russian (1934) and Japanese (1943); the remainder covers the 40-year span 1944-1984, which saw a number of post-humous publications, reprintings, and translations of Sapir's writings.

5. *Concluding Remarks*

No attempt has been made in this introduction to do justice to Sapir's inter-disciplinary contributions to scholarship. Such an appraisal would require, it seems to me, the collective effort of several *érudits* in fields such as linguistics, ethnology, sociology, psychology, and probably a variety of other subjects. It was in part the need for such an effort that underlay the plan to have a conference on Sapir and his work in Ottawa in October 1984. The material brought together in this volume authored by distinguished scholars past and present in the fields of anthropology and language study should offer at least some impressions, and informed ones at that, of Sapir's scientific genius. No apology is offered for the bias in this collection in favour of Sapir's residence in Canada, given the scant information usually found in the American literature on this most productive period of Sapir's scholarly career, while he held this "exceptionally favourable position in Ottawa" (Lowie in this volume, p.124; cf. also Darnell, pp.174-76).

NOTES

1) Note that I have not reprinted the various bibliographies of Sapir's scholarly output appended to the obituaries of Boas (1939:59-63), Benedict (1939:469-77), and the addenda to a 1938 list in Edgerton (1940:463-64), since the present volume contains a much more complete and updated listing (pp.197ff.). Only the bibliographical footnote in Swadesh (1939:134n) has been retained for illustrative purposes.

2) For the record I am listing a number of brief reviews of Sapir's *Language* not in-cluded in the References; I owe knowledge of these to Philip Sapir. Thus there appeared anonymous notices in the following newspapers and magazines: *New York Evening Post* (14 Nov. 1921), *Boston Herald* (27 Nov. 1921), *Boston Evening Transcript* (8 Dec. 1921) – which suggests that Sapir's book appeared in print in November 1921 – and in *Times Literary Supplement* (18 May 1922), *Notes & Queries* (20 May 1922), *The Smart Set* (22 May 1922), *The Spectator* (27 May 1922) – which seems to indicate that it appeared in Britain early in May 1922. Further notices were published in *Journal of Education*

(Nov. 1922), *The Freeman* (22 Feb. 1922), and also signed by initials only in *Detroit News* of 8 Jan. 1922 (T.L.M.) and *New Statesman* of 1 July 1922 (L.A.M.). That journalist friends of Sapir's jumped into the act may be gathered from Harrold's (1922) review, which was the basis of an editorial in the *Toronto Daily Star* (27 Feb. 1922); another Canadian journalist, unlike Harrold (1889-1945), who lived in Ottawa, apparently stationed in Toronto was John Daniel Robins (1889-1952) — cf. his review of Sapir's book in *The Canadian Forum* (Sept. 1922); interestingly enough, Robins wrote a 296-page thesis at the University of Chicago in 1927, i.e. during Sapir's professorship there, on *Color Words in English.* (See also footnote 4 below.)

3) There do not appear to have been many reviews of Sapir's *Language* in Continental Europe; apart the one by Meillet (1922), I know only one by the Dutch Anglicist Etsko Kruisinga (1879-1944) and the Belgian sociologist-historian Daniel Warnotte (1871-1949), who included it in a "Science du langage" rubric in a sociological journal (cf. Kruisinga 1925 and Warnotte 1922). However, owing to the kind offices of Philip Sapir I received copies of letters dated 30 Dec. 1921 and 16 Feb. 1922, respectively, which the distinguished Danish Anglicist Otto Jespersen (1860-1943) and the great Swedish Sinologist Bernhard Karlgren (1889-1978) sent to Sapir thanking him for the presentation of copies of *Language.* But it does not appear that either of the two scholars commented on the book in print.

4) It is interesting to note that three (out of four) of the persons Sapir's mentions in the preface of *Language*, namely, Kroeber, Lowie, and the literary scholar Jacob Zeitlin (1883-1937), wrote reviews; the only who didn't was Wilson Dallam Wallis (1886-1970). Another non-linguistic scholar writing a review of *Language* was Arthur F.J. Remy (1871-1954) of Columbia University (Remy 1922).

5) This view is echoed by Hjelmslev (1939:77), who points out that "it should not be forgotten that even if Sapir is almost constantly speaking in psychological terms, there is in his conception no trace of real psychologism", and that "[t]he psychological terminology is a garment that can easily be stripped off without in the least affecting the results."

6) However, Hymes has not, to my knowledge, written a paper especially devoted to Sapir which could have been included in the present volume, though he has presented Sapir's ideas on a number of occasions, including in his tributes to Kroeber in 1960 and Swadesh in 1971 (reprinted in Hymes 1983, on pp.245-72 and 273-330, respectively).

7) Cf. the Addenda to Sapir's bibliography in this volume (pp.211ff.), for details.

8) Actually only the 1925 paper was included in the Joos volume, most probably because of the 'mentalism' evident especially in Sapir's (1933) paper; typically, a German anthology, *Beschreibungsmethoden des amerikanischen Strukturalismus* ed. by Elisabeth Bense, Peter Eisenberg & Hartmut Haberland (Munich: Max Hueber, 1976), includes a translation of Sapir's 'Sound Patterns' paper (pp.49-63).

9) Such an evaluation (favoured by Kroeber in 1959; cf. this volume, p.133) will have to await the publication of the bulk of Sapir's poems, many of which were circulated among friends only. It should be done by someone thoroughly familiar with Sapir's life (since many of the poems are autobiographical in nature) and the period in which they were written. This would require an effort to recapture the atmosphere of the literary circles of the time, including those in Ottawa, where Sapir was an active member of the local literary scene exchanging letters with the Ottawa novelist Magde Macbeth (1878-1965) and

the better known Ottawa-born poet Duncan Campbell Scott (1862-1947), who was, like Sapir, a civil servant in Ottawa eventually rising to the position of deputy super-intendent-general for Indian Affairs. As is evident from the bibliography in the Mandelbaum volume (cf. Sapir 1949.614-16), the bulk of Sapir's poetry was written during his Ottawa period 1917-25 and his first couple of years in Chicago, where his poetic pen began to run dry following his marriage, in 1926, to Ottawa-born Jean Victoria McClenagan (1899-1979). For a recent appreciation of Sapir's poetry, cf. the paper by Richard Handler, "The Dainty and the Hungry Man: Literature and anthropology in the work of Edward Sapir", *Observers Observed: Essays on Ethnographic Fieldwork* (= *History of Anthropology*, vol.1), ed. by George W. Stocking, 208-231. Chicago: Univ. of Chicago Press, 1983; see also the same author's note, "Sapir's Poetic Experience", in *American Anthropologist* 86.416-17 (1984).

REFERENCES*

Allen, Robert J(ohn). 1970. *The Work and Thought of Edward Sapir in Anthropology: An analysis.* An Honors Paper presented to the Faculty of the Department of Anthropology, Franklin and Marshall College, Lancaster, Pennsylvania, 20 April 1970, ii, 107 typed pp.

————. 1974. "The Individual, His Culture and His Rights". *The Journal of Intergroup Relations* 3:4.3-12.

Benedict, Ruth (Fulton). 1939. "Edward Sapir". *American Anthropologist* 41.465-77. (Pp.465-68 repr. in this volume, pp.15-18.)

Bernier-Montminy, Hélène. 1976. "La recherche anthropologique au Musée National du Canada, 1910 à 1925". *Bulletin of the Canadian Ethnology Society/Société d'Ethnologie Canadienne* No.1 (Dec.1976), 28-50. (Rev. version published in *Historiographia Linguistica* 11:3.397-412 [1984].)

Bloomfield, Leonard. 1922. Review of Sapir (1921). *The Classical Weekley* 15. 142-43 (13 March 1922)). (Reprinted in this volume, pp.45-47.)

Boas, Franz. 1939. "Edward Sapir". *IJAL* 10.58-63. (Pp.58-59 repr. in this volume, pp.3-4.)

Bradley, Henry. 1923. Review of Sapir (1921). *The Queen's Quarterly* 30:4. 389-94.

Bright, James W(ilson). 1922. Review of Sapir (1921). *Modern Language Notes* 37:3.188-92 (March).

*) This bibliography contains a few items not referred to in the introduction but which had been read in its preparation. *IJAL* stands for "International Journal of American Linguistics".

––––––. 1971. *Bright's Old English Grammar and Reader.* Ed. by Frederick G(omes) Cassidy & Richard N. Ringler. New York: Holt, Rinehart & Winston.

Cain, Michael. 1980. "Edward Sapir and Gestalt Psychology". *Anthropological Linguistics* 22.141-50. [Cf. the reply by Murray (1981b).]

Chomsky, Noam. 1951. *Morphophonemics of Modern Hebrew.* M.A. Thesis, Univ. of Pennsylvania. (Published, New York: Garland, 1979.)

Cole, Douglas. 1973. "The Origins of Canadian Anthropology, 1850-1910". *Journal of Canadian Studies* 8.33-45.

Cole, Fay-Cooper. 1952. "Eminent Personalities of the Half Century". *American Anthropoligist* 54.157-67.

Collinson, W(illiam) E(dward). 1924. Review of Sapir (1921), together with Saussure (^{2}1922). *Modern Language Review* 19.253-55.

Darnell, Regna (Diebold). 1976. "The Sapir Years at the National Museum, Ottawa". *The History of Canadian Anthropology: Proceedings of the plenary session of the Canadian Ethnology Society* ed. by James Friedman, 98-121. Hamilton, Ont.: Canadian Ethnology Society. (Rev. version in this volume, pp.159-78.)

Davis, Jack L. 1976. "The Whorf Hypothesis and Native American Literature". *South Dakota Review* 14:2.59-72.

De Angulo (y Mayo), Jaime. 1922 "A New View of Language [= Review of Sapir 1921]". *The Canadian Bookman* (May 1922), p.170.

Dürbeck, Helmut. 1975. "Neuere Untersuchungen zur Sapir-Whorf Hypothese". *Linguistics* No.145.5-45.

Edgerton, Franklin. 1940. "Edward Sapir". *The American Philosophical Society Yearbook 1939.*460-63. (Pp.460-62 repr. in this volume, pp.5-7.)

Ferry, Marie-Paule. 1970. "Sapir et l'ethnolinguistique". *Langages* No.18: *L'ethnolinguistique* ed. by Bernard Pottier, 14-21. Paris: Didier/Larousse.

Gipper, Helmut. 1976. "Die Sapir-Whorf Hypothese: Verbalismus oder Wissenschaft: Eine Entgegnung auf die Kritik Dürbecks". *Linguistics* No.178.25-46.

Goldberg, G[eorge?].1922. "An Exclusive Art [= Review of Sapir 1921]". *Christian Science Monitor* (1 Feb. 1922).

Greenberg, Joseph H(arold). 1951. Review of Sapir (1949). *American Anthropologist* 52.516-18. (Repr. in this volume, pp.66-68.)

––––––. 1971. *Language, Culture, and Communication: Essays by Joseph H. Greenberg.* Ed. by Anwar S. Dil. Stanford, Calif.: Stanford Univ. Press.

Gregores, Emma. 1953. Review of Sapir (1949). *Filología* (Buenos Aires) 2.210-20.

Guxman, M(irra) M(oiseevna). 1954. "E. Sapir i ètnografičeskaja lingvistika". *Voprosy Jazykoznanija* 3:1.110-27.

Haas, Mary R(osamond). 1953. "Sapir and the Training of Anthropological Linguists". *American Anthropologist* 55.447-50. (Repr. in this volume, pp. 115-18.)

—————. 1976. "Boas, Sapir, and Bloomfield". *American Indian Languages and American Linguistics: The Second Golden Anniversary Symposium of the Linguistic Society of America* ed. by Wallace L. Chafe, 59-69. Lisse/Holland: Peter de Ridder Press.

Harris, Zellig S(abbettai). 1951. Review article on Sapir (1949). *Language* 27.288-333. (Repr. in this volume, pp.69-114.)

—————. 1968. "Sapir, Edward. II: Contributions to Linguistics". *International Encyclopedia of the Social Sciences* 14.13-14. New York: Macmillan & Free Press.

Harrold, E(rnest) W(illiam). 1922. Review of Sapir (1921). *The Ottawa Citizen* of 16 Feb. 1922. [Adapted under the title of "The Wonders of Speech" in the *Toronto Daily Star* on 22 Feb. 1922.]

Hayashi, Tetsuro. 1984. "Edward Sapir in Japan: A survey of translations, 1940-1983". *Historiographia Linguistica* 11:3.461-66.

Hjelmslev, Louis. 1939. "Edward Sapir". *Acta Linguistica* 1.76-77.

Hockett, Charles F(rancis). 1954. "Two Models of Grammatical Description". *Word* 10.210-31.

Hoijer, Harry. 1941. "Methods in the Classification of American Indian Languages". Spier et al. 1941.1-14.

—————. 1946. "Introduction". *Linguistic Structures of Native America.* By Harry Hoijer et al. (= *Viking Fund Publications in Anthropology*, 6), 9-29. New York: Wenner-Gren Foundation for Anthropological Research.

—————. 1951. "Cultural Implications of Some Navajo Linguistic Categories". *Language* 27.111-20.

—————. 1954. "Sapir-Whorf Hypothesis". *Language and Culture: Conference on the interrelationship of language and other aspects of culture* ed. by H. Hoijer, 92-105. Chicago: Univ. of Chicago Press. (Repr., 1967.)

Hooton, Earnest A(lbert). 1940. "Edward Sapir". *Proceedings of the American Academy of Arts and Sciences* 74:6.157-59 (Nov. 1940).

Hymes, Dell H(athaway). 1970. "Linguistic Method in Ethnography". *Method and Theory in Linguistics* ed. by Paul L(ucian) Garvin, 249-311. The Hague: Mouton. (Repr., with revisions, in Hymes 1983.135-244.)

—————. 1983. *Essays in the History of Linguistic Anthropology.* Amsterdam

& Philadelphia: John Benjamins. [Cf. the review by Murray (1984).]

Jespersen, Otto. 1922. *Language: Its nature, development and origin.* London: Allen & Unwin.

Jessel, Levic. 1978. "Whorf: The differentiation of language". *International Journal of the Sociology of Language* 18.83-110.

Jenness, Diamond, 1939. "Edward Sapir". *Transactions of the Royal Society of Canada* for 1939, 3rd series, 33.151-53 (1940). (Repr. in this volume, pp.9-11.)

Koerner, E(rnst) F(rideryk) Konrad. 1977. "The Humboltian Trend in Linguistics". *Studies in Descriptive and Historical Linguistics: Festschrift for Winfred P. Lehmann* ed. by Paul J. Hopper, 145-58. Amsterdam: John Benjamins.

Kroeber, A(lfred) L(ouis). 1922. "A Study of Language [= Review of Sapir (1921)]". *The Dial* 72:3.314-17. (Excerpted in this volume, p.51.)

––––––. 1984[1959]. "Reflections on Edward Sapir, Scholar and Man". This volume, pp.131-39.

Kruisinga, Etsko. 1925. Review of Sapir (1921). *English Studies* 7.177-79.

Lakoff, Robin T(almach). 1972. "Another Look at Drift". *Linguistic Change and Generative Theory: Essays from the UCLA conference on historical linguistics in the perspective of transformational theory* ed. by Robert P. Stockwell & Ronald K.S. Macauley, 172-98. Bloomington & London: Indiana Univ. Press.

Léon, Pierre, Henry Schogt & Edward Burstynsky, eds. 1977. *La Phonologie. 1: Les écoles et les théories.* Paris: Klincksieck.

Lowie, Robert H(arry). 1919. Review of Sapir (1916). *American Anthropologist* 21.75-77. (Repr. in this volume, pp.39-41.)

––––––. 1923. Review of Sapir (1921). *Ibid.* 25.90-93. (Repr. in this volume, pp.43-46.)

––––––. 1984[1956]. "Comments on Edward Sapir, his Personality and Scholarship". This volume, pp.21-30. [For Lowie (1965), see the footnote on p.31.]

Malkiel, Yakov. 1976. "What Did Edward Mean dy *Drift*?". *Romance Philology* 30.622 (1976-77).

––––––. 1981. "Drift, Slope, and Slant: Background of, and variations upon, a Sapirian theme". *Language* 57:3.535-70.

––––––. 1984[1959]. "The Prospects of a Sapir Renaissance in Linguistics". *Historiographia Linguistica* 11:3.389-96.

Mandelbaum, David G(oodman). 1949. "Introduction". Sapir (1949).v-xii.

––––––. 1968. "Edward Sapir. I: Contribution to cultural anthropology".

International Encyclopedia of the Social Sciences 14.9-13. New York: Macmillan & Free Press.

McCawley, James D(avid). 1967. "Sapir's Phonologic Representation". *IJAL* 33.106-111. (Repr. in this volume, pp.153-58.)

Meillet, Antoine. 1922. Review of Sapir (1921), together with Jespersen (1922) and Vendryes (1921). *Bulletin de la Société de Linguistique de Paris* 23:2. 1-9, especially pp.6-8.

Mikuš, Radivoj Franciscus. 1953. "Edward Sapir et la syntagmatique". *Cahiers Ferdinand de Saussure* 11.11-30.

Murray, Stephen O(mar). 1981a. "The Canadian 'Winter' of Edward Sapir". *Historiographia Linguistica* 8.63-68.

———. 1981b. "Sapir's Gestalt". *Anthropological Linguistics* 23:1.8-12. [= Reply to Cain (1980).]

———. 1983. *Group Formation in Social Science*. Edmonton, Alberta: Linguistic Research, Inc. [Chap.V, "Sapir" (71-86).]

———. 1984. Review article on Hymes (1983). *Historiographia Linguistica* 11:3.449-60.

Newman, Stanley S(tewart). 1951. Review of Sapir (1949). *IJAL* 17.180-86. (Repr. in this volume, pp.59-65.)

Pike, Kenneth L(ee). 1984. "Some Teachers who helped Me". *Historiographia Linguistica* 11:1.493-95.

Preston, Richard J(oseph). 1966. "Edward Sapir's Anthropology: Style, structure and method". *American Anthropologist* 68.1105-1128.

———. 1980. "Reflections on Edward Sapir's Anthropology in Canada". *Canadian Review of Sociology and Anthropology* 17:4.367-74. (Rev. version in this volume, pp.179-84.)

Prokosch, Eduard. 1922. Review of Sapir (1921), together with Schrijnen (1921). *Journal of English and Germanic Philology* 21:2.353-57 (April 1922).

Remy, Arthur F(rank) J(oseph). 1922. Review of Sapir (1921). *The Literary Review of the New York Evening Post* of 6 May 1922.

Robins, John D(aniel). 1922. Review of Sapir (1921). *The Canadian Forum* 2:24.762 and 764 (Sept.1922).

Russell, Loris S. 1961. *The National Musuem of Canada 1910-1960*. Ottawa: Department of Northern Affairs and National Resources, v, 37 pp.

Sapir, Edward. 1907. "Herder's 'Ursprung der Sprache'". *Modern Philology* 5.109-142. (Repr. in *Historiographia Linguistica* 11:3.355-88 [1984].)

———. 1912. "Language and Environment". *American Anthropologist* n.s. 14. 226-42. (Repr. in Sapir 1949.89-103.)

—————. 1916. *Time Perspective in Aboriginal American Culture: A study in method.* (= *Canada, Department of Mines; Geological Survey, Memoir,* 90 = *Anthropological Series,* 13.) Ottawa: Government Printing Bureau.

—————. 1921. *Language: An introduction to the study of speech.* New York: Harcourt, Brace & Co. [= Howe]. (Also published with Oxford Univ. Press and in London: Humphrey Milford, [1922].)

—————. 1925. "Sound Patterns in Language". *Language* 1.37-51.

—————. 1929. "The Status of Linguistics as a Science". *Language* 5.207-214.

—————. 1933. "La réalité psychologique des phonèmes". *Revue de Psychologie normale et pathologique* 30.247-65. (English version first published in Sapir 1949.46-60.)

—————. 1949. *Selected Writings of Edward Sapir in Language, Culture and Personality.* Ed. with an introduction by David G. Mandelbaum. Berkeley & Los Angeles: Univ. of California Press.

Sapir, Edward & Morris Swadesh. 1932. *The Expression of the Ending-Point Relation in English, French, and German.* Ed. by Alice V[anderbilt] Morris. Baltimore, Md.: Waverly Press for the Linguistic Society of America.

—————, —————. 1939. *Nootka Texts: Texts and ethnological narratives with grammatical notes and lexical materials.* Ibid.

—————, —————. 1946. "American Indian Grammatical Categories". *Word* 2.103-112. [For 1953, 1955, and 1960 publications as well as 1966 and 1978 reprints of the 1932 and 1939 studies, see Addenda to Sapir's Bibliography in this volume, pp.211-17.]

Saussure, Ferdinand de. 1922. *Cours de linguistique générale.* Publié par Charles Bally & Albert Sechehaye avec la collaboration de Albert Riedlinger. 2e édition. Paris: Payot.

Schrijnen, Josef. 1921. *Einführung in das Studium der indogermanischen Sprachwissenschaft.* Heidelberg: Carl Winter.

Sommerfelt, Alf. 1952. Review of Sapir (1949). *Norsk Tidsskrift for Sprogvidenskap* 16.465-67.

Spier, Leslie. 1939a. "Edward Sapir". *Science* 89.237-38. (Repr. in part in this volume, pp.13-14.)

—————. 1939b. "Edward Sapir". *Man* 39.92-93.

—————, A(lfred) Irwing Hallowell & Stanley S(tewart) Newman, eds. 1941. *Language, Culture, and Personality: Essays in memory of Edward Sapir.* Menasha, Wis.: Edward Sapir Memorial Fund.

Swadesh, Morris. 1961. "The Culture Historic Implications of Sapir's Linguistic

Classification". *A William Cameron Townsend en el vigésimo quinto aniversario del Instituto Lingüístico de Verano*, 663-71. México, D.F.: Instituto Nacional de Anthropologià e Historia. (Repr. in this volume, pp.141-52.)
————. 1971. *The Origin and Diversification of Language*. Ed. by Joel Sherzer. With a foreword and an article on "Morris Swadesh: From the first Yale school to world prehistory" by Dell Hymes. Chicago: Aldine-Atherton; London: Routledge & Kegan Paul.

Trager, George L(eonard). 1951. Review note on Sapir (1949). *Studies in Linguistics* 9:1.18-19.
————. 1959. "The Systematization of the Sapir-Whorf Hypothesis". *Anthropological Linguistics* 1:1.31-38.

Van West, John. 1974. *The History of Anthropology in Canada*. Toronto: Dept. of Anthropology, Univ. of Toronto, mimeographed, 47 pp.

Vendryes, Joseph. 1921. *Le Langage: Introduction linguistique à l'histoire*. Paris: La Renaissance du Livre. (Repr., with a bibliographical supplement, Paris: Albin Michel, 1950.)
————. 1925. *Language: A linguistic introduction to history*. Transl. from the French by Paul Radin. New York: Alfred A. Knopf; London: Kegan Paul, Trench, Trübner & Co. (Repr., New York: Barnes & Noble, 1951; London: Routledge & Kegan Paul, 1952.)

Vennemann, Theo. 1975. "An Explanation of Drift". *Word Order and Word Order Change* ed. by Charles N. Li, 269-305. Austin: Univ. of Texas Press.

Voegelin, C(harles) F(rederick). 1942. "Sapir: Insight and rigor". *American Anthropologist* 44.322-24.
————. 1952. "Edward Sapir". *Word Study* 27:4.1-3. (Repr. in this volume, pp.33-36.)
————, and F(lorence) M. Voegelin. 1963. "On the History of Structuralizing in 20th Century America". *Anthropological Linguistics* 5:1.12-37.

Warnotte, D(aniel). 1922. Review of Sapir (1921), together with Vendryes (1921). *Revue de l'Institut de Sociologie* (Brussels) 2:2.309-314 (March), esp. pp.312-13.

Woolfson, A. Peter. 1970. "An Explanation of Sapir's Concept of Language in the Light of Ethnological Theory and Piagetian Developmental Psychology". *Language Sciences* No.11.8-10 (August 1970).

Zeitlin, Jacob. 1922. Review of Sapir (1921). *The Nation* (New York, 8 March 1922).

PART I

Obituaries and Biographical Sketches, 1939-1952

Edward Sapir (New Haven, 1936)

EDWARD SAPIR*

FRANZ BOAS

With the death of Edward Sapir which occurred on the fourth of February passed away one of the most brilliant scholars in linguistics and anthropology of our country. Born in Germany on January 26, 1884, he was taken by his parents to America when five years old.

After obtaining the Bachelor's degree of Columbia College in 1904, he continued in the graduate school, devoting himself first to the study of Germanics. Soon his interests broadened and he acquired knowledge in a wide field of linguistics. This brought him into contact not only with Semitic languages but also with the many languages of American Indians and indirectly with anthropology.

In 1905, while still a student at Columbia University, he studied the language and customs of the Wishram, a tribe living on lower Columbia River. The grammatical results of this investigation were published in the Handbook of American Indian Languages, while the text appeared as the second volume of the Publica- tions of the American Ethnological Society.

In 1906, while still at Columbia, he made a study of the language of the Takelma Indians of Oregon, planned as part of the general Handbook of American Indian Languages published by the Bureau of American Ethnology. The grammar resulting from these studies showed his understanding for unusual forms of linguistic expression.

In 1907 and 1908 he went to California where he undertook linguistic field studies among the Yana Indians, the results of which were published in 1910 by the University of California. Later on he returned to this subject in 1922, 1923, and 1929. After a year he came back to Columbia University, where he obtained the degree of Doctor of Philosophy. Even before this he was called to the University of Pennsylvania, where he was instructor from 1908-1910 and where he published the Takelma Texts on which his grammar was based. While in Philadelphia, he had the opportunity to study Paiute with a native resident in that city, the results of which were not published until 1931, the first thorough study of one of the important languages of the Shoshonian Group. This led to a careful comparison of Nahuatl and Southern Paiute, published by the Société des Américanistes of Paris in 1913 and 1915.

In 1910 he was called to Ottawa to organize anthropological work under the auspices of the Geological Survey which had carried on incidental anthropologi-

* Repr., with permission of the Editor and The University of Chicago Press, from *International Journal of American Linguistics* 10.58-59 (1939).

cal work under the direction of George M. Dawson. His principal work in Canada related to the natives of the west coast of Vancouver Island and to the Athapascan tribes. Particularly the latter were the center of his attention for many years and his own studies as well as, in later years, those of his students constituted much of what we know about this widely scattered group. After the first few years, largely owing to the World War, interest of the Canadian government in anthropological and linguistic matters waned and he accepted a call to the University of Chicago in 1925, first as associate professor of anthropology, then in 1927 as professor of anthropology and general linguistics. In 1931 he received a call both to Columbia and Yale Universities, and accepted the call to Yale, where he served as professor of anthropology and linguistics until his death.

Only his outstanding field studies can be mentioned here. He summarized his general views on linguistics in his excellent short book "Language", 1921, which undoubtedly has had a strong influence on linguistic science. His interest was primarily historical, and with a phenomenal knowledge of a wide field of facts he combined a rare intuition. The strictness of phonetic methods and the general adoption of phonemic principles in the study of primitive languages are largely due to him. His attempts of elucidating earlier relationships of American languages among themselves and with Asiatic languages show his interest in the historical problem. It is still doubtful how far earlier relationships can be reconstructed, but the problem remains with us and will always challenge our attention. His last published paper on glottalized consonants in a number of languages and the application of his results to Indo-European are brilliant examples of his methods.

The presence of a Gwabo native from West Africa in the United States gave him the opportunity to make a careful study of the musical pattern of the language. The grammar which he worked out in cooperation with Dr. George Herzog still awaits publication.

His anthropological publications are less numerous, but important. The linguistic material collected by him contains, naturally, much anthropological information, but he also paid attention to more general problems. Such are embodied in his papers on "Terms of Relationship and the Levirate," on "Time Perspective in Aboriginal American Cultures," on "Culture, Genuine and Spurious". In later years his interest was centered on problems of personality.

His early death has deprived us of one of the leaders on both linguistic and anthropological thought. Those who knew him personally, his willingness to give liberally of his knowledge and ideas, will miss him keenly. His work will live not only in his writings but also in the students he has trained and among whom he has established methods of conscientious painstaking work.

EDWARD SAPIR*

FRANKLIN EDGERTON

Edward Sapir died on February 4, 1939, aged 55 years and a few days. Born at Lauenburg, Pomerania, January 26, 1884, he came to this country with his parents in 1889. He studied at Columbia University, which granted him the degrees of A.B. (1904), A.M. (1905), Ph.D. (1909), and honorary Sc.D. (1929). He was Research Assistant in Anthropology in the University of California, 1907-8; Instructor in Anthropology in the University of Pennsylvania, 1908-10; Chief of the Division of Anthropology of the Geological Survey, Canadian National Museum, Ottawa, 1910-25; Associate Professor of Anthropology, 1925-27, and Professor of Anthropology and General Linguistics, 1927-31, in the University of Chicago; Sterling Professor of Anthropology and Linguistics in Yale University since 1931. A bibliography of his more important scholarly publications down to 1937, prepared by himself, was printed in the journal *Psychiatry* 1:154ff. (February 1938). It omits book reviews, and a few other minor publications (chiefly of early date). It also omits his poems. Yet it includes (with the supplement) 112 items, among them about ten substantial books. Besides the American Philosophical Society (elected in 1937), he was a member of the National Academy, and of the American Academy of Arts and Sciences; a corresponding member of the Société des Américanistes de Paris, and of the Reale Accademia delle Scienze di Bologna. He was an active member of the American Anthropological Association, the Linguistic Society of America, the American Folklore Society, and the American Oriental Society; he had held the Presidency of the first three of these.

He was married in 1911 to Florence Delson, who died in 1924; and again in 1926 to Jean V. McClenaghan, who survives him. Two sons and a daughter by the first marriage, and two sons by the second, also survive.

His bibliography suggests one of his most striking characteristics, his versatility. One of the greatest linguistic scholars of

* Reprinted, with the permission of the American Philosophical Society, Philadelphia, from *The American Philosophical Society Yearbook 1939* (1940), pp. 460-463.

the world, he was also a profound student of ethnology, folklore, sociology, religion, psychology, and even psychiatry. He had musical and poetic gifts; he wrote on "Representative Music" and "The Musical Foundations of Verse," and published a good deal of original poetry. The title of one of his articles, "Language as a Form of Human Behavior," is characteristic of his philosophic approach to linguistic studies, and of not a little of what he wrote. What are called the "broader aspects" of linguistics, the philosophy, psychology, and sociology of language, engaged his attention very insistently. But not to any neglect of the formal side, of the bed-rock facts, the basic data of language. Aided by exceptional facility of acquisition and retentive memory, both of which aroused the wonder and envy of his colleagues, he was able to amass and keep in mind, and to produce on a moment's notice, vast stores of detailed facts about an unbelievable number of languages in many parts of the earth. Yet, as has been said, language was only one of many interests to him, although certainly the first (to which he invariably returned after many excursions). Many of us tend to be slightly suspicious of one who seems to know so much about so many things; and this suspicion is only enhanced if he not only seems to control the facts, but is able to arrange them with apparent facility and artistic perfection and to relate them to one another, as Sapir always could. There may be a touch of envy in this attitude. Unable to cover so much ground ourselves, we are ready to ask whether breadth has not been won at the expense of depth. But while such suspicion may sometimes be justified, I never heard of anyone who thought it justified in the case of Sapir. He seemed able to meet every one of us on our own grounds, to see the minutiae of many provinces as with a magnifying glass, and at the same time effortlessly to survey the whole terrain.

To this rare capacity for combining brilliant theorizing with profound learning he added a third quality, which made him one of the greatest of teachers and the most fascinating of personal associates: an ability to present the product of that knowledge and thought, however abstruse and technical it might be, in simple, lucid, and effective words. He wore his intellectual greatness easily and gracefully, like a well-fitting garment. No one was overawed by it; on the contrary, he constantly drew into the circle of his interests many who were attracted at first as much by his personality as by the subject.

To evaluate properly his achievements in linguistics alone would be impossible in this brief notice, and I do not feel competent even to discuss what he did in other fields of learning. His book on "Language: an Introduction to the Study of Speech" (1921) contains many original and stimulating ideas; one of the most influential has proved to be the concept of "drift" in linguistic change, —independent development of related dialects in similar directions. This book, and many of his articles, are things which, while extremely valuable to linguistic scientists, are also of great interest to laymen. The bulk of his linguistic publications, however, consists of more severely technical studies. He was a pupil of Franz Boas, the dean of Americanists and founder of a new school and method of investigation of unrecorded languages. Sapir always recognized with full appreciation his debt to this great scholar and teacher; who would, however, I believe, not only call Sapir his greatest pupil, but also acknowledge that he played an important part in developing the method, which is sometimes spoken of under their joint names. Products of this phase of his work appear in a large body of original texts in Indian languages, with interpretations and grammatical analyses. The same method has been applied by Sapir himself to African languages, and by others to other fields. In more recent years Sapir turned his attention to active cultivation of older linguistic branches: Semitic, Indo-European, Sinitic, Tibetan, and others, always with brilliant and stimulating results. He was one of the leading exponents of what is called the "laryngeal hypothesis" in Indo-European phonology, which is now promising to revolutionize our conventional views of that subject. He began an intensive study of Tocharian, a little-known Indo-European language once spoken in Central Asia. He left behind him a large mass of notes on this subject, which it is hoped may some day be worked over and made available to science. They contain many highly original views, very important if demonstrable; for instance, Sapir believed that he could show extensive inter-borrowings between Tocharian and Tibetan, which was geographically near to it.

His all too early death deprives us of one of the greatest figures in American humanistic scholarship. That he was not only a scientist of the first rank, but also an artist, seems to me significant. These were not two separate sides of his nature; he was an artist in science, or a scientist in art—a thoroughly integrated personality in any event. Possibly this may in part explain why many of us do not think it going too far to call him a genius.

Edward and Florence Sapir with first-born son,
Michael (Ottawa, 1913)

EDWARD SAPIR
(1884 - 1939)*

DIAMOND JENNESS

O N February 4, 1939, Edward Sapir, who had been elected a Fellow of the Royal Society of Canada in 1922, died at New Haven, Connecticut, at the early age of 55 years. By his death science lost one of its most brilliant anthropologists and philologists, and the academic world a most inspiring teacher.

Sapir was born in Lauenburg, Germany, on January 26, 1884, but he migrated with his parents to New York when he was five years old. On graduating from Columbia University in 1904 he immediately began the studies that were to make him the foremost authority on the languages of the American Indians. His earliest researches, carried out while he was on the staff, first of the University of California, then of the University of Pennsylvania, dealt with the languages of the Yana, Takelma, Shoshone, and Southern Paiute tribes of the western United States. In 1910, when he was appointed Chief of the newly-created Division of Anthropology in the National Museum at Ottawa, he transferred his energies to the Canadian Indians, commencing with the Nootka tribe on the west coast of Vancouver Island. The two short papers on those Indians which he printed in the *Queen's Quarterly* display remarkably deep insight; but his voluminous manuscripts on their language and social life still await publication.

From the Nootka he turned to the Indians of the Mackenzie River basin and northern British Columbia, the Athapaskan tribes, whose dialects he subjected to a rigid analysis along the lines that had been thoroughly tested with the Indo-European languages of the Old World. Not only did he prove that these Athapaskan dialects were genetically connected with two apparently very dissimilar languages, Haida and Tlinkit, on the Pacific Coast, but he reconstructed a large vocabulary of ur-Athapaskan roots and tried to relate them to ancient root-forms in the Sinitic languages spoken throughout China, Tibet, and Siam. Had he succeeded he would have established the first certain link between a language spoken in the New World and one spoken in the Old. The manuscripts he left behind him actually carried him a

* Reprinted, with permission of The Royal Society of Canada, Ottawa, from *Proceedings of the Royal Society of Canada, 1939*, 3rd series, Vol. 33 (1940), pp. 151-53.

long way towards that goal; but the task was too great for one man to accomplish single-handed, if for no other reason than because it depended on parallel researches in eastern Asia.

It was during his residence in Ottawa that Sapir became interested in philosophy and psychology, especially in those phases that were concerned with the expression of thought in speech; and within the space of two months, using only a few hastily-scribbled notes, he dictated a revolutionary text-book on Language which has been accounted the profoundest treatise on the subject yet published—too profound, indeed, to be recommended to the uninitiated layman. Literature and poetry were his chief distractions; he gave a course on English literature before a local Ottawa society, and he was a regular contributor to the poetry columns of such magazines as the *New Republic, Nation,* and *Poetry.* His love of music (he was an accomplished pianist) found expression in the composition of a sonata and other pieces; none of which, however, did he attempt to publish.

In spite of his great productivity during this period, Sapir was not satisfied. Family troubles pressed heavily on him, and he missed in Ottawa the society of fellow-linguists and psychologists with whom he could discuss the problems that interested him most. Consequently in 1925, when his first wife died after a prolonged illness, leaving him with three small children, he gladly accepted a professorship of Anthropology and Linguistics in Chicago University. There he was able to give full scope to his extraordinary gifts as a teacher and lecturer. Both there, and later at Yale University, to which he was called in 1931, he gathered round him a brilliant company of linguistic students from all parts of the world whom he fertilized with new ideas and sent out to carry on the researches which he himself had not the time to continue. One student, from China, took up his Athapaskan problem, and after spending a summer among the Indians of the Mackenzie River basin, returned to his homeland to pursue the investigations from the Chinese angle. Sapir himself was able to make a notable contribution to Sinitic scholarship by exposing the Tibetan relationship of Tocharian, a language spoken in Central Asia during the 1st millenium A.D. that had been brought to light by the excavations of Sir Aurel Stein.

These six years in Chicago were perhaps the happiest in Sapir's life. It was there he married his second wife, Jean McClenaghan, who not only relieved him of all domestic worries, but helped him in his psychological studies. He was in constant demand within and without the university as a lecturer, for he spoke fluently without preparation, and what he said was always stimulating. The writer has seen him enter a hall filled with tumultuous children ranging in age from six years to twenty, and with only three scraps of paper, one white, one yellow, and one black, hold them spellbound for an hour while he discoursed, simply and clearly as only a great scholar can discourse, on human races and their differences.

Sapir found Yale more difficult than Chicago, because he was burdened with administrative duties such as he had always disliked. Along with these duties, and with his teaching and lecturing, he still kept up the linguistic studies that lay nearest to his heart; and he even planned a field season in China during his academic year of furlough. Overwork exacted its toll, however, at the very beginning of his sabbatical year, and he fell a victim to the heart trouble that two years later occasioned his death.

EDWARD SAPIR, PH.D., Sc.D.
1884 - 1939 *

HARRY STACK SULLIVAN

O NE of the fine minds of the Western world passed into history on February fourth. The Sterling professor of anthropology and of linguistics at Yale, past president of the Linguistic Society of America and of the American Anthropological Association, trustee of the William Alanson White Psychiatric Foundation, member of the National Academy of Sciences, of the American Academy of Arts and Sciences, of the Royal Society of Canada, the American Philosophical Society, the Ethnological Society, the Folk Lore Society, Société linguistique de Paris, Société des Américanistes de Paris, Reale Accademia della Scienze de Bologna; a great linguist, the foremost cultural anthropologist, Edward Sapir leaves but shadowy marks of his genius in the distinguished scholars who gained their orientation and inspiration in contact with him.

His creative work, begun in 1906 in the analysis of American Indian languages, was but moving towards its zenith in his far flung exploration of the relations of culture and personality when his heart disorganized in the Fall of 1937. The span of his interests was far too wide to let him rest in semi-invalidism, he was too vital to accept the biologically inevitable. He lived in an ever-expanding world of human potentiality. He could not take his own necessity very seriously. The collaborative research which chiefly interested him having been deferred, he resumed his university teaching in 1938. The high seriousness and personal zeal that had characterized his thirty years of academic work were not to be lain aside. The final overstrain came some two months later.

Edward Sapir's linguistics was the study of verbal symbols in action. The culture that interested him as an anthropologist was dynamic, the growing, shifting patterns that appear in people as they live among their kind. He was a social psychologist and a psychiatrist. His analytic gifts joined with the rarest of synthetic creativeness, a broad scholarship, great energy, fine sensibilities, a kindly patience, exquisite sensitivity. He was one of the most articulate of men, a poet, a musician, an intellect that evoked reverence, a personality unendingly charming, a genius largely wasted on a world not yet awake to the value of the very great.

* Reprinted, with permission of the Editor and the William Alanson White Psychiatric Foundation, Washington, D.C., from *Psychiatry: Journal of the biology and pathology of interpersonal relations* [now subtitled: *Journal for the study of interpersonal processes*] 2:2. 159 (May 1939).

EDWARD SAPIR*

LESLIE SPIER

[. . .]

His ethnographic studies were, for the most part, incidental products of his linguistic work. But this gave them a distinctive quality, namely, a constant illumination from linguistic insights. This approach marks his principal contribution to ethnological method, "Time Perspective in Aboriginal American Culture" (1916). His published ethnographic reports are few and brief, but a deftness and incisiveness make them models of description. His two little papers on the Takelma of Oregon, for example, are marvels of succinct presentation and put to shame many a more pretentious monograph. It is therefore regrettable that he left incomplete his magnificent collection of materials on Nootka, Yana and Hupa.

Dr. Sapir's major published contribution, however, lies in the field of language. His control of the perfected techniques of Indo-European and Semitic philology was extended into the realm of primitive languages. Lexical and grammatical contributions, ranging from Hebrew and Tocharian to American Indian Uto-Aztecan, Hokan, Athapascan and Wakashan, attest his extraordinary fertility. The soundness of these analyses can not be challenged. Beyond this, though fully recognizing independent developments, his emphasis on "drift" – the idea that languages differentiated from a common base will show parallel modifications – led him to suggest genetic connection in families previously regarded as distinct.

The more unique contribution lay, not in structural nor historical phases, but in language as a psychologic-symbolic phenomenon. In the first place, he offered in "Language" (1921) a new approach of broad philosophic sweep. Pointing out that the traditional classification of languages relates properly only to their techniques, he emphasized the more fundamental characterizations of conceptual types and degrees of synthesis. The primary concern is with basic concepts, their radical or relational, pure or concrete nature, and the mechanisms

* Excerpt from the author's obituary notice in *Science*, vol.89 No.2307 (17 March 1939), pp.237-38.

for their expression. Essentially, this is emphasis on language as thought rather than as form.

His studies of the interrelations of psychiatry and culture are closely allied to this. Here he was concerned that psychiatry and psychoanalysis should profit from a study of variant cultural matrices and that cultural behavior as mechanism for thought and living should be understood in terms of psychological experience. When chairman of the Division of Anthropology and Psychology, National Research Council (1934-35), he had opportunity to lay the groundwork for coordinated studies along these lines, which may be expected to bear future fruit.

His most striking personal characteristics were a crystalline quality of thought and speech and an ever-present kindliness. The artistry of his effortless verbal performances, his articulateness, was a delight. It is no accident that half his writings are groups of poems, literary and musical criticism, showing the same heightened sensibility to nuances of sound and meaning, the same intuitions, that fertilized his linguistic and psychiatric work.

No life can be long enough to accomplish the program he set for himself, but we can only regret that his proved so brief.

EDWARD SAPIR*

RUTH BENEDICT

THE death of Edward Sapir on February 4, 1939 removes from American linguistics and anthropology one of their most brilliant and challenging students. His long illness, after his breakdown in the summer of 1937, had schooled his friends and his students to the hardly faced fear that his work might be prematurely ended, but the alternating succession of hope and despair proved finally to be no adequate preparation for the news of his death.

Sapir was born on January 26, 1884 in Lauenburg, Germany, and his parents when he was five years old brought him with them to America when they emigrated to this country. A child of New York's East Side, he could depend on no inherited advantages of birth or position. His gifts, however, opened for him the best education available, and he won scholarships at Horace Mann and later at Columbia College where he graduated in 1904 at the age of twenty. He immediately continued graduate work in Germanics and Semitics, and with Boas in primitive languages and anthropology. After one year of graduate work he undertook his study of the language of the Wishram on the lower Columbia River, the texts appearing in 1909 as the second volume of the Publications of the American Ethnological Society. The following year he went to Oregon to study the Takelma language, the difficulties of which made his grammar, presented as his doctoral dissertation, a particularly brilliant achievement. There was no period of apprenticeship in Sapir's linguistic work; his phonetic and morphological gifts are as apparent in this boyhood work as in that of a student of long and arduous experience. Immediately also, in 1907, the appearance of his two papers on Takelma ethnology in the *Anthropologist* and in the *Journal of American Folklore,* showed his insight into the culture of a then unguessed-at area.

Kroeber had just become assistant professor at the new department of anthropology at the University of California and for a year, 1907–08, Sapir was assistant in that department, preparing his Yana texts. When no permanent place was made for him there, he went for two years to the

* Reprinted, with permission of the American Anthropological Association, Washington, D.C., from *American Anthropologist* 41.465-68 (1939).

University of Pennsylvania, first as fellow and then as instructor. His work on the Southern Paiute was done in Philadelphia, the first thorough study of a Shoshonean language, and a piece of work he often referred to as his "best." Neither grammar nor texts appeared until 1930, a delay which was grievous to him, but the historical implications of his investigations he discussed carefully in the 1913 and 1915 articles published in Paris. These papers substantiated the existence of the Uto-Aztecan linguistic stock which had previously been posited.

These were lean years in Sapir's life and he often spoke of the financial hardships. They were, however, the period of most concentrated achievement in his life, and his year in California especially was a favorite memory. After two years in Pennsylvania he was called in 1910 to Ottawa as chief of the newly established Division of Anthropology under the Geological Survey of Canada. This same year he married Florence Delson, his cousin, and his three children of this marriage, Michael, Helen, and Philip, were all born in Ottawa during the fifteen years he remained there. His first field-work under the Canadian auspices was among the Nootka Indians of Vancouver Island, and this work greatly influenced his own thinking in ethnology, but he never prepared either the ethnology or the grammar for publication. This was the time also of his work on Sarcee and other Athabascan languages of Canada. His interest had shifted; he was devoting himself to the study of linguistic change and to the study of genetic relationships among languages not hitherto classified together. His intensive studies of various Athabascan languages, continued in later years with a highly refined study of Navaho, gave him the material with which to explore processes of linguistic change with rigorous methodology and to construct an Ur-Athabascan language in the best philological manner. Trained as he was in the methods of Indo-Germanic philology he applied these methods to the study of primitive linguistic stocks, establishing phonetic shifts and characterizing specific sound patterns which dominated the phonetic variety of a given language. In his detailed Athabascan work mere superficial resemblances did not constitute, for him, a basis upon which to build theories of genetic relationships; he trusted rather to carefully verified and regular phonetic shifts. The Athabascan linguistic reconstruction led him to posit the Na-Dene linguistic group, composed of Athabascan, Tlingit, and Haida. He also contributed substantially to the discussion of the Penutian and Hokan stocks then recently proposed by Kroeber and Dixon. His latest classification of American Indian languages, that published in 1929 in the *Encyclopaedia Britannica*, 14th edition, goes in certain cases beyond proved and documented relationships, and any final evaluation can be made only after intensive research upon the languages in question.

The call to Chicago University in 1925 was most welcome to Sapir. He had been isolated from linguistic and anthropological contacts for many years, and had fallen victim to lassitude. He had rescued himself to the extent of writing his book on Language in 1921, but his gifts as teacher and lecturer had been unused for a decade or more; his intellectual interests, now centering themselves more and more upon psychological problems of culture, had had no stage on which to display themselves. His personal life had been disrupted by the long illness and death of his wife, and he was most restless.

The position at Chicago was one he was uniquely qualified to adorn. The Department of Anthropology had been recently established under Fay-Cooper Cole, and Sapir immediately attracted serious students both in linguistics and ethnology. No one was a more delightful and fluent speaker; his most casual lectures and occasional papers were full of felicities and insights. In Chicago he was in great demand to speak to groups of all kinds outside the University and he was stimulated as he had not been for years before. In his classes too he was able for the first time to train serious students of linguistics, to ground them in phonetic recording and in methods of linguistic analysis. Few teachers are able to communicate the kind of intellectual excitement with which Sapir filled those first students working with him in the classroom or in the field on the phonetics or the grammar of Navaho.

The call to Chicago marks also the beginning of the period, which continued to the end of his life, of a major interest in semantics. Language is a system of communication, but, after all, how accurate is the communication between two people? Many varying associations with the word are possible and many varying affectual responses. Is communication achieved and in how far can this be studied? This problem led him into an intensive study of the English language and of abortive verbal communication in English.

There was close relation between this problem and his growing interest at this time in problems of personality and culture. The possibilities in this field had first begun to preoccupy him when he read Jung's *Psychological Types* and Ogden's and Richards' *Meaning of Meaning* during his last years at Ottawa, and the course he gave at Columbia University in the Summer Session just before taking his post in Chicago was brilliant evidence of his immediate use of such material in connection with culture. His approach to the problem was always through the individual, and sociological approaches he either regarded as self-evident or as threatening the autonomy of the self. As he was fond of saying, "There are as many cultures as there are individuals in the population" and he was dissatisfied with sociological generalizations. His strong conviction that the individual was uniquely important in cultural studies, however, did not lead him to train students to explore cultures through intensive observation of a series of divergent individuals in their sociological matrix; it led him rather to the disparagement of sociological studies and to the belief that the solution of the problem lay in the use of techniques of individual psychology and particularly of psychoanalysis. Certainly his skepticism of generalizations about culture was salutary, and his efforts to bring psychiatry and ethnology closer together for their mutual enrichment are significant for the future.

Sapir's six years at Chicago were the happiest of his life. He married Jean McClenaghan there in 1926 and their first son, Paul, was born there. In 1931 he was called to Yale and accepted the Sterling Professorship in Anthropology and Linguistics. In 1934 he was elected to the National Academy.

During Sapir's professorship at Yale his research in languages transcended the territory usually cultivated by the linguistic scholar in Anthropology. His studies in Indogermanics and Semitics resulted in insights of singular importance which were fully appreciated by linguists in these fields, and which were embodied in brief but carefully documented papers. Among the most significant was the discovery of a relationship between Tibetan and Tocharian. In these studies he brilliantly applied the phonemic approach which he had been instrumental in developing and which already has proved a source of fresh vigor to the discipline of linguistics.

He continued at Yale to occupy himself with psychological problems of anthropology, and under the auspices of the Division of the Social Sciences of the Rockefeller Foundation he was enabled to gather together a group of foreign students holding exchange fellowships in this country for a year's study of the Impact of Culture on Personality. In this seminar the members made use of their own life experiences in different European and Eastern countries. As Chairman of the Division of Psychology and Anthropology of the National Research Council he also established the Committee on Personality and Culture, at first under the chairmanship of his friend, Dr. Harry Stack Sullivan, and later of Lloyd Warner.

Even in an anthropological journal an appreciation of Edward Sapir is incomplete without mention of him as a poet. The same sensitivity and the same gifts of expression which made him a poet made him also a great linguist, and shaped his keen understanding of the content of speech—the poetry of native ritual, the vigor of a primitive oration. For many years his poetry appeared constantly in *The New Republic*, *The Nation*, *Poetry*, and similar magazines. He once made a selection of those he would like to retain and it is a loss that they have never been published in book form.

Few men in academic life have been so brilliantly endowed as Professor Sapir, and the loss which linguistics and anthropology have sustained in his death cannot be measured. To those who have been his friends, his death leaves a vacancy which can never be filled.

EDWARD SAPIR*

MORRIS SWADESH

Edward Sapir died in his fifty-sixth year on February fourth. The heart condition of which he died had been diagnosed about five years before but caused serious trouble for the first time in the summer of 1937 when Sapir was in Ann Arbor teaching in the Linguistic Institute. The enthusiasm and energy which he put into his teaching and scientific discussion and his cordiality in social contact with colleagues and students sapped his strength and brought on a heart attack. During the few previous years while under a doctor's regimen of general quiet and relaxation, his intellectual enthusiasm could not be held within the restraints which his physical condition demanded.

Sapir was born in Lauenburg, Germany, January 26, 1884. When he was only four, his father, Jacob Sapir, migrated to the United States to carry on his profession of cantor. Edward Sapir early showed scholarly ability, musical sense, and literary talent, and won a four-year Pulitzer fellowship for study in Columbia University. He became interested in linguistic science and took a master's degree in Germanic. About this time he came into contact with Franz Boas, dean of American anthropologists and virtually the initiator of strict scientific method in American linguistics. Boas had a profound influence on Sapir, and particularly impressed upon him the need for a broad knowledge of languages of varying structures. He has told us how he came away from a conference with Boas impressed that he had everything to learn about language. For every generalization he had before believed was certain and exceptionless, Boas could summon indubitable contrary examples from American Indian languages he knew. Sapir was also impressed with the possibilities of inductive study of living languages by phonetic recording from native speakers. This led him into the field at least fourteen times to study such languages as Chinook (Wishram dialect), Yana (three dialects), Tlingit, Nootka, Sarcee, Kutchin, Ingalik, Hupa, Navaho, Southern Paiute. In addition, he made use of incidental opportunities to add to his first-hand knowledge of particular languages

* Reprinted, with permission of the Linguitsic Society of America and the Editor, from *Language* 15.132-35 (1939).

whenever he met a speaker of some new language. His work on Jabo
of Africa was done with a native, Blooah by name, who was found by
some anthropology students working in a bowling alley in Chicago.
Typical of his constant desire to observe linguistic phenomena, when a
Lithuanian American student once dropped into his office at Yale, he
inquired about the inflectional accents and asked him to pronounce
words which illustrated the contrasting types. He was then interested
to note that the native Lithuanian, though he had not been aware
before that there were two different ways of accenting a word, was able
to recognize a difference that would hardly have been noticed by a
non-native.

He also did a tremendous amount of reading. As a result of his
constant interest and study, he probably had a greater knowledge of
specific linguistic phenomena than ten or more ordinary linguistic scientists. We have lost this treasury of linguistic knowledge, this accumulation of facts in the mind of one man who was at the same time most
competent to draw upon their theoretical significance. But he has
shown the way to others, particularly to his students. He has demonstrated the value and the possibility of having a quantity of data as a
basis from which to generalize and as a background for the approach to
specific problems. Some will say that the faculty of retaining and being
able to use so much knowledge belongs only to genius, but Sapir's attitude was that such knowledge can be coordinated under a general
understanding of linguistic science. He who has a sound command of
linguistic theory can retain a quantity of specific facts to support his
theories and to aid him in the constant refinement of his understanding
of linguistic phenomena.

Sapir's interests in cultural anthropology and in psychology were
completely integrated with his interest in linguistics. He early came to
see linguistics as a social science, and social science was to him completely linked with the operations of the personality. He felt that the
abstraction of language science from the social setting deprived it of
considerable vitality. His own mind was so capable of dialectic thinking, of keeping track of all the various factors in a situation, that he was
impatient of those who approached a problem by arbitrarily ruling out
consideration of certain factors. He himself set no restrictions on his
thinking, but was always ready to bring in new aspects that had heuristic value.

The bibliography given in Psychiatry 1.154–7 (1938) (which does not include his poems) gives an indication of the breadth of his scholarship.[1] The acuity of his analysis is evident in each of them.

The whole of Sapir's spirit cannot be told in terms of scientific achievement. We must mention too his great belief in human rights. He resented oppression and discrimination against groups and violations of individual justice. As a Jew, he was keenly aware of anti-semitism in American educational institutions and resisted every official action that seemed to involve this issue. But he was not ethnocentric in his sense of social justice and fought equally hard for any individual who was unjustly treated.

Sapir took his doctor's degree in anthropology at Columbia in 1909, was a research assistant at California for a year (1907-8) and held a fellowship and an instructorship at Pennsylvania from 1908 to 1910. He then went to Ottawa to be Chief of the Division of Anthropology of the Geological Survey of Canada and held that position for fifteen years. In 1925 he went to Chicago as Associate Professor of Anthropology and Linguistics. In 1927 he became full Professor. In 1931 he went to Yale as Sterling Professor of Anthropology and Linguistics and as Chair-

---

[1] The wide range of his work on American Indian Languages has been summarily indicated above. From the other titles may be selected for special mention here: The Musical Foundations of Verse, JEGPh 20.213-22 (1921); Language, an Introduction to the Study of Speech, New York, 1921; The Grammarian and his Language, Am. Mercury 1.149-55 (1924); Sound Patterns in Language, LANG. 1.37-51 (1925); A Study of Phonetic Symbolism, Journ. Exper. Psych. 12.225-39 (1929); Male and Female Forms of Speech in Yana, Donum Nat. Schrijnen 79-85 (1929); The Status of Linguistics as a Science, LANG. 5.207-14 (1929); Totality, LANG. MONOGR. 6 (1930); The Concept of Phonetic Law as tested in Primitive Languages by Leonard Bloomfield, Methods in Social Science 297-306 (1931); Notes on the Gweabo Language of Liberia, LANG. 7.30-41 (1931); The Function of an International Auxiliary Language, Psyche No. 44.4-15 (1931); The Expression of the Ending-Point Relation in English, French, and German (with Morris Swadesh, edited by Alice V. Morris), LANG. MONOGR. (1931); La Réalité Psychologique des Phonèmes, Journ. de Psych. 30.247-65 (1933); Hittite *hapatis* 'vassal' and Greek ὀπᾶδος, LANG. 10.274-9 (1934); κίβδα a Karian Gloss, JAOS 56.85 (1936); Internal Linguistic Evidence suggestive of the Northern Origin of the Navaho, Am. Anthrop. n.s. 38.224-35 (1936); Hebrew *'argāz*, a Philistine Word, JAOS 56.272-81 (1936); Greek ἀτύζομαι, a Hittite Loanword, and its Relatives, LANG. 12.175-80 (1936); Tibetan Influences on Tocharian, I, LANG. 12.259-71 (1936); Hebrew 'helmet', a Loanword, and its Bearing on Indo-European Phonology, JAOS 57.73-7 (1937); Glottalized Continuants in Navaho, Nootka, and Kwakiutl (with a note on Indo-European), LANG. 14.248-74 (1938); Nootka Texts (with Morris Swadesh), Special Publications of the Linguistic Society, William Dwight Whitney Linguistic Series (1938).

man of the newly founded Anthropology Department. He was a member, regular or honorary, of a number of anthropological and linguistic societies here and abroad; he was president of the Linguistic Society in 1933, and of the Anthropological Society in 1938. He held several other offices at different times in these societies and served on the committees of research councils, including the National Research Council and the American Indian Committee of the American Council of Learned Societies. Among the special honors conferred in recognition of his achievements were memberships in Sigma Xi, the American Academy of Arts and Sciences, and an honorary degree of Doctor of Science at Columbia.

He leaves a widow, Mrs. Jean McClenaghan Sapir, and five children —Herbert Michael, Helen, Philip, Paul, and David, the first three by a former marriage with Florence Delson, who died in 1924. A host of students, colleagues, and friends also mourn him. We regret the loss to descriptive and comparative linguistics and ethnology, to cultural theory, to social psychology. But more than that, we who are scientists and regard science as a thing of prime value, have it brought home to us at such a time as this how much character is worth. We regret the loss to science but feel poignant sorrow at the passing of a man who was honest and just, who sincerely respected the personal worth of all whom he had dealings with, and who had the human feeling and courage to fight against injustice and discrimination.

EDWARD SAPIR*

DAVID MANDELBAUM

When Edward Sapir died on February 4, 1939 science lost one of its most luminous personalities. World famous as a brilliant linguist, a gifted anthropologist and keen psychologist, Sapir has left many spheres of scholarship bereft of a truly great inspiration. The broad range and depth of his interests are widely recognized but it may not be generally known that Sapir was also concerned with Jewish problems. His writings in this field are relatively few and scattered but, brief as they are, they reach to the heart of the matter. Years ago he was able to foresee the rise of rabid nationalisms, the current difficulties of Zionism and the impending travail of Jewry. It is well in times like these to review his thoughts and judgments concerning the course of Jewish life. Before doing so, let us briefly outline the salient facts of his career.

Edward Sapir was born in Lauenburg, Pomerania (January 26, 1884) of orthodox Jewish parents. When five years old he was brought to the United States where his father filled the triple role of *shohet*, rabbi and cantor in New York synagogues. Sapir's abilities were manifested early and scholarships were awarded to him at Horace Mann School and at Columbia University, where he was graduated at the age of twenty. He went on to pursue graduate study of Germanic and Semitic languages but soon allied himself with the linguistic and anthropological researches carried on by Franz Boas among primitive peoples. After a year with Boas he went out to study the language of the Wishram Indians of the state of Washington and in the following year worked with the Takelma Indians of Oregon. His first papers, published in his early twenties, are no apprentice fumblings, but models of clarity and keen analysis.

After receiving the Ph.D. at Columbia in 1909 he taught for a while

* Reprinted, with permission of the Editors and the author, from *Jewish Social Studies* 3: 131-40 (1941).

at the University of Pennsylvania (1909-10) and in 1910 was appointed Chief of the Division of Anthropology in the Geological Survey of Canada. He married his cousin, Florence Delson, in the same year and his three children of this marriage were born in Ottawa. Sapir's fifteen years in Canada were burdened with administrative duties and somewhat dulled by isolation from stimulating scientific contacts but they did provide ample opportunity for field work with many Indian tribes. After the long illness and death of his wife Sapir left Ottawa to become professor of anthropology and general linguistics at the University of Chicago. At Chicago there was at last scope for the exercise of his great talents. His classes were filled with students from many departments of the University; he was in demand as a lecturer for groups in the city; he was able to train scholars to carry out the methods and concepts of linguistic analysis which he had developed. He married Jean McClenaghan in 1926; their first son was born in Chicago, the second in New Haven where Sapir had accepted the Sterling Professorship in Anthropology and Linguistics. The call to Yale was most attractive. The terms of the appointment were so favorable that Sapir was able to set up one of the great centers of anthropological and linguistic work in the country. During his years at Yale from 1931 until his death, he continued to exert an important influence on the development of both linguistic and anthropological science. While he was on a leave of absence in 1938 a series of heart attacks checked his career and the same ailment a year later ended it.

It is no difficult task to give his measure as a scholar in official terms. His position at Yale, an honorary Sc.D. from Columbia, membership in the National Academy of Sciences, elections to the presidency of the American Anthropological Association, of the Linguistic Society of America and many other honors attest that his colleagues awarded the highest available distinctions to Edward Sapir. It is more difficult to indicate what Sapir meant to those who knew him and his work. For he was more than an inspired scholar, he was an inspiring person. Listening to him was a lucid adventure in the field of ideas; one came forth exhilarated, more than oneself. Diamond Jenness, Sapir's successor at Ottawa, relates how he once saw Sapir enter a hall filled with tumultuous children, " . . . and with only three scraps of paper, one white, one yellow, one black, hold them spellbound for an hour while he discoursed, simply and clearly as only a great scholar can, on human races and their differences."

He contributed to many areas of knowledge, but his chief academic interest was linguistics. He had a truly phenomenal knowledge of languages; it was not unusual for him to quote from thirty or more languages in the course of a single impromptu lecture. This command of linguistic fact gave substance to his penetrating and revolutionary insights into the functioning and history of languages. The modern science of linguistics, with its strictness of method and reliance on phonemic principles, was to a very significant extent moulded by him. The papers he wrote on cultural anthropology are often only by-products of linguistic researches but each is a gem of clear presentation and incisive analysis. His most considerable work in this field, *Time Perspective in Aboriginal American Culture*, is essentially a philosophical assay of anthropological method. It is full of deep insights; a casual sentence may present a conclusion which distinguished scholars are only now, some twenty-five years later, reaching after long study.

In later years Sapir became much interested in the problem of personality development, of the interplay between culture and personality. Widely read in psychiatry and psychoanalysis, he paved the way toward a fruitful union of the disparate disciplines of psychology and anthropology. His few papers on these subjects are direction-finders for the development of a meaningful social psychology. The same sensitivity to verbal nuance and human motivation which made Sapir so gifted a scholar and scientist enabled him to write poetry. His poems were published over a period of many years in such journals as *The Nation, Poetry, The Dial*. His versatility extended to yet another of the arts. An able pianist, he had composed a sonata and other musical works.

Sapir's students were sometimes so awed by the immensity of his knowledge and the keenness of his intellect that they were literally abashed in his presence. But once they overcame their own timidity they found in Sapir the most sympathetic of mentors, the kindliest of men. If one of us was able to present a striking new idea or fresh and valid evidence to revise an old concept he was always ready, even eager, to take it up and carry it forward. He had no vested intellectual interests. It is through his students that Sapir's work must be carried on. His writings are all too few, though his bibliography includes upwards of two hundred fifty titles.

Many of the postulates which were so graphically presented in lectures he never put on paper. The deft scalpel of his wit could cut through the enveloping maze of cultural form to reveal the founts of human behavior. He could explain his explorations so clearly, in such resplendent phrases, that we felt ourselves, with him, heroes in the world of ideas. An eminent psychiatrist recently remarked that Sapir was an intoxicating man. That he was. And the stimulus of his life and work will continue to enliven many of us for a long time to come.

During his years at Yale Sapir lent his support to the work of the Yiddish Scientific Institute and actively furthered the program of the Conference on Jewish Relations. He was one of the founders of the Conference and served as a vice-president of the organization from its inception to his death. Sapir was also a member of the committee which launched *Jewish Social Studies* and was a member of the editorial council of the journal. In conversation he would occasionally tell how profoundly Judaism had affected his life. During childhood he rebelled against it. The interminable regulations, the binding restrictions of orthodoxy seemed unnecessary, intolerable. The discipline was a burden to the sensitive child and he hated it. But as he grew older he came more and more to appreciate the grand plan of life that lay beneath the irksome petty details. Toward the end of his life he turned to the linguistic and ethnological study of the Talmud and in it he found a reflection of all his interests, of his life principles. In the study of the Talmud, as in his other academic studies, he found the sheer pursuit of scholarship a constant delight. "Don't you feel," he once said to Rabbi M. L. Zigmond (who was writing a thesis on American Indian ethnobotany), "that when you become engrossed in a problem of pure scholarship it is like taking a long, cool drink of water on a very hot day?"

A single word in a biblical text, an unusual turn of phrase, would lead him to follow a train of investigation which would wind up in a whole new vista of linguistic knowledge. Thus the Hebrew word ארגז "coffer, casket," (I Samuel 6. 8, 11, 15), posited a problem because of its context, infrequency and lack of genuine Semitic cognates. Sapir suggested that it was a loan word from the Philistine language, which originally meant "the box of a cart." The likeness between *argaz* and such words as Latin *arca* made it clear, he stated, that, "It is entirely possible, and

even probable, that the Anatolian-Aegean linguistic group of which
Philistine is an offshoot is an Indo-European group (of 'pre-Greek
type?')."[1] Similarly, Sapir tried to show that כובע "helmet," and the
place-name *Siddîm* (Genesis 14.3), are loan words from the Hittite.[2]

A paper published in 1915 still remains one of the best linguistic
studies of Yiddish. In it Sapir points out that the Judeo-German dialects
have developed in comparative isolation from the main body of German
vernaculars since the beginning of the sixteenth century. They have
been influenced by various Slavic tongues as well as by Hebrew. Yiddish
is like English in that it has developed in isolation and has been subject
to extensive foreign influence, but shows less effect of this influence than
does English since its basis has remained thoroughly German and its
foreign accretions are of secondary importance. In this article Sapir gives
many examples of the manner in which Yiddish has preserved certain
archaic features which have disappeared in modern German. For example, Yiddish has not levelled Middle High German î and ei into ai, but
has kept them apart as ai and e, respectively; e.g., *vais*, "white," *ix vés*,
"I know" (from MHG *wîz* and *ich weiz*, respectively; contrast modern
literary German *weiss* for both). In the same way an old dative singular
in -en of weak feminines (MHG *der zungen, der mitten*, but modern
German *der Zunge, der Mitte*) is preserved in stereotyped phrases like
in dr mitn drin, "right in the midst of it." In the case of *zamd*, "sand," an
old Indo-Germanic m has been preserved that has in practically all other
Germanic dialects been assimilated in n (cf. ἄμαθος, "sand," from **samad-
hos*). The old imperative *lâ* ("let") survives in phrases like *ló mir* (or
ló mix), "let me" (contrast modern German *lass mich*). In some other
respects Yiddish has developed much faster than modern German and is
more aberrant than the standard literary language. The great frequency
of final voiced stops and spirants in Judeo-German is a feature which is
entirely foreign to the main body of Germanic dialects but is paralleled
by a similar development in English and Swedish.[3]

The refreshment and joy which Sapir derived from his studies in

[1] *Journal of the American Oriental Society*, vol. lvi (1936) 279.

[2] *Journal of the American Oriental Society*, vol. lvii (1937) 73-77; *American Journal of
Semitic Languages and Literatures*, vol. lv (1937) 86-88.

[3] "Notes on Judeo-German Philology," in *Jewish Quarterly Review*, n.s. vol. vi (1915)
231-64.

Jewish linguistics were only one phase of the good which he knew could be gained from a knowledge of Judaic writings. For he felt, as he put it, "... the necessity of having a cultural background if one is to be oneself."[4] His acquaintance with the manner and principles of Jewish life helped to buttress and integrate his own world-view. Not that Sapir was ever content to gloat over the inventory of the historic achievements of Jewry, as some Jewish scholars seem to do. He believed that the past of the people is important only insofar as it serves as the mould of the present. Both gold and dross may be cast in the same mould. What we are and shall be, rather than what we as Jews have been, was of prime importance to Edward Sapir. He put the matter succinctly in a review of Paul Radin's *Monotheism among Primitive Peoples.* Sapir wrote,

> "... we can see more clearly that it means little or nothing to be proud, or to refrain from being proud, of the supposedly distinctive contributions that Judaism has made to religious thought and feeling. Psychologically, monotheism is not a Jewish trait, no more than it is any other kind of national trait. Historically, it so chanced that the particular form of monotheism that had been developed by the Jews proved stimulating in the further development of other forms of monotheism in alien lands. The cultural and spiritual significance of monotheism, as of every other pattern of conduct, is not implicit in itself but depends altogether on what sustenance living human beings may derive from it, or, to speak more accurately, may put into it. Monotheism as such is neither good nor bad, neither high nor low, precisely as a sonnet as such is neither good nor bad or as parliamentary government as such is neither high nor low. And surely a dead monotheism is not a greater spiritual force than a live polytheism ..."[5]

The historic heritage of Judaism may be an empty, meaningless shell, or a rich, rewarding vessel, depending on what the living inheritors put into it, how they use it. Those Jews who dare to press forward into uncharted sectors of the universe of ideas, those who brave social pressure to protest against injustice and misery, those who are the shock troops against the bastions of reaction—those Jews are filling the old chalice of Judaism with fresh life-giving vigor and are fulfilling their historic status as Jews.

[4] *Menorah Journal*, vol. xii (1926) 217.
[5] *Menorah Journal*, vol. xi (1925) 527.

Edward Sapir was always an explorer of ideas. He would not hesitate to plot the true position of a concept, as he saw it, no matter how contrary were the views of others. This is not the place to tell of the new directions he found in science. Let us take an example from his role in Jewish affairs. At a time when the very word assimilation was anathema to most Jewish leaders Sapir took the platform with some rather rabid writers and orators to state the case for assimilation. It is to be noted that Sapir never argued that assimilation was the solution for all Jews, nor that it was a generally preferable course. He simply stated what any anthropologist could see, that some measure of assimilation was inevitable. A review of Ludwig Lewisohn's *Israel*, in which he gave his views on this subject, is worth quoting at some length.

"Mr. Lewisohn is very bitter about the assimilationists. Assimilation, he thinks, has been tried and found wanting in America no less than in Germany. But he seems to overlook some very simple facts and to refrain from certain very simple reflections. In the first place, when in the history of mankind has ethnic assimilation been a comfortable or an easy process? Had Mr. Lewisohn taken a bird's eye view of human relations, instead of seeing the Jewish Problem as the utterly unique thing which it is not, he would have realized the inevitability of conflict, now overt and sanguinary, now peaceful but insidious, between any two cultures or religions or peoples that offer as many points of difference as do the Jews and the traditions and peoples they have come into such close contact with. But instead of envisaging this conflict as a perpetually insoluble one, as a sort of fatal conundrum of history, he would, furthermore, have made the less dramatic but far more sober observation that the psychological distance which separates the Jew from the non-Jew today is, by and large, perceptibly less great than it has ever been. Ku Klux Klans and pogroms and the stiffening of Jewish disabilities here and there do not prove that assimilation is impossible, but they prove that it is a far less easily consummated process and a more tortuously winding one than some idealists would like to have it. They reiterate, in short, one of the annoying truisms of history. Mankind has never been unyielding, it has merely been stubbornly disposed not to yield.

"Mr. Lewisohn is quite wrong, I believe, in ruling out assimilation as a solution of the Jewish problem. It is, patently, a very possible and a very excellent one in thousands of individual cases—in spite of the embarrassing fact that many highly educated Jews or very wealthy Jews are debarred from clubs that are deemed desirable of entry. But he is perfectly correct in finding also another solution, for there is no reason whatever to believe that but one solution was preordained. For one thing, it is altogether likely that large masses of Jews will continue to lead a somewhat distinctive life in the midst of other people. This too is a 'solution' as such things go in that flux of human affairs which always refuses to reach the particular equilibrium desired by those who decide on the course of events. For another, the Zionist experiment to which Mr. Lewisohn pins his hopes is an admirable solution insofar as it satisfies the aspirations of many thousands of courageous Jews, inspired by a number of distinct motives. One gains nothing by closing one's eyes to facts and by declaring, out of the rhetorical fervor of one's preference, this or that turn to be the right and only solution. For there is not one Jewish problem, there are many—keenly personal ones of all sorts, and varying group problems conditioned by local circumstances, economic and cultural."[6]

Implicit in these words we may find something of the unresolved tragedy of every sensitive individual whose knowledge of humanity imparts a degree of true clairvoyance. He can see man's career in its broad sweep; he knows that culture goes on, even if men and nations and races disappear; he can trace the stream of history circuitously winding, now toward, now away from the ends he would want to attain. Yet he himself is part of that stream, the current carries him along with all his fellow men, he must struggle and sacrifice to turn the current though in his mind's eye he can see that the turning point is still far ahead—perhaps farther than his own limited strength can reach.

The pat answers and convenient explanations which comfort others bring small solace to him, though he may recognize how great a boon such doctrines can be to many men. Thus, in the Lewisohn review, Sapir wrote of Zionism,

"It is just a little difficult to see how such a movement as Zionism, actuated as it is by the reawakening of the spirit of Jewish nationalism, is to keep itself unalloyed by the necessities and foibles that attend any nationalist undertaking. Perhaps Jewish nationalism, as Mr. Lewisohn would have us believe, is a permanently broadminded and self-sacrificing

[6] *Menorah Journal*, vol. xii (1926) 214-18.

faith, perhaps there *is* an abiding something that is different and finer about the temper of Zionism, an idealism made local through necessity rather than through choice. But the gentle sceptic, fed on history and on a sad belief in the essential sameness of human psychology in every nook and cranny of the world, can only shake his head with that bitter-sweet smile that is at least as Jewish a symbol as the clear-eyed confidence of the nationalist."

The dilemma which arises out of an intuitive vision of the future and from the inescapable participation in the present is in no sense a peculiarly Jewish characteristic, nor one which is confined to any one time, or place, or people. But it has troubled many Jews, perhaps is an innate problem of the Jewish way of life. Judaism has always extended its allegiance to something beyond provincial and parochial walls, yet has always found itself operating within such walls. Let me quote one final paragraph from Sapir's review of *Israel* to illustrate this.

"It seems to me that if there is anything distinctive about the temper of Jewish thought today, it is that it has largely transcended the limits of any localism, however vast and powerful. This temper has been as often the subject of abuse as of favorable comment. Jewish 'disloyalty' and 'negativism,' however, are but terms of disparagement for a spirit that is abroad in the world today and which it is the 'mission' of the Jew—if the romantic philosopher of history must give him a mission—to foster as best he can. This spirit runs counter to the current nationalism which is perhaps more articulate than truly vital. It is not so much a destroyer of folk values as a solvent of them. It refuses to make a fetish of any localism or lineage but insists on utilizing the cultural goods of all localisms and of every lineage for a deeply personal synthesis."

Here then is the way out of the dilemma, the answer to the puzzle. If we are clear about where we want to go—where our Jewish traits would lead us, if you like, then we need have no qualms or fears about working through and working with the social forces and forms about us. Wisdom and vision need not make impotent philosophizers of us all. Let them rather give us added force to act as do men who know where they want to go.

For a long time Sapir's attitude toward Jewish problems was that of the anthropologist whose training admits him to a seat in the press box of the human universe. He saw Jewish matters steadily and saw them whole, as befits a scientific observer. During his latter years, however, he began to feel that a place at the observation post does not exclude one from a share in the play on the field. He became more and more engrossed in and concerned with the problems of being a Jew and with the turmoil of modern events. Sapir's analysis of man's culture led him to affirm the genius of a social group. "It remains true that large groups of people everywhere tend to think and to act in accordance with established and all but instinctive forms, which are in large measure peculiar to it. The question as to whether these forms, that in their interrelations constitute the genius of a people, are primarily explainable in terms of native temperament, of historical development, or of both is of interest to the social psychologist, but need not cause us much concern."[7]

To my way of thinking, Edward Sapir expressed the genius of his people in its finest aspect. Jews are, in a sense, born ethnologists. By virtue of their dual participation in two cultural spheres, that of Judaism and that of their environing society, they are often made sensitive to differences in the forms of culture. They recognize the mannerisms and mores of social behavior for what they are worth—as a means to an end. Hence they are apt to handle the formal ways of culture with solemn respect, yet not be taken in by them. Their ultimate allegiance is to the basic meanings which they recognize beneath the swathings of convention.

So did Sapir evaluate form and meaning in the study of man. Perhaps he was so enamored of linguistics because it is in this most mathematical of social studies that his intuitive hunches as to fundamental formulae beneath formal differences can most definitely be clinched. The span of his life was cut short before he was able to demonstrate the proof of many of his ideas. It is the task of his students to clothe these brilliant intuitions with fitting fact.

---

[7] "Culture, Genuine and Spurious," in *American Journal of Sociology*, vol. xxix (1924) 406.

EDWARD SAPIR*

C. F. VOEGELIN

American anthropology has enjoyed a number of giants dispropor-
tionate to the number of its practitioners. The brightest of these in
the memory of living anthropologists is Edward Sapir ; his brightness
was so conspicuous that hypercritical contemporaries would sometimes question whether so brilliant a light could last long. No one
questioned his solidity, however. Both in terms of solid training and
in terms of solid publications, there was nothing ' light ' about
Sapir ; he was a ' heavyweight ' in the best sense of the term. It may
have been felt as something of a contradiction that any mortal
could—at the same time—be so much of a ' heavyweight ' and so
very, very bright, with a brightness that we associate with youth and
poetry and innocence.

Long ago, when we were discussing these qualities, the present
writer was told by an older colleague that Sapir (who had just then
accepted a job at Yale in both Anthropology and Linguistics) was
overcommitted by his double-barreled job, that he had indeed over-
responded to the opportunities of his job while at Chicago, that he
would never recover the productive phase of the life he had led in
Canada. My older colleague concluded comfortably that ten years
after Sapir's death, graduate students in anthropology would question
why Sapir's contemporaries were so enthusiastic about him ; they
would ask what all the excitement was about . . . Now more than ten
years have elapsed since Sapir died (February 4, 1939), and now
graduate students in anthropology read *The Selected Writings of
Edward Sapir* (published by the University of California Press in

* Reprinted, with permission of G. & C. Merriam Co., Springfield, Mass., publishers
of the Merriam-Webster dictionaries., and the author, from *Word Study* 27, No.4 (April
1952), pp.1-3.

1949), wishing, as many have told me, that they might have known Sapir in person. The peculiar power of stimulating intellectual excitement which Sapir possessed is, as the record shows, still preserved in his writing.

Graduated from Columbia University in 1904 at the age of twenty, Sapir's first graduate work was in Germanics specifically, and more generally in the ancient Indo-European languages. It was Franz Boas who gave him the opportunity to study American Indian languages. For some half dozen predoctoral and postdoctoral years, Sapir studied the Wishram language, spoken in Washington ; Takelma, spoken in Oregon (the subject of his Ph.D. dissertation) ; Yana, spoken in California ; and Paiute, spoken in Utah. These half dozen student years were marked by great phonetic virtuosity, enormous bursts of energy, great hopes. Since the first fresh years of his linguistic experience were spent among languages spoken in the Western states, it is no wonder that the young Sapir longed for an academic post in the West. The middle-aged Sapir always spoke of California with a certain nostalgia—California, the center of more linguistic diversity than was to be found in any other part of the world then available to an academic linguist. How Sapir could be delighted with linguistic diversity is shown in his most readable (and only) book, a decade later—*Language*, published in 1921.

If Sapir viewed his West Coast experience as something he would like to have continued most of his life, it forms a strange contrast to the next phase of his life—his Canadian years. They were sad years, the years from 1910 to 1925 spent as chief of the Division of Anthropology in the Canadian National Museum at Ottawa—years of scholarly solitude and hard though not frustrating work—years of yearning for friendship. The yearning was reflected in long visits from former fellow graduate students, such as Paul Radin, and in frequent visits to New York friends and to that stern teacher, Franz Boas. This yearning may also have been an indirect stimulus for Sapir's poetry and for his musical studies, most of which were done in Ottawa.

Sapir's life was not episodic but rather integrative. Once he had experimented with poetry and music, the subtle and the dramatic never left him. For example, his early work in comparative Uto-Aztecan was as conservative as any work in comparative Indo-

European and also, it was stated in a conservative, scholarly style. After his intensive and deeply personal experiences in writing poetry, Sapir made dramatic comparisons among widely (or as some thought, wildly) divergent languages. Where his predecessor, Powell, counted a half hundred separate language families in North America, Sapir counted a half dozen. His observations were subtle as well as dramatic ; he could discover identities in forms marking personal actors among Algonquian languages of the Great Lakes and in Yurok and Wiyot of California. Though these languages showed few other immediate similarities, Sapir boldly postulated a genetic relationship.

During these personally unhappy but professionally productive years, Sapir's early liking for the West Coast was continued in the languages he chose to study—all west of the continental divide (Nootka as well as Na-dene languages) ; yet all about the Great Lakes and within sight of Ottawa were Algonquian languages which were certainly relevant to Sapir's wide-flung comparisons. He scarcely looked at these. Often, he would stay in his study to write methodological papers, such as the early reviews of psychoanalysis, or his monograph called the *Time Perspective*, which attempts to transfer techniques used in historical linguistics to the advantage of cultural data.

When Sapir left his Ottawa study in 1925, he went to the Great Lakes—to the University of Chicago. But he continued his field trips to western Indians—to the Navaho of the Southwest and to the Hupa of California. All the energy of Sapir's youthfulness, his playful virtuosity, and his pleasure in exhibiting it, returned to him in Chicago. For example, he transcribed for the edification of graduate students a most difficult African language, and solved tonal problems with breath-taking accuracy and speed. Here in Chicago (surrounded for the first time by students) was Sapir at the beginning of his middle age but no longer sedate as in his Canadian years. With a wide audience in literary circles as well as in anthropology, with a national reputation as the most brilliant of all living anthropologists (both for his linguistic work and his fresh theoretical writings), Sapir regained the exuberance of his student days, and their hope.

Sapir went to Yale in 1931 and was followed by most of his Chicago students, and by students from other universities, most of whom already had their doctorates. A small company of postdoctoral fellows in New Haven appreciated Sapir in a more subdued but no less sincere fashion than did his beginning graduate students in Chicago. Such beginners were conspicuously absent at Yale ; and though Sapir continued presenting linguistic seminars for his post-doctoral fellows, his large seminars were devoted to his innovations in anthropological theory—to the impact of culture and personality. The published papers from this period are, in certain parts, unrhymed poems. His theory was not limited to culture and personality, but included semantics. Sapir returned to the ancient Indo-European and Semitic problems of his youth also. It was during the Yale period, particularly, that Sapir became consciously interdisciplinary.

At Yale, Sapir was stimulating as well as stimulated, but no one has seriously suggested that he was happy in New Haven. If he was unable to recapture all his youthful and Chicago exuberance all the time, he could nevertheless be momentarily exuberant—as when his old friend Harry Stack Sullivan would come up from Washington. If he was unhappy, we have much to blame besides the town and gown ; the economic depression was unabated from 1931 to 1939, and Sapir suffered emotionally perhaps more than did postdoctoral fellows at the meager job opportunities for young scholars. If a New England Indian were brought to New Haven for linguistic study, Sapir would be only mildly interested ; even when western Indians, Nootka or Navaho, were brought to town, he was too busy to give as much time as he formerly did to his special field. The theoretical direction of Sapir's thoughts were away from pure linguistics toward culture and personality. Convinced that we live in a semihostile world, Sapir could not escape the conclusion that it is a median number of personalities which make it hostile. As for culture, Sapir could never bring himself to embrace her visible forms as he could those of language. No one has quite understood why, but all are agreed that a man who was by nature exuberant and boyishly happy was less than happy at the end of an extraordinarily brilliant and extraordinarily short life.

PART II

Comments on Sapir's Work, 1919 - 1953

Edward Sapir (Ottawa, 1913)

REVIEW OF *TIME PERSPECTIVE* (1916)*

ROBERT H. LOWIE

Philosophical papers on anthropological matters are rare on this side of the Atlantic, and accordingly Dr. Sapir's essay on the logic of culture-historical studies has met with a warm reception among those of his colleagues who share his interest in theoretical problems. By far the greater part of the paper is devoted to inferential evidence for a temporal arrangement of cultural events; and as might be expected from the author's special lines of work the testimony of physical anthropology is dealt with rather briefly, while considerable space is granted to that of ethnology and proportionately still more to linguistics. This is surely exactly as it should be, since a scholar's most valuable methodological points must develop from his personal experience in the handling of data.

It seems to me accordingly that the linguistic section (pp. 51–85) will prove the most fruitful part of Dr. Sapir's contribution and I wish it were greatly expanded. Here he expounds methods that have proved significant in Old World investigations, but have hitherto remained strangely unfamiliar to the majority of American ethnologists. His demand that field-workers in studying a department of culture should also determine the range and nature of the correlated vocabulary (p. 62) will certainly be welcomed with hearty applause. In his discussion of differentiation the author shows the independence of judgment and constructive boldness that characterize his work in this domain. He insists on a proper weighting of differences before drawing chronological conclusions. Thus, all the Central and Eastern Algonkian languages are considered jointly equivalent to the Arapaho or the Blackfoot branch of the family, whence it is inferred that the pristine home of the stock lies considerably to the west of its present geographical center (p. 80). A corresponding argument is applied to the Athapascan case and to the Eskimo (p. 81 f.).

The ethnological part (pp. 13–51) suffers from a certain degree of formalism. Dr. Sapir recounts all the various methods that have actually been employed in inferring time sequences and his recital partakes somewhat of the enumeration of permissible syllogisms in a textbook of

* Reprinted, with permission of the American Anthropological Association, Washington, D.C., from *American Anthropologist* N.S. 21.75-77 (1919).

logic.   However, this tendency is balanced by the stimulating discussion of specific instances.   The author has evidently sought to draw illustrations from all the principal areas of North America and in view of their range it is not surprising to find a number of errors of detail.   For example, the Mandan can hardly be described as a predominantly agricultural people (p. 27) and the Sun dance was not wholly lacking among the Omaha (p. 49) since their communal hunt embraces a highly distinctive feature of the ceremonial complex, though in an unusual setting.

Considering the place of survivals in the history of our science, the extreme brevity of treatment doled out to them (p. 24) is surprising, even if Dr. Sapir were tempted to take a wholly negative attitude towards the method.

Dr. Sapir's position with reference to certain moot-questions is of interest.   He anticipates in some measure Dr. Wissler's recently expressed ideas on the correlation of race, language, and civilization (p. 11).   He rises in defence of native testimony and is pleased to refer to my own attitude as one of "lofty scepticism" (p. 7).   I must protest that it has all the vulgarity of common sense.   If the same ceremonial complex, e. g., is shared by the Sarsi, Blackfoot, and Crow and each of these peoples insists that it originated with them, it is difficult to reconcile these statements.   The fact that one of them must be correct does not establish the methodological validity of accepting native tradition as history.   No one doubts that traditions going back a hundred years ago or so may contain worth while historical information, though it is astonishing what a slight impression significant events make on the aboriginal consciousness even within so brief a span of time.   As soon as we go back further, we find that relatively advanced tribes like the Zuñi concoct schemes that canno ꞏbe harmonized with objective evidence.   When, finally, we consider that even so eminently historical a people as the Chinese, who possess written records, cannot be trusted absolutely beyond 800 B.C., it would be somewhat rash to accept the testimony of North American Indians in matters involving equal or greater periods.

On the other hand, I find myself in hearty accord with the author in regard to the subject of culture areas (p. 44 seq.).   All that he has to offer on this point merits careful study.   He is certainly warranted in insisting that the culture areas established descriptively as classificatory devices are not chronologically equivalent and require sequential evaluation.   Further we should not ignore the possibility of other than the conventional groupings.   It is true that by stressing material factors, which involve an adjustment to the geographical environment, Wissler has demonstrated a considerable stability of the cultural centers. But when the emphasis is shifted, a different result may appear. Thus, by envisaging the intangible totality of cultures rather than their separate elements Kroeber comes to divide the tribes of the Pacific slope of North America as one unit from the entire remainder of the continent. A grouping on the basis of social organization would certainly produce novel results, which would be somewhat similar but by no means coterminous with those arrived at if attention were concentrated exclusively on kinship terms. Or, taking again the customary point of view for comparison, I have long felt that the Southern Siouan tribes should be linked with the Central Algonkian rather than with the typical Plains people.

These hints must suffice to indicate the importance of Dr. Sapir's paper. Since practice is still better than theory, most readers will clamor for a sequel in which the various methodological principles and cautions shall find application to a concrete problem.

CANADA

DEPARTMENT OF MINES

HON. P. E. BLONDIN, MINISTER; R. G. McCONNELL, DEPUTY MINISTER.

GEOLOGICAL SURVEY

MEMOIR 90

No. 13, ANTHROPOLOGICAL SERIES

Time Perspective in Aboriginal American Culture, A Study in Method

BY

E. Sapir

OTTAWA
GOVERNMENT PRINTING BUREAU
1916

No. 1635

REVIEW OF *LANGUAGE* (1921)*

ROBERT H. LOWIE

Three distinct types of public may be considered by the writer of a treatise on the fundamentals of language—the nondescript general reader, the ethnologist, and the specialist in linguistics. It is true that since few ethnologists are more than laymen in the field of language, the first two classes largely coincide. Nevertheless, the theoretically-minded students of culture will view linguistic phenomena with a peculiar interest and must inevitably draw some parallels between the problems arising in this sharply demarcated province of the social heritage and in the grand totality of culture; and accordingly they may be legitimately reckoned of a separate category.

In the reviewer's opinion Dr. Sapir felicitously solves the problem of appealing to this triple audience. Regarded from the point of view of the laity, his book represents a remarkable achievement in popularization on a very high plane. Relying to an appreciable extent on examples culled from English speech, he succeeds in illustrating the more important processes operative in the history of language. Even the complete novice, provided he is willing to devote some concentrated thinking to the task, will gain a considerable insight into the psychological and historical determinants affecting the growth of speech-forms. He will probably learn with astonishment what far-reaching changes in morphology can be initiated by a sound-shift; and with presumably even greater amazement, how varied are the means by which thought may be symbolically represented in speech, what totally different aspects of reality may be singled out for distinction by different languages. New vistas of another order are likely to rise before him: the relations of thought and speech, of literary style and its linguistic basis, will appear in a new light, while time-honored fallacies, such as those of a close connection between race and language, or between linguistic types and definite stages of civilization, will fade away.

* Reprinted, with permission of the American Anthropological Association, Washington, D.C., from *American Anthropologist* N.S. 25.90-93 (1923).

The theoretically minded ethnologist will find many of his own problems illustrated in novel fashion within the linguistic field—especially so far as they belong to the historical category. Is there such a thing as orthogenetic evolution in culture? Well, in its linguistic compartment, at any rate, Dr. Sapir discovers a definite "drift"—a tendency, moreover, that may persist in languages long after their separation from the parental stock (p. 184), though certainly there is no mystic agency that impels speech towards a predetermined goal: English may become more and more analytic without assuming the character of Indo-Chinese (p. 180). Of tremendous significance in the light of the blatant proclamations of Professor Elliot Smith and the Graebnerian school, are the author's observations on linguistic parallels. Speaking of the principle of concord as noted in Chinook and Bantu, he remarks (p. 122):

It is impressive to observe how the human mind has arrived at the same form of expression in two such historically unconnected regions.

Again (p. 152 f.) he discovers noteworthy similarities between Takelma and Greek,

languages that are as geographically remote from each other and as unconnected in a historical sense as two languages selected at random can well be.

Quite generally, we are told that

broadly similar morphologies must have been reached by unrelated languages, independently and frequently (p. 128);

through what elusive instrumentalities remains a question for the future. But as their variety demonstrates, the formal patterns of languages are quite arbitrary, as much so as, say, certain mythological conceptions; and what applies to the one department of culture must be held to obtain for the other until the champions of the "historical" schools deign to prove the contrary. Those of us, therefore, who while fully alive to the importance of diffusion are not convinced of the impossibility of independent evolution in a limited way will take no small comfort from Dr. Sapir's findings. Another side of his historical thinking will be discussed below.

Speaking tentatively and under correction concerning the professional linguist's attitude, I feel that his attention will be arrested by a number of distinctive features in the book before us. First of all, it has a definitely anthropological orientation. Dr. Sapir, starting from a mastery of the philological technique elaborated and perfected in the Indo-Germanic domain has extended its principles through original field-studies to the languages of American Indians, while simultaneously keeping abreast of the corresponding labors of, say, Meinhof in Africa and of Father Schmidt in the Southeast Asiatic field. The significance of this characteristic becomes clearer when we compare Dr. Sapir's volume with its namesake, still more recently published by Professor Jespersen. There is much sanity in the few pages the Danish scholar devotes to the tongues of primitive peoples, but after all they provide only the border embellishment for the fabric of his philosophy of speech. His ideas, in other words, were formed by researches in the familiar channels and merely found subsidiary exemplification in more exotic spheres. Sapir's views, on the contrary, are cast in a single mould; they are the outcome of a broad-gauge survey of language as such, whether spoken by primitive or lettered peoples.

It must, accordingly, be of peculiar interest to students of language to familiarize themselves with the more general notions evolved on the basis of so wide an inquiry as underlies this little book, even though its space limitations allow no more than a brief exposition, precluding scientific demonstration. Two points merit special attention—the author's classificatory scheme, and his views on the interrelations of distinct languages.

As for the former, it may again be well to contrast Sapir's book with Jespersen's. Jespersen no less than Sapir rejects the traditional tripartite scheme of isolating, agglutinative, and inflectional categories (*Language*, pp. 76–80) but his conclusion that "the structural diversities of languages are too great for us to classify them comprehensively" bears the unsatisfactoriness of all unqualified agnosticism. Sapir, proceeding from a provisional to a revised tabulation of the concepts denoted by grammatical processes (pp. 92 f., 106 f.), groups languages according to their expression of these concepts. The basic query he propounds is, whether a language keeps "the basic relational concepts . . . . free of an admixture of the concrete"; and this leads to a dichotomy into pure-relational and mixed-relational languages. Each of the resulting categories is, then, subdivided into a simple and a complex class, these sub-types being distinguished by the absence or the use of inseparable elements in building up concrete ideas. The conventional terminology, however, is not wholly discarded but merely degraded to the rank of an auxiliary device for characterizing an agglutinative or other trend.

I confess myself wholly incompetent to appraise the value of this scheme, which I must add in justice to its author is put forward in quite undogmatic fashion (p. 153). However, I am impressed by the provisional historical evidence cited in favor of the proposition that we are here dealing with phenomena coming nearer the essentials of speech than those envisaged by earlier classifiers and I shall eagerly await the verdict of those entitled to a professional judgment. Should Dr. Sapir's views stand sustained, it is quite clear that they would constitute a landmark in the progress of linguistic science.

Finally, a word or two must be devoted to Dr. Sapir's ideas on historical relationships. To put the matter briefly, he accepts of course the borrowing of foreign words, admits the diffusion of phonetic features "over a continuous area in somewhat the same way that elements of culture ray out from a geographical center" (p. 213), but finds no historical evidence for any but superficial outside influences on morphology (p. 217). This, however, leads to a dilemma, for as a matter of fact important structural traits are distributed over major areas, where they are shared by languages differing so widely as to be reckoned genetically unrelated by orthodox science. Dr. Sapir contends that while some resemblances may be interpreted as due to independent evolution, as set forth above, this explanation no longer holds when the parallels are of too specific a nature. In that case it is necessary to revise the received classification and to shift the boundaries staked out for linguistic families, in other words to regard as genetically connected certain stocks hitherto treated as distinct. Our guide in the re-formulation of the historical grouping must be "contrastive perspective"—the comparative weighting of similarities and dissimilarities obtaining among a series of progressively more divergent languages (pp. 217–220).

It must not be supposed that the somewhat heretical position maintained by Dr. Sapir on historical interrelationships is put forward in obtrusive fashion. Those who know how definitely he adheres in more technical publications to the view outlined will admire the self-restraint exercised in compressing deep-seated convictions within the narrow compass of three pages. Such reverence for the general reader is not common among writers of popular works. This reserve, however, is only typical of the entire book, which is noticeably free from crotchetiness. Indeed, rarely is such freshness of outlook coupled with such judgment and taste. An Attic flavor pervades the volume as a whole. I know of no general work put forth by American anthropological scholarship of which we have more reason to be proud.

REVIEW OF *LANGUAGE* (1921)*

LEONARD BLOOMFIELD

This book is in every way to be commended to the general reader. The presentation is zestful; on the score of clearness no reader will complain who realizes that he must contribute some effort if he wants to learn things. In matters of human conduct, such as speech, we are so much under the spell of fetishes and tabus that no writer can spare us hard work, if we are to wrench ourselves away from these and acquire a scientific outlook. Although Dr. Sapir says in his Preface (iii) that his main purpose is to show "what I conceive language to be", the general reader may be assured that the book is dependable, for the author's conception is evidently the result of wide study and scientific experience.

For the specialist also Dr. Sapir's book is of interest, for it contains not only those general statements upon which all students of language are agreed, but also well-grounded expressions of opinion upon matters still under discussion. As regards these latter, Dr. Sapir in almost every instance favors those views which I, for one, believe to be in accord with our best knowledge of speech and of the ways of man. As Dr. Sapir gives no bibliography, one cannot say how much of his agreement with scholars who have expressed similar views is a matter of independent approach. For instance, on page 57 the author develops what he justly calls "an important conception",—the "inner" or "ideal" phonetic system of a language: it is exactly the concept of *distinctive features* developed by the school of Sweet, Passy, and Daniel Jones (see, for instance, the Principles of the International Phonetic Association [London, 1912], or, for the practical application, S. K. Chatterji's Brief Sketch of Bengali Phonetics [London, 1921], especially 3). The same concept was developed (independently, I think) by Franz Boas (Handbook of American Indian Languages, 16) and by de Saussure (Cours de Linguistique Générale [Paris, 1916]). It is a question of no scientific moment, to be sure, but of some external interest, whether Dr. Sapir had at hand, for instance, this last book, which gives a theoretic foundation to the newer trend of linguistic study.

* Reprinted, with permission of the Editor of *The Classical World,* from *The Classical Weekly* 15.142-43 (13 March 1922).

This newer trend affects two critical points. We are coming to believe that restriction to historical work is unreasonable and, in the long run, methodically impossible. One is glad to see, therefore, that Dr. Sapir deals with synchronic matters (to use de Saussure's terminology) before he deals with diachronic, and gives to the former as much space as to the latter. The second point is that we are casting off our dependence on psychology, realizing that linguistics, like every science, must study its subject-matter in and for itself, working on fundamental assumptions of its own; that only on this condition will our results be of value to related sciences (especially, in our case, to psychology) and in the light of these related sciences in the outcome more deeply understandable. In other words, we must study people's habits of language—the way people talk—without bothering about the mental processes that we may conceive to underlie or accompany these habits. We must dodge this issue by a fundamental assumption, leaving it to a separate investigation, in which our results will figure as data alongside the results of the other social sciences. Dr. Sapir is here again in the modern trend; his whole presentation deals with the actualities of language rather than with hypothetical mental parallels. Especially well put is the following passage (9–10):

> From the physiologist's or psychologist's point of view we may seem to be making an unwarrantable abstraction in desiring to handle the subject of speech without constant and explicit reference to that basis. However, such an abstraction is justifiable. We can profitably discuss the intention, the form, and the history of speech, precisely as we discuss the nature of any other phase of human culture—say art or religion—as an institutional or cultural entity, leaving the organic and psychological mechanisms back of it as something to be taken for granted. . . . Our study of language is not to be one of the genesis and operation of a concrete mechanism; it is, rather, to be an inquiry into the function and form of the arbitrary systems of symbolism that we term languages.

Where Dr. Sapir falls short in this respect, he does only what all the rest of us have done. His definition of the sentence, for example (36), goes right back to the irrelevant subject-and-predicate notion of logic[1], and is controverted by his own material, especially by his illuminating analysis of an English sentence (92–93), which is a good example of real linguistics. Had Dr. Sapir taken Meillet's definition (Introduction à l'Étude Comparée des Langues Indo-européennes[3], [Paris, 1912], 339), he would have had a definition in terms of linguistics—a definition, that is, in accord with the

---

[1] Compare (98): "In every intelligible proposition at least two of these radical ideas must be expressed, though in exceptional cases . . .".

first thirty-five pages of his book, with the whole tendency of his exposition, and, in particular, with his description of the *word*, which he himself seems to distrust, saying (35), "In practice this unpretentious criterion does better service than might be supposed", an apology which is really a powerful proof of correctness. I wish to quote with approval in this connection this statement (13–14), "From the point of view of language, thought may be defined as the highest latent or potential content of speech, the content that is obtained by interpreting each of the elements in the flow of language as possessed of its very fullest conceptual value", and with approval to refer to such passages as that on the parts of speech (123–124). On the other hand, such questions as "What, then, are the absolutely essential concepts in speech. . . ?" (98), and such a passage as that on page 126 are out of accord with the author's own method in concrete problems. Such classifications as are attempted in the tables on pages 106–107 and 150–151 are similarly irrelevant, and are, indeed, invalidated by the author's own reservations. Like the rest of us, Dr. Sapir still pays tribute to aprioristic speculation which steals upon us in the guise of psychology; as his own approach is scientific, these false generalizations stand out from the rest of the discussion. Dr. Sapir has less of them than his predecessors; whoever is interested in the progress of our science will welcome his book as a forward step.

It is important, in the expansion of our science to its just province, that we should not commit the obvious fault of losing the historical accuracy of our predecessors; accordingly one regrets an error of principle in the historical part (190), where the author speaks as if the contrast of vowels in *foot* : *boot* were a matter of sound-change now in progress. Of course sound-change while in progress does not show itself to us in this or any other way; the contrast in question is due to a sound-change dated about 1700, followed by varying distribution of the resultant forms in Standard English (see Wyld, History of Modern Colloquial English, 238 f.). The understanding of the process of sound-change—of immense "diagnostic value" for psychology, ethnology, and, indeed, all forms of human science —is our most valuable heritage from the purely historical linguistics of the nineteenth century. It represents the phase of work in which our predecessors refrained from premature psychologic interpretation, and it is probably premature psychologic interpretation which leads Dr. Sapir to ignore this result[2]. This is hardly worth mentioning, were it not that we

---

[2] Similarly, the statement about the umlaut-plural of German *Tag* (204) is wrong: it occurs in a number of dialects, and has parallels in Middle High German.

who conceive of a science of human speech must not justify a criticism with which rule-of-thumb workers are only too ready.

The chapter on How Languages Influence Each Other (205–220) is especially suggestive and interesting. The last chapters, however, which discuss the relation of language to other phases of human conduct, yield scant results (221–235, 236–247), because these other phases are as yet little known to science. "Race", for instance, is not a scientific concept, but a popular notion developed in rationalization of certain inter-ethnic contacts. And, as to other such matters, what can be said in the way of science, when (242) the style of Mr. George Moore receives praise?

LANGUAGE

AN INTRODUCTION TO THE STUDY
OF SPEECH

BY

EDWARD SAPIR

NEW YORK
HARCOURT, BRACE AND COMPANY

A STUDY OF LANGUAGE*

A. L. KROEBER

... there is much in the chapter on Types of Linguistic Structure, a subject in which philologists have for a century been at their most logical, prejudiced, hard and fast, ineffective, and worst, with a classification into isolating, agglutinative, and inflective types — compartments that accommodate perhaps thirty per cent of the languages of mankind. [...]

Sapir's own classification, which follows these thrusts, is too finely integrated a conception to be mutilated in abbreviation here. One does not pack the delicate structure of an organism into a sentence, nor try to convey the quality of a great painting in a twenty-stroke sketch. The professionals will have their reaction to this new approach — unless they find it most convenient to ignore altogether. How far Sapir's scheme will stand permanently, only time can tell.
[...]

The general reader will be even more interested in the chapter on Language, Race and Culture; and writers, in the final one on Language and Literature. This last starts off with a fascinating search for the causes that make one piece of literature reasonably translatable, and another — a ballad of Swinburne, for instance — so hopelessly baffling in any but its original medium. Sapir finds the reason in two levels of which speech is composed: a generalized, latent layer, and an upper one in which the particular conformation of each language inheres. Literature that moves chiefly in the upper stratum is as good as untranslatable. Yet every language, being a medium of its own, exacts in some measure a style peculiar to it. [...]

There is not a diacritical mark in this book, yet its philology is sound; not a foot-note reference, yet it is scholarly; not a page that is difficult for an interested layman, yet it opens new paths of thought. A rare felicity pervades it, a freedom from the hackneyed; and its balance equals its spontaneity. It is unique in its field, and is likely to become and long remain standard.

* Excerpted from "A Study of Language [= Review of Sapir's *Language*]", published in *The Dial: A monthly review and index of current literature* 72:3 (New York, March 1922), pp.314-17; here: p.316-17.

Selected Writings of
Edward Sapir
in Language, Culture and Personality

EDITED BY DAVID G. MANDELBAUM

1949
Berkeley and Los Angeles
UNIVERSITY OF CALIFORNIA PRESS

REVIEW OF *SELECTED WRITINGS* (1949)*

HARRY HOIJER

Edward Sapir (1884–1939), an outstanding anthropologist and linguist, died before he had the opportunity to assemble his writings in many fields into definitive book-length works. As a result, only his major work, *Language: An Introduction to the Study of Speech* (New York: Harcourt Brace, 1921), has any considerable circulation. All else that he wrote must be searched out of various more or less obscure periodical publications, and has necessarily remained almost unknown to all but a few specialists in the disciplines to which Sapir contributed. The volume under review should correct this situation, for it very adequately fulfills the editor's objective, that is, "to present, in accessible form, those of Sapir's writings which carry the gist of his thought" (p. xi). Dr. Mandelbaum divides his book into three parts, entitled "Language," "Culture," and "The Interplay of Culture and Personality," respectively. The first part on language has three sections, "The Nature of Language," "Studies of American Indian Languages," and "Studies of Indo-European and Semitic Languages," and takes up somewhat more than half the book. The second part (on culture) is similarly divided: "The General View," "American Indians," and "Literature and Music," while the last part requires no sub-division. Mandelbaum has written an excellent introduction, a brief sketch of Sapir's life and work, and has also provided each part and section of the book with a short preface, in which he relates the papers reprinted to others not included. There is also a complete bibliography of all of Sapir's writings, scientific, popular, and literary, but there is unfortunately no index.

Though the book contains many of Sapir's papers on non-linguistic subjects, we shall discuss only his linguistic contributions, and leave for others a review of his anthropological work. In linguistics, in-

* © 1951 by The Regents of the University of California. Reprinted from *Romance Philology* 4:4.311-15 (May 1951), by permission of The Regents.

disputably Sapir's main interest, his work is remarkable, both for its contribution to our knowledge of many obscure and so-called primitive tongues, mainly of aboriginal America, and for its theoretical and methodological importance. Sapir collected field data, some of which is very detailed, on more than seventeen American Indian languages and one West African tongue, and published a number of noteworthy articles in both the Indo-European and Semitic fields. Though Boas, Sapir's teacher, is quite properly called the first truly scientific student of American Languages, Sapir must be credited with the significant achievement of consolidating and outlining the basic problems, historical and structural, which the field affords. To him also must go the credit for encouraging and training students, first at the University of Chicago (1925–1931) and later at Yale University (1931–1939). Nearly all the outstanding scholars who are today active in American Indian linguistics owe their education, directly or indirectly, to Sapir.

Sapir's field studies of American Indian languages cover a wide range of highly diversified idioms. Where the Indo-European or Semitic scholar works in large part within the boundaries of a single language family, Sapir's efforts took him into languages belonging to many distinct stocks, some of which are probably as far apart as Indo-European and Sinitic. He published two full length monographs, one on Takelma of the Penutian stock (his doctoral dissertation) and the other on Southern Paiute of the Shoshonean stock, which are still unsurpassed as models of descriptive methodology. His work on Yana (Hokan stock), Nootka (Wakashan stock), and Navaho (Athapaskan stock), contained in collections of texts and a large number of articles, is equally good, though only a portion of these data have been published. Finally, we find a number of shorter collections of data, represented in brief articles on Chinook, Wishram, Tutelo, Comox, Chimariko, Haida, Sarcee, and Gweabo (Jabo), a West African language. It should be noted that most of these idioms belong to distinctive stocks or widely divergent branches of larger linguistic families. In addition to the unpublished data on Yana, Navaho, and Nootka already mentioned, Sapir left much more, primarily on the Athapaskan languages, Sarcee, Hupa, and Kutchin.

But Sapir did not confine himself alone to purely descriptive studies. He contributed significantly to the problem of classifying American Indian languages, in particular those of North America. Here Sapir struck out boldly, suggesting, and often documenting, genetic relationships of wide scope. His more famous papers along this line are, first, a series linking the widespread Shoshonean family of the Great Basin to Aztec of the Valley of Mexico, and proposing a still more remote tie-up between these and Tanoan, a Pueblo group; second, a paper suggesting that the Athapaskan languages of Canada, the Pacific coast, and the American Southwest are ultimately relatable to Tlinkit and Haida of the North Pacific coast; third, a long paper documenting certain fundamental structural parallels between the Hokan languages of California, the Coahuiltecan of Texas, and Subtiaba-Tlappanec of Nicaragua; and fourth, a pair of papers containing the suggestion that Wiyot and Yurok of California are remote outliers of the great Algonkin family, found for the most part east of the Mississippi. Finally, Sapir worked out a highly tentative and largely impressionistic classification of all North American Indian languages, which reduced some fifty-odd families to six major groups, a work which illustrates, more than any other, Sapir's phenomenal control of linguistic data. More important, all of these papers on historical problems illustrate Sapir's extraordinary insight into the fundamentals of diverse linguistic structures, which enabled him to perceive and describe parallelisms and similarities, even where these are heavily overlaid by later developments peculiar to each language.

This flair for comparative studies and analytical insight led Sapir to one of his most interesting theoretical formulations, that of linguistic drift. This concept was first presented systematically in his book *Language*, but is illustrated over and over again in the historical papers referred to above, some of which appeared earlier than the book. Briefly, Sapir defines the concept as follows. Calling attention to individual variations in speech within a given language community (*Language*, pp. 157–160), he goes on to say:

If individual variations 'on a flat' were the only kind of variability in language, I believe we should be at a loss to explain why and how dialects arise, why it is that a linguistic prototype gradually breaks up into a number of mutually unintelligible languages. But language is not merely something that is spread out in space, as it were—a series of reflections in individual minds of one and the same timeless picture. Language moves down time in a current of its own making. It has a drift. If there were no breaking up of a language into dialects, if each language continued as a firm, self-contained unity, it would still be constantly moving away from any assignable norm, developing new features unceasingly and gradually transforming itself into a language so different from its starting point as to be in effect a new language (*Language*, pp. 160–161).

If the historical changes that take place in a language, if the vast accumulation of minute modifications which in time results in the complete remodeling of the language, are not in essence identical with the individual variations that we note on every hand about us, if these variations are born only to die without a trace, while the equally minute, or even minuter, changes that make up the drift are forever imprinted on the history of the language, are we not imputing to this history a certain mystical quality? ... And if this drift of language is not merely the familiar set of individual variations seen in vertical perspective, that is historically, instead of horizontally, that is in daily experience, what is it? Language exists only in so far as it is actually used... What significant changes take place in it must exist, to begin with, as individual variations. This is perfectly true, and yet it by no means follows that the general drift of language can be understood from an exhaustive descriptive study of these variations alone. They themselves are random phenomena ... The linguistic drift has direction. In other words, only those individual variations embody it or carry it which move in a certain direction, just as only certain wave movements in the bay outline the tide. The drift of a language is constituted by the unconscious selection on the part of its speakers of those individual variations that are cumulative in some special direction (*ibid.*, pp. 165–166).

The concept is then illustrated at some length from English and other Indo-European languages in the remainder of the chapter (pp. 167–182), illustrations too long to include here. The curious reader may also find the notion of drift illustrated in "The Hokan Affinity of Subtiaba in Nicaragua," a paper unfortunately omitted from the volume under review, but easily available in the *American Anthropologist*, XXVII, 402–435, 491–527. No one of Sapir's students, except possibly the late B. L. Whorf, has further applied the concept of drift, and none have developed its theoretical implications. It remains, nevertheless, an historical concept of exciting potentialities, not only for linguistics but as well for the study of culture generally.

Though Sapir's earlier work in linguistics tended to center on descriptive and historical studies, he later began to write on some more general problems of linguistic theory. A few of these problems are treated in *Language* (see especially chaps. IV, V, and VI), but others find only partial exploitation in brief articles. Sapir laid the foundations of much of modern phonemic theory in the following two articles, included in the volume under review: "Sound Patterns in Language" (pp. 33–45) and "The Psychological Reality of Phonemes" (pp. 46–60). Another article, "A Study of Phonetic Symbolism" (pp. 61–72), outlines an experimental approach to the study of speech sounds and their primary symbolic values. Data pertinent to the task of creating an international language are examined in "The Function of an International Language" (pp. 110–121), "Grading: A Study in Semantics" (pp. 122–149), and in two longer papers not included by Mandelbaum: "Totality" (Linguistic Society of America, *Language Monographs*, No. VI, 1930) and "The Expression of the Ending-Point Relation in English, French, and German" (Linguistic Society of America, *Language Monographs*, No. X, 1932). Interest in problems bordering the fields of linguistics and psychology resulted in "Speech as a Personality Trait" (pp. 533–543), "The Unconscious Patterning of Behavior in Society" (pp. 544–559), and "Language as a Form of Human Behavior" (*The English Journal*, XVI [1927], 421–433).

Sapir also found time to make linguistics better known to social scientists generally and to elucidate the many ways in which the scientific study of language can be of material aid in solving problems in both the understanding and the history of human cultures. The book *Language* was written for the layman rather than the specialist, and chaps. X and XI on "Language, Race, and Culture," and "Language and Literature," respectively, are still authoritative in their field. Similarly useful introductions to linguistic science are found in his articles in the *Encyclopedia of the Social Sciences* on "Communication," "Dialect," "Language," and "Symbolism." An outstanding review of linguistic techniques for the study of culture history may be found in "Time Perspective in Aboriginal American Culture: A Study in Method" (pp. 389–462, see especially pp. 432–459), which is still a "must" for beginning students in anthropology. Other papers on the relation of language to culture and to cultural anthropology include "Language and Environment" *American Anthropologist*, XIV [1912], 226–242), "Abnormal Types of Speech in Nootka" (pp. 179–196), and "The Status of Linguistics as a Science" (pp. 160–166).

But it is quite impossible to do justice to Sapir's brilliant scholarship merely by listing his papers. To get the full flavor of his work, one must read the selections themselves, as fresh and to the point today as when they were written. Each contribution, however brief, never fails to suggest new lines of approach to linguistic problems and to open new avenues of research. And it is in this provocative and stimulating faculty that Sapir served linguistics best, both in his writings and in his classroom teaching. For his work goes on in the researches and writings of his students and students' students, who today are following the numerous lines of research and study he opened to them.

Dr. Mandelbaum has performed an important and useful service in bringing Sapir's papers together and so encouraging and making easy a re-study of the main bulk of his work. There is little doubt that those who dip into this collection, if they are at all concerned with linguistic or anthropological problems, will go on to study the papers which had to be omitted for lack of space. An editor can scarcely hope for a better response.

Sapir's residence during 1915-16 at 67 Aylmer St., Ottawa

Sapir's residence during 1917-20 at 1 Findlay Ave., Ottawa

REVIEW OF *SELECTED WRITINGS* (1949)*

STANLEY NEWMAN

The task of selecting a representative collection of Sapir's writings would tax the judgment of any editor. For in spite of Sapir's short life, his monographs, articles, and reviews flowed in a voluminous and steady stream over a productive period of nearly thirty-five years. His writings encompassed a wide range of topics in several distinct disciplines. And the quality of his writing was maintained at a level of originality and richness that was just as steady as its volume. Sapir did not seem to experience the ups and downs of inventiveness that normally plague a writer. Even in a brief review, where he would ostensibly be discussing a specific book, his fresh insights illuminated a circle of new problems with unsuspected significance.

In spite of the difficulties involved in choosing a representative group of Sapir's writings, David Mandelbaum has performed the task with admirable skill and sensitivity. Prefacing the volume is a brief introduction, presenting the salient facts of Sapir's life and the main characteristics of his personality.

The selections are grouped into three major parts: Language, Culture, and The Interplay of Culture and Personality. The first two parts are each subdivided into three topical sections. A short editor's preface, introducing each part or section, points out some of the themes and the significance of the constituent papers. In these prefaces and in the introduction Mandelbaum shows a keen understanding of the recurring motifs that were manifested in Sapir's thinking and wide-ranging curiosity. The book ends with a bibliography of Sapir's scientific papers and other prose writings, compiled by Leslie Spier, and a separate bibliography of Sapir's poems, prepared by his son, Philip.

Half of the book is given over to the part on Language, which comprises three sections: The Nature of Language, Studies of American Indian Languages, and Studies of Indo-European and Semitic Languages. The first section contains twelve papers which include: articles which were originally published in *Language* and might be classed as general linguistics; several papers stressing the psychological and cultural aspects of language, those which appeared in psychological journals, in the *American Anthropologist*, or in the *Encyclopaedia of the Social Sciences*; one of his articles, "The Concept of Phonetic Law as Tested in Primitive Languages by Leonard Bloomfield," dealing with comparative linguistic methods; one of his contributions to the problems of an international auxiliary language; and one of his semantic studies, the paper on "Grading."

In the second section are reprinted six of Sapir's papers in the field of American Indian languages. His descriptive studies are not represented here, for the book, after all, is primarily aimed at a non-linguistic audience. Even in this section the emphasis is peripheral to linguistics in its narrowest sense. Two of the papers, "Abnormal Types of Speech in Nootka" and "Male and Female Forms of Speech in Yana," deal with linguistic devices characterizing certain socially defined groups in these two cultures. The Nootka article takes up the problem of the historical development of these abnormal types of speech, which resemble speech defects but function as mocking forms or as styles of speech identifying certain folktale characters. The historical perspective is emphasized more thoroughly in "Internal Linguistic Evidence Suggestive of the Northern Origin of the Navaho," which illustrates how comparative linguistic

* Reprinted, with permission of The University of Chicago Press, the author, and the editor, from *International Journal of American Linguistics* 17.180-86 (1951).

data can be utilized to reconstruct the history of group migrations. The possible similarities in the phonological development of glottalized continuants in several unrelated languages are examined in "Glottalized Continuants in Navaho, Nootka, and Kwakiutl (with a note on Indo-European)." The "note" of some half-dozen pages is a succinct presentation of Sapir's views on the Indo-European laryngeal hypothesis. The section also includes a study in comparative linguistics, "A Chinookan Phonetic Law," and the contribution to linguistic classification, "Central and North American Languages."

The third section, Studies of Indo-European and Semitic Languages, contains four papers and one review. Here Sapir's interests were principally in comparative and etymological problems.

The 13-page bibliography prepared by Spier, which contains some 300 entries, provides a clear story of the range of Sapir's publications and the shifts in his interests. The first ten years, from 1906 through 1915, were primarily devoted to descriptive studies in American Indian languages. During this time he published texts, vocabularies, descriptive sketches or fragments on Kwakiutl, Chinook, Yana, Wishram, Wasco, Takelma, Ute, Paiute, Nootka, Tutelo, Chasta Costa, Comox. Toward the end of this period another aspect of American Indian linguistics was brought into focus. Sapir's background of training in Semitic and in Indo-European comparative linguistics were now applied to American Indian languages. In 1913 he, published the first of his papers on "Southern Paiute and Nahuatl, a Study in Uto-Aztekan," the other two in the series appearing in 1915. This substantial study of nearly a hundred pages represents, as far as I know, the first application to American Indian languages of the comparative method based upon the analysis of systematic phonetic correspondences and directed toward the reconstruction of the sound system in a parent lan-

guage. During these years he also published some of his Algonkian studies as well as his paper on "The Na-dene Languages, a Preliminary Report." It is a revealing commentary on Sapir's character that when he wrote an article, nearly twenty years later, demonstrating the application of the comparative approach to American Indian languages he entitled it "The Concept of Phonetic Law as Tested in Primitive Languages by Leonard Bloomfield."

The period of 1916 through 1925, which covered the last ten years of his fifteen-year stay in Ottawa, brought significant new currents into the broadening stream of his interests. He continued, though less intensively, to publish descriptive studies in American Indian languages. The full-length grammar of Takelma appeared in this period, based upon data collected some ten years earlier. His detailed and meticulous description of Southern Paiute, not published until 1930, was completed in 1917. He also wrote descriptive articles on Nootka, Yana, Kutenai, Chimariko, Haida, Sarcee. Comparative linguistics drew more of his attention than it had previously, but his interest turned increasingly toward structural comparisons rather than phonological analyses. He kept on publishing comparative studies in Athabascan and Algonkian, and it was during these years that he wrote all of his articles on the Hokan problem and his one paper on Penutian.

Sapir's contributions to American Indian linguistics should correct the impression that he was a writer who produced only one book, *Language*, with the remainder of his work appearing in the form of brief articles. It is true that he had a special flair for condensing a problem or a point of view in the ten-to-twenty-page article which is the favored literary form of scholarly journals. But he did not by any means confine himself to this form. He also wrote many longer articles, and he produced about a dozen monograph-length or book-length grammars, text collections, and comparative studies in American Indian languages.

But, in addition to his linguistic work in the American Indian field, Sapir's writings during this period reveal the new trend that was to become the absorbing interest of his life. He began to venture beyond the strict confines of linguistics and to seek new perspectives for the phenomena of language that would relate it to other forms of human behavior. About half of his monograph of 1916, *Time Perspective in Aboriginal American Culture: A Study in Method*, discusses the types of linguistic evidence which can be utilized for reconstructing culture history. His book *Language*, published in 1921, contains sections and chapters which show the same tendency to explore wider problems. But the book should be regarded as merely an evidence of his early attempts in this direction, for he later abandoned or completely restated many of the problems discussed in its pages, such as the relation between language and thought, or the characteristics of language as a form of art—an idea in which he was apparently stimulated at the time through his reading of Croce.

In 1925 he wrote his first article on an international auxiliary language. The same year saw the publication of "Sound Patterns in Language," the first article, I believe, in which he used the term "phoneme." To Sapir the phoneme concept was significant, not so much as a methodological tool for the linguist, but rather as a powerful and clear demonstration of the unconscious patterning of human behavior. Essentially, he attempted to show in this article that speech sounds cannot be fruitfully understood as a mere set of articulatory motor habits: two languages "may have identical sounds but utterly distinct phonetic patterns; or they may have mutually incompatible phonetic systems, from the articulatory and acoustic standpoint, but identical or similar patterns."

One can gain some notion of the new sources of stimulation and vitality that entered Sapir's work during the 1916–1925 period by examining his writings outside of linguistics. Ethnological papers continued to appear as before. But in 1917 he published reviews of Freud's *Delusion and Dream* and of Oskar Pfister's *The Psychoanalytic Method*. These were the first indications in his writings of an interest that was to continue throughout his life. Articles and reviews on music and literature also began to appear during these years. And in 1917 he began to publish poetry, whose volume and whose significance to his thinking should not be overlooked. He published one book of verse and over a hundred poems or groups of poems in many literary journals of Canada and the United States. These were no amateurish effusions which he tossed off now and then in his lighter moments. In fact, it might be said of Sapir that he could not approach any task in the true spirit of an amateur or a dilettante. He worked at poetry with the same unrelaxing energy and incisiveness of mind that characterized his efforts in linguistics or ethnology.

His experience with poetry had a distinctive influence upon his prose style. Sapir was always a competent writer of expository prose. Even his earliest papers show that he never lacked the ability to write the clear, precise, well-organized, though somewhat colorless prose characteristic of the better academic writings. But his prose from about 1920 began to take on new dimensions. One can notice a growth in the apparently effortless and graceful fluency of his expression. Certain verbal habits peculiar to poetry invaded his prose. Even passages pulled out of context from his later writings are eminently quotable, for he became skillful in the use of the packed phrase, the vibrant word, the familiar image reset in an unfamiliar context to evoke fresh and unsuspected implications of a theme.

His writing continued to be clear and

ordered in its conceptual exposition, but he emphasized more and more the control of evocative overtones in any topic he discussed. He set out to capture, not only the intellects of his readers, but their feelings and attitudes as well, and anyone who knew Sapir can have little doubt that he did this with utter frankness and a full consciousness of what he was doing. Instead of continuing to master the one style of conventional academic writing, he became adept at handling many styles. He preferred to play a variety of stylistic tunes in one and the same article, shifting imperceptibly from a sober argument, to an imaginative play with words and concepts, to an interlude of wit and humor—and Sapir became increasingly fond of indulging in passages of academic leg-pulling—back to the sober line of argument again. It is this breadth and variety in his control over language which gives his writing its color and refreshing vitality.

The implications of Sapir's holistic use of language—his attempt to write for the reader as a person rather than as a disembodied intellect—were realized more fully in his publications after he returned to the United States in 1925. He practically stopped writing descriptive and comparative studies in American Indian languages. Most of the few American Indian papers which appeared were apparently based upon previously collected materials and merely edited for publication during this period. He became more interested in utilizing this data to illustrate socially and psychologically significant modes of behavior in language. Several entire articles were written in this vein, such as "Nootka Baby Words" (1929), "Male and Female Forms of Speech in Yana" (1929), "Two Navaho Puns" (1932), his earlier papers dealing with the kinship systems of several American Indian languages, and his "Abnormal Types of Speech in Nootka" (1915). Throughout many articles he drew upon his American Indian linguistic data for ex-

amples to pinpoint a broader theme. This technique—the presentation of concrete examples, followed by an explanation of their meaning and significance in a more inclusive frame of reference—became a favorite mode of exposition with Sapir.

This period saw a revival of his earlier interest in historical and comparative studies of the Indo-European and Semitic languages. The Hittite problem stimulated him to examine Hittite-Indo-European relationships and to publish several papers on his results. In one article he traced certain influences of Tibetan on Tocharian, which he believed to be a "Tibetanized Indo-European idiom." He had additional data on the Tocharian-Tibetan problem, and early in his career he had collected Sinitic materials in exploring Sinitic-Nadene relationships. But this article, which appeared in 1936, three years before his death, is the only published account of his Sinitic studies, most of which still remain in his unpublished files.

He also continued publishing articles on the problems of an international constructed language. And it was during this period that he wrote his three papers in the field of semantics—*Totality, The Expression of the Ending-Point Relation in English, French, and German,* and "Grading, A Study in Semantics."

The bulk of his articles after 1925, however, reflected his primary interest in pushing language study beyond the conventional boundaries of linguistics. Some of his general articles during these years—"Philology" (1926), "Communication," (1931), "Dialect" (1931), "Language" (1933), "Symbolism" (1934)—outlined the multiple facets of linguistic phenomena as they impinge on problems of individual and group behavior. This point of view was presented in a programmatic manner in "The Status of Linguistics as a Science" (1929), whose purpose, in spite of its title, was "not to insist on what linguistics has already accomplished, but rather to point out some of the connections between linguistics and other scientific disciplines." In this paper he stressed the strategic importance of linguistics for the methodology of social science. In the concluding sentences of this article he wrote:

Better than any other social science, linguistics shows by its data and methods, necessarily more easily defined than the data and methods of any other type of discipline dealing with socialized behavior, the possibility of a truly scientific study of society which does not ape the methods nor attempt to adopt unrevised the concepts of the natural sciences. It is peculiarly important that linguists, who are often accused, and accused justly, of failure to look beyond the pretty patterns of their subject matter, should become aware of what their science may mean for the interpretation of human conduct in general. Whether they like it or not, they must become increasingly concerned with the many anthropological, sociological, and psychological problems which invade the field of language.

The content of language was, to Sapir, significant as "a symbolic guide to culture." "We see and hear and otherwise experience very largely as we do because the language habits of our community predispose certain choices of interpretation." The individual's behavior in language was also important as symptomatic of his personality, and this theme he discussed in detail in "Speech as a Personality Trait" (1926). But it was the evidence of form in language which impressed Sapir as having the deepest implications for an understanding of human behavior. Linguistic form was a patterned phenomenon; in the individual or the group these formal configurations were adhered to or recreated unconsciously and intuitively. Sapir unceasingly hammered at this theme in his articles, whether written for linguists, psychologists, or social scientists. In "The Unconscious Patterning of Behavior in Society" (1927), a paper which appeared in a symposium addressed primarily to psychologists, Sapir used linguistic data as his prize exhibit, but he also attempted to show that unconscious patterning was characteristic of non-linguistic

forms of behavior as well. He translated this concept into psychoanalytic terms, though perhaps with his tongue in his cheek, when he wrote in an earlier book review of the need for discovering a social psychology of "form-libido." In short, language provided the clearest and most easily described evidence of the fundamental human tendency to mold behavior into unconscious patterns of form.

The reader who is aware of this guiding theme in Sapir's thinking will also be aware that it is somewhat arbitrary to divide Sapir's writings into the categories of 1) Language, 2) Culture, and 3) The Interplay of Culture and Personality. In editing the volume of selected writings, Mandelbaum set up these three categories as a necessary convenience, serving to organize the material into conventionally recognized fields and to highlight the diversity of Sapir's contributions. But to Sapir these were not separate fields, and his writings, particularly during the last 15 or 20 years of his life, explain and reiterate his reasons for considering them as an indissolubly fused whole. The danger of this division is that the unwary linguist may, in the first place, read the papers in Part One headed "Language" and find a good deal that seems to be peripheral to his discipline. As a matter of fact, about half of these papers were originally published outside of linguistic journals or sources. In the second place, the too-busy linguist may fail to read the other parts of the volume and thus miss a number of papers that are just as relevant to linguistics. Part Two, "Culture," contains the *Time Perspective* paper, the last half of which—some forty pages—gives a concentrated presentation of the methods for using linguistic evidence to work out time perspectives. This paper should be required reading for students in linguistics, as it is for most students of ethnology. Similarly, in Part Three such papers as "Speech as a Personality Trait," "Symbolism," and "The Unconscious Patterning of Behavior in

Society" should not be by-passed by the linguist.

At the time that Sapir was seeking to expand the horizons of language study beyond the linguist's traditional universe of discourse, history played a cruel trick on him by directing linguistics into contrary channels. Under the influence of Bloomfield, American linguists in the 1930s turned to an intensive cultivation of their own field, sharpening their methodological tools and rigorously defining the proper limits of their science in terms of what Trager has identified as "microlinguistics." They became increasingly efficient microlinguists. Certainly no one can deny that this involutionary trend has given linguistics a disciplined clarity and power of analysis that it never had before. But it is equally true that this trend carries with it the seeds of an ever-narrowing parochialism. And it was Sapir's main purpose to make linguistics a more cosmopolitan member of the community of sciences.

The recent arguments over "mentalism" may have obscured Sapir's position on the relation of linguistics to the other sciences of human behavior. He was as thoroughly committed as Bloomfield to the view that a valid linguistic science must be a coherent and self-consistent body of concepts. It must not look for extra-linguistic formulations to support or, still worse, to validate its findings. Modern linguists are and should be particularly sensitive to the fallacies of trying to find an external deus ex machina to explain the phenomena of their science, for Nineteenth Century linguistics was heavily overburdened with vain speculations, often indulged in by otherwise sound linguists, who philosophized and psychologized about evolution, race, climate, national character, and whatnot as determinants of linguistic facts.

Sapir's policy in seeking interdisciplinary linkages between linguistics and psychology was simply to present linguistic formulations and to allow psychologists, of whatever brand, to make their own reinterpretations. Many of his articles were addressed to psychoanalysts and psychiatrists, for he saw that the operations of the unconscious as manifested in language could provide data of particular interest to these specialties. In "The Status of Linguistics as a Science" he pointed out that the configurated character of language, which "develops its fundamental patterns with relatively the most complete detachment from other types of cultural patterning," should have a special value for Gestalt psychologists. He spoke to experimental psychologists in their own lingo in "A Study in Phonetic Symbolism," where he reported the results of his use of experimental techniques in studies of sound symbolisms.

In making this manifold approach to psychologists Sapir realized that, if linguistics is the body of formulations made by professional linguists, then psychology is the body of formulations made by psychologists. He did not try to select or construct a linguist's psychology, which, like a psychologist's version of linguistics, would be neither fish nor fowl, but a spurious body of doctrine irrelevant to both disciplines. This is not merely a matter of good manners, of the linguist's being gentleman enough not to muscle in on the psychologist's territory. It is the much more serious matter of recognizing that the consistency and integrity of any science must be maintained by the trained workers in that field, not by outsiders who may sometimes feel they can view the field with godlike omniscience. The failure to recognize this has frequently put a stop to fruitful communication between disciplines.

Sapir's approach to this delicate interdisciplinary problem is especially important at this time, because there are signs that a renewed effort in this direction is now being made. Fruitful results can be achieved if interested linguists and specialists in the other sciences of human behavior are willing to respect and to try to understand one another. This type of endeavor is, of course, fraught with misunderstandings and disillusionments. But it is the only way in which linguists and other specialists can cooperate to find concrete problems in which both can contribute and to formulate concepts relevant to both fields. Because Sapir understood the necessity of this approach, his linguistic writings are particularly meaningful to non-linguists. Papers of this type are predominant in Mandelbaum's selection, and it may turn out that Sapir's major contribution in the long run will be as the linguists' spokesman to psychologists and social scientists. Although Sapir used linguistic methods and procedures with consummate skill, he was an artist rather than a scientist in this regard. It was Bloomfield who formulated the methods of linguistic science into a clearly defined and tightly coherent body of doctrine.

Linguistics has been fortunate indeed in claiming two men of this stature of genius, who could provide such utterly different and complementary impulses to their field. The one might be considered the centripetal force in linguistics; the other's impulse was decidedly centrifugal. One pointed the way to a more intensive and logical analysis of linguistic phenomena; the other indicated the broader perspectives within which linguistic science could contribute to a richer understanding of human behavior.

REVIEW OF *SELECTED WRITINGS* (1949)*

JOSEPH H. GREENBERG

Selected Writings of Edward Sapir in Language, Culture, and Personality. Edited by DAVID G. MANDELBAUM. (xv, 617 pp., $6.50. University of California Press, Berkeley and Los Angeles, 1949.)

Anthropology, as well as the social sciences in general, owes a debt of gratitude to David Mandelbaum for satisfying the long-felt need of a representative collection of the scientific writings of Edward Sapir. The present volume, although of necessity encompassing only a fraction of the total output of so productive a scholar as Sapir, gives an ample and well-balanced presentation of his varied contributions in linguistics, ethnology and personality studies. Understandably, each reader will miss some particular contribution which strikes him as especially significant or characteristic. Thus, the present reviewer would have liked to see included at least one article illustrative of Sapir's methods in establishing linguistic relationships, for example, the Algonkin-Ritwan paper or that on the Hokan affinities of Subtiaba. In spite of such inevitable individual disagreements, I believe that Mandelbaum has chosen judiciously and with a lively perception of the varied interests and backgrounds, linguistic, ethnological and psychological, which the reader of Sapir will bring to his works.

The volume is divided into three parts, Language, Culture, and The Interplay of Culture and Personality, of which the first part, on language, not too surprisingly occupies approximately half of the six-hundred odd pages. This first part, like the others, has a number of subdivisions, each of which is accompanied by prefatory remarks on the part of the editor. In this case the subdivisions are: The Nature of Language, Studies of American Indian Languages, Studies of Indo-European and Semitic Languages. Among the well-known articles which appear in this section are: Sound Patterns in Language, the article "Language" in the *Encyclopedia of the Social Sciences*, Internal Linguistic Evidence Suggestive of the Northern Origin of the Navaho, Central and North American Indian Languages (containing Sapir's famous and often misunderstood classification into six superstocks) and Tibetan Influences on Tocharian (likewise sometimes misunderstood as implying a genetic relationship between these two languages).

Sapir's contributions to formal linguistics, both in its synchronic and diachronic aspects were fundamental. The unifying element which pervades Sapir's approach to the subject-matter of language is his conception of language as an organized struc-

* Reprinted, with permission of the American Anthropological Association, Washington, D.C., and the author, from *American Anthropologist* 52.516-18 (1950).

ture, both functionally on a particular time plane, and as a constantly reintegrating system in process of continuous change. In the field of phonology the basic structural unit is the phoneme, and if today its position is assured, this triumph is to a considerable degree the result of Sapir's influence. To superficial view it may appear that contemporary trends in formal linguistic studies are not along lines laid down by Sapir. I cannot help but see in the present-day extension of structural methods to the areas of morphology and syntax a well-nigh inevitable expansion of methods implicit in Sapir's view of language as a systemic pattern. Indeed, this view is already contained in Boas' linguistic approach with its transcendence of Indo-European grammatical categories and its application of ethnological insight to the analysis of the morphological structure of language. Nor is the present-day tendency toward methodological rigor and the creation of a special symbolism for the statement of linguistic facts essentially foreign to Sapir's thought. A glance at the article "Grading: a Study in Semantics" in the present volume shows Sapir ready to apply a specially invented symbolism as an aid in analysis and a method of presenting conclusions.

Sapir's achievements in historic linguistics rest largely on the application of the well-tested methods of Indo-Europeanist linguistics to the field of American Indian languages, but much also derives from Sapir's feeling for linguistic structure on the historical level. Thus the process of language change has a general coherence which we may characterize by Sapir's term "drift." Just as a certain aspect of a culture may be seized upon and elaborated until eventually a new and transformed systemic integration emerges, so also in the field of language. Thus, an exceptional form, descriptively of little moment in the present stage of a language, may bear witness to a former widespread process and provide the clue to a distant and unsuspected relationship. Sapir's application of such insights to the problems of the classification of American Indian languages is well-known.

The second part of the present collection concerns Culture; the best-known papers in this section are "Time Perspective in Aboriginal American Culture" and "Culture, Genuine and Spurious." Important as were Sapir's contributions to formal linguistics, in the long view it is probable that his analyses of the interrelationships of language and the rest of culture will have greater significance for anthropology as a whole. The treatment of this intricate subject-matter in "Time Perspectives" is, of course, classic. On rereading, one discovers that even at the present time there is literally nothing of importance that can be added to the sections on the employment of linguistic data in historical reconstruction. Much of the methodology described here remains for future application on a more intensive scale than has been practiced in the past.

The essay, "Culture, Genuine and Spurious," has considerable timeliness in view of the prominence which problems of value are now assuming in anthropological discussion. With this essay, too, a new motif, all but absent in the purely linguistic section, makes its appearance and becomes more prominent as the volume proceeds. This is Sapir's emphasis on individual personality. His interest in this sphere, which led him to pioneer in the field of personality and culture, appears to arise, in large measure, from his perception of the contrast between the values inherent in his own personality and those dominant on the American scene. It is this contrast which lends a certain poignancy to much of the later writings in this volume. An anthropology which omitted consideration of such matters would hardly seem adequate to one of Sapir's perceptiveness in this field.

The last section of the book, devoted to this topic of the interplay of personality and culture contains such well-known papers as "Why Cultural Anthropology Needs the Psychiatrist," and "The Emergence of the Concept of Personality in a Study of Culture." This latter essay seems to the present reviewer to contain Sapir's ripest views on the subject. It is remarkable for its even-handed appreciation of both historical and functional factors in the investigation of personality and, as such, it can hardly fail to exert a beneficial influence.

Much else, that cannot be discussed within the compass of a review, has of necessity been passed over here, Sapir's treatment of language and personality, the delightfully illuminating articles on Custom, Fashion and Symbolism in the *Encyclopedia of the Social Sciences*, and many other topics.

The present volume contains, in addition, a complete bibliography both of Sapir's scientific writings and of his poetry. I believe that its appearance will further stimulate existing interest in Sapir's work and widen the influence of his thought. David Mandelbaum has thus performed a signal service in making available in convenient form so many of the writings of a truly unique figure in American anthropology.

REVIEW ARTICLE ON *SELECTED WRITINGS**

ZELLIG S. HARRIS

This volume brings together some of the most important material in linguistics and in the social studies which touch upon linguistics. The writings of Edward Sapir are invaluable for their complete grasp of linguistics, for their approach to language and culture and personality, for the wonderful working of data which they exhibit. We all know what a never-ending source of learning and delight this was to Sapir's students and friends. Now it becomes available to those who would learn today, to whoever can appreciate both subtlety and independence of thought.

In going through the articles reprinted here, I was impressed with how well they read after all these years: how much was still new or freshly put in the articles I had never read before; how much more I could see now in the articles which I had already read in the original publication. The work is in no way dated. Aside from further organization of morphological analysis, Sapir's linguistic analysis is equal to the best that has yet been done, and his understanding of language as a system is better than anything in the field. In personality studies there has been more recent work along the lines that Sapir foreshadowed, but no superior formulation has superseded his. Quite the contrary: the deepest understandings of the interrelation of culture and personality are still to be found in his writings. And as for culture, Sapir's comments are a breath of fresh air not only because of their intrinsic worth, but also because they bear the imprint of an era when social criticism and understanding went farther than today: in the debunking carried out by the intellectuals during the gilded twenties, and in the left liberalism with which many Americans responded during the thirties to the undisguised inadequacy of their own social structure.

The articles selected for this volume give an excellent coverage of Sapir's three specialties, and every reader will appreciate not only the trouble that Mandelbaum went to in putting the book together, but also the wisdom of Mandelbaum's selection. The items are arranged under three headings: Language (The nature of language; Studies of American Indian languages; Studies of Indo-European and Semitic languages), Culture (The general view; American Indians; Literature and music), and The interplay of culture and personality; with a complete bibliography of Sapir's writings appended. Perhaps the most interesting articles are these: Language (from the Encyclopedia of the Social Sciences); Sound patterns in language; Communication (also from the ESS); The function of an international auxiliary language; Central and North-American languages (from the Encyclopaedia Britannica); Internal linguistic evidence suggestive of the northern origin of the Navaho; Culture, genuine and spurious; Fashion (from the ESS); Time perspective in aboriginal American culture; Cultural anthropology and psychiatry; The unconscious patterning of behavior in society; Why cultural anthropology needs the psychiatrist; Psychiatric and cultural pit-

* Reprinted, with permission of the Linguistic Society of America, Washington, D.C., the author, and the editor, from *Language* 27.288-333 (1951).

falls in the business of getting a living; The emergence of the concept of personality in a study of cultures.

The importance of all these reprinted articles makes it even clearer than before
that Sapir's unpublished material should be made available. There are many
unpublished notes and lists of comparisons in American Indian languages. These
have first claim, but everything else should also be collected and arranged.
As examples of the most important, we might mention Sapir's Yana dictionary
materials and his Comparative Wakashan note books, both of which are in
Morris Swadesh's hands; the latter he is now editing for the Library of the
American Philosophical Society. We need have no concern about whether it
would be fair to Sapir's memory to publish his unfinished work. The material
contains contributions which should not be lost; and Sapir himself prepared an
early paper, Grading, for·publication in a relatively unfinished state.

We will consider here the material in all three sections of the present volume,
both because the treatment and approach in the culture and the personality
sections is similar to that in the linguistics section, and because linguists should
know the whole Sapir and should understand how he combined his' interests
in language, in culture, and in personality.

1. LANGUAGE

1.1. DESCRIPTIVE LINGUISTICS: PROCESS; ANALYSIS IN DEPTH. Sapir puts the essential statements of modern linguistics in postulational or definitional form:
'Not only are all languages phonetic in character; they are also phonemic'; and
morphemes are 'conventional groupings of such phonemes' (8–9).[1] But by the
side of this, we find his characteristic approach in depth. Phonemes are presented
not as a classification of phonetic events or types, but as the result of a process
of selection: 'Between the articulation of the voice into the phonetic sequence
... and the complicated patterning of phonetic sequences into ... words, phrases,
and sentences there is a very interesting process of phonetic selection and generalization.' And concerning the phonemic constituency of morphemes we find:
'the limiting conditions [of morphemes] may be said to constitute the phonemic
mechanics, or phonology, of a particular language.' The term 'limiting conditions' aptly relates the range of morpheme construction to the range of phoneme
combination.

Sapir thus sees the elements of linguistics and the relations among them as
being the results of processes in language. The descriptive structure of a language can, of course, be regarded as the result of many processes of change, as
de Saussure pointed out in his example of the cross section of a tree-trunk in
relation to the growth and vertical axis of the tree.[2] This kind of interest appears
in Sapir's Glottalized Continuants, and will be discussed below.

Process or Distribution. Sapir, however, also used this model of an 'entity as

---

[1] Page numbers refer directly to the volume under review, without specifying the particular article involved. I would like to call attention to Stanley S. Newman's very interesting review of this book, IJAL 17.180–5 (1951), in which there is some explanation of
Sapir's unusual style of writing.

[2] Ferdinand de Saussure, Cours de linguistique générale 125.

a result of process' within descriptive linguistics proper. Consider, for example, those environmental ranges by virtue of which two sound types never contrast: say the fact that in a certain language no morpheme contains two vowels in succession; and that in any word which contains one morpheme ending in a vowel, followed by a second morpheme beginning with a vowel, a glottal stop is pronounced between these two vowels. When we speak in terms of distribution and classification, we would say that no morpheme contains the VV sequence, and that all morphemes which end in V before consonant or juncture have alternants ending in V? before vowel (before any following morpheme which begins with a vowel). Hence the VV sequence never occurs across morpheme junction, just as it doesn't occur within a morpheme. In contract with this, Sapir would say that no two vowels could come together (within a morpheme), and that when a particular morpheme conjunction would have the effect of bringing two vowels together a glottal stop comes in as a protective mechanism to keep them apart. This kind of model appears in much of Sapir's grammatical work and in the work of some of his students, as for example in Newman's handsome analysis of Yokuts.[3]

We can consider this simply as a method of description, an alternative to our present formulations, which we make in terms of the classifying of occurrences. The process model has the advantage of being more dramatic, and often of reflecting the actual historical changes (the inter-morphemic glottal stop may well have been a later development).[4] It has the greater advantage of opening the way to a more subtle descriptive analysis—something always dear to Sapir's heart—by giving a special secondary status to some parts of the descriptive structure. For example, we may be missing something when we say innocently that VV does not occur across morpheme boundary (while V?V and VCV do): the V?V which we find there may not be fully equivalent to the VCV which result from morphemes ending in -VC plus morphemes beginning in V- (or from -V plus CV-); for one thing, these VCV alternate with -VC and V- when their morphemes occur separately, whereas the V?V alternate with -V and V-; for another, the frequency of V?V (differently from VCV) may be much greater in those positions where morpheme boundaries can occur than in other positions.[5] On the other hand, the process model has the disadvantage of bringing into descriptive analysis a new dimension—the relations of one distribution to another distribution—which does not fit well into the algebraic character of the present bald statements of distribution. There is need for further elaboration

[3] Stanley S. Newman, Yokuts language of California (New York, 1944).

[4] Cf. Sapir's article on glottalized continuants (225–50), and Henry M. Hoenigswald, Sound change and linguistic structure, Lg. 22.138–43 (1946).

[5] To make this more explicit: Suppose all word-initial morphemes have two or more syllables (vowels). Then the probability of finding ? rather than some other consonant after the FIRST vowel of a word is related simply to the frequency of the medial glottal stop. The probability of finding ? after the SECOND vowel is related to the frequency of the glottal stop (medial and at the end of morphemes) plus the frequency of morphemes which end with a vowel (and of morphemes which begin with a vowel). However, the probability of finding other consonants (not ?) after the second vowel is related merely to the frequency of those consonants medially and at morpheme-end.

of descriptive techniques, in order to make room for such refinements among our direct distributional statements.

The Process and its Result. We can also consider the use of the process model as an activity of the linguists who use it; and we can then say that aside from such personality reasons as may have dictated Sapir's use of it, it also occupies a determinate position from the point of view of the history of science. It seems to constitute a stage in the separation of descriptive method both from historical analysis and from the older psychologizing of grammatical forms. The older grammars did not distinguish descriptive from historical statements, so that the history of the glottal stop at word boundary would have been combined with the statement of the absence of vowel sequences there. The older grammars assigned reasons for speech forms: people said VʔV (with 'intrusive glottal stop') in order to avoid VV which they did not otherwise pronounce.[6] Finally, the older grammars frequently failed to distinguish morphological from phonological considerations, so that the morphophonemic fact about VʔV appearing for -V + .V- would be given together with the phonemic fact about the absence of VV. The formulations in terms of process give expression to all this while at the same time separating descriptive linguistics from the rest. This is achieved by the dual character of these formulations: the 'process' of protecting the cross-boundary -V + V- yields the 'result' that VʔV occurs.

The process section of this formulation takes cognizance of such factors as were brought out by the older linguistics (or by Sapir's interest in descriptive detail); the result section gives the distributional statement as an item in a separate science of distributions.[7]

Process in Language Structure. The process model led to a characterization of linguistic structures in terms of the types of process involved in them. A grammar was viewed as consisting of so much prefixation and suffixation, so much internal change or reduplication, used at such and such points.[8] Much of what was called process concerned the changes in or near a given form as its environment varied. For example, there is an internal change in *knife* (to *knive-*) when *-s* 'plural' appears in its environment. There is another internal change in *sing* (to *sang*) which can occur without any change in environment: *You sing well* ∼ *You sang well*. (But if we vary the environment to *I like to* ( ), we exclude *sang* and find only *I like to sing*.) There is a process of suffixation that adds *-ed*

---

[6] How different Sapir's psychologism is from this will be discussed in Part 3 below. For the moment, it is worth noting that Sapir's grammatical formulations stayed within linguistic categories. In descriptive linguistics he would not say that people inserted a glottal stop so as to avoid the sequence VV, but that the glottal stop constituted, in respect of medial VV, a 'protection' (in cross-boundary position) of that non-occurrence of VV. The primacy of medial VV over the cross-boundary case is maintained, but in terms of the structure rather than in terms of people's intervention in their own speech behavior.

[7] We can say that the use of base forms in morphophonemics—as in Leonard Bloomfield's Menomini morphophonemics, TCLP 8.105–15 (1939)—is a further step from history or process toward purely distributional statements.

[8] It is interesting that Bloomfield's work, which (as suggested above) represents a later stage in this particular development, presents phonemes no longer as the result of process but as direct classification, whereas the morphology is still largely described in terms of process. Cf. the chapters on phonology and on morphology in his book Language.

to many English words without any accompanying change in environment, or when the environment is changed to include *yesterday*, but never directly after *will* or *to: I walk, I walked, I walked yesterday, I will walk, I want to walk.* Today we would say that *knife* and *knive* are alternants of one morpheme, and that the internal change there is a morphophonemic alternant of zero (other morphemes, like *spoon*, have no change before -*s*). We would say that *sang* consists of *sing* plus some other perfectly respectable morpheme, and that this other morpheme (change of /i/ to /æ/) is an alternant of the morpheme -*ed*.

To speak only of the presence of internal change, suffixation, reduplication in a language is to tell merely what is the phonemic history of a morpheme and its neighborhood, as the morpheme is tracked through its various environments. To speak only of the fact that some nouns have alternant forms before -*s* (or that some nouns before -*s* are complementary to other nouns not before -*s*), and that -*ed* has various alternant forms, is to give bare distributional statements with the merest nod to the phonemic composition of the morphemes.

To speak of internal change and suffixation and the like as occurring under particular environmental conditions is to give a detailed distributional statement of morphemes as phonemic groupings. This last can be described as a combining of today's distributional interests with the interest in process of Sapir (and, in morphology, Bloomfield) and various European linguists; it is a direction of development which would be fruitful in the present stage of linguistics. It would be fruitful because linguistics has at present one technique for stating the relation of phoneme to morpheme (morphemes are arbitrary combinations of phonemes) and another for stating the general relation of morpheme to utterance (utterances are composed of stated distributions of morphemes). To take greater cognizance of the phonemic composition of morphemes is to come nearer to the direct relation of phoneme to utterance (utterances are composed of stated distributions of phonemes). This goal will presumably never be reached, because there will always be arbitrary elements in the phonemic composition of morphemes. But if we can make general statements about part of this field, as by noting when the morphemes or alternants consist of added new phonemes or of repeated phonemes or of exchanged phonemes, we leave less that is arbitrary and outside our generalized statements.

1.2. LINGUISTIC STRUCTURE: PATTERN. Sapir's greatest contribution to linguistics, and the feature most characteristic of his linguistic work, was not the process model but the patterning of data. Both of these analytic approaches were of course used by many linguists beside Sapir, but Sapir made major contributions to both lines of development. For patterning we have, first of all, his famous Sound patterns in language (1925), which is reprinted here on pages 33–45. Here he pointed out that what is linguistically significant is not what sounds are observed in a given language but under what linguistic circumstances (i.e. in what distribution) those sounds occur. The phraseology of course is pre-phonemic, but (or since) the article is one of the cornerstones of phonemic analysis.

Sapir's search for patterns pervaded not only his phonemic but also his morphological work, as anyone would know who saw him working over his large charts of Navaho verb forms. His morphological patterning may be seen in his analysis of paradigms in his book Language (Ch. 5), and in his Navaho work, and in his published and unpublished American Indian material. His phonemic patterning is amply evident in the articles reprinted in this volume.

Since the original appearance of his articles, patterning has become an everyday matter for linguistics. Phonemic analysis seems quite obvious today. Morphological analysis is more procedural now than in Sapir's book Language (1921). Some of the earliest organized work in morphophonemic patterning was carried out by Sapir[9] or under his influence.[10]

Today the distinction between phonemic and morphophonemic patterns is quite prominent. In La réalité psychologique des phonèmes (1933; English version printed here on pp. 46-60), Sapir includes both kinds without explicit distinction. Phonemic examples (from native responses) are: writing /ḥi/ in Nootka for phonetic hɛ, ɛ being the allophone of i after h (54); reconstructing the Southern Paiute allophone p when post-vocalic -βaʻ 'at' was experimentally pronounced after pause (49; initial p and post-vocalic β are positional variants of each other); writing [p'] with prior release of oral closure and ['m] with prior release of glottal closure equivalently as /p̓/ and /m̓/, because the distributional features of [p'] and ['m] are equivalent (56-7; both occur at syllable beginning where clusters do not occur, neither occurs at syllable end where other types of consonants occur, plus a morphophonemic equivalence). Morphophonemic examples (from native responses) are: recognition of the difference between the phonemically identical Sarcee /dìní/ 'this one' and /dìní/ 'it makes a sound' based on the form of the stem before suffixes, e.g. /-í/ 'the one who', where we find /dìná·ʼ/, /dìnítʻí/, morphophonemic stem nítʻ (52-3); writing Nootka morphemic s-s (with morpheme boundary between them) as morphophonemic ss, and phonetic [V̆s·V] as containing phonemic /s/—[s·] being the allophone of /s/ after short vowel and before vowel—even though this ss is phonemically /s/: in the morphophonemic writing tsiˑqšitʻlassatlni 'we went there only to speak' (containing 'as 'to go in order to' and sa 'only') the ss is phonemically identical (and phonetically equivalent) with the /s/ of /tlasatl/ 'the stick that takes an upright position on the beach'—phonetically [tlas·atl] and with morphemic boundary tla-satl (54-5).

Language Classification. The variegated kinds of patterning, once recognized, invited attempts at some kind of organization. To organize the patterns of each language into a total structure of that language, and to investigate and compare the kinds of structuralization, was not possible until much more work had been done around these patterns. What was done instead by Sapir and others was to classify patterns (case system etc.) and to classify language types on this basis. To a large extent this was what Sapir did in his famous classification of (North) American Indian languages into six major groups (169-78). It is clear from the considerations explicitly presented by Sapir in this article (and also from the difficulty of conceiving any discoverable genetic relation among some of the

---

[9] In Sapir and Swadesh, Nootka texts 236-9 (Philadelphia, 1939).

[10] As in Morris Swadesh and C. F. Voegelin, A problem in phonological alternation, Lg. 15.7 (1939; written some years earlier).

families, for example in the 'Hokan-Siouan' group) that this classification is structural rather than genetic, though in many cases it suggests possible genetic connections that can be supported by further research.

Sapir also proposed a general method of classifying languages on the basis of types of grammatical patterning (in his book Language), but neither he nor others followed it up. For since there was no organizing principle for all patternings, such as would arise out of an analysis of the full possibilities of linguistic patterning and of their structural interrelations, the classification work was a useful but temporary way of noting what formal features occur in languages, and which of them occur together. The classification results could not in themselves be used for any further work, except to suggest distant genetic relationships as in the American Indian classification. (In contrast, if a fully organized—though not necessarily one-dimensional—classification of complete language structures is ever achieved, the results would be useful for understanding the development of linguistic systems, for discovering the limitations and further possibilities of language-like systems, etc.) The piling up of research in distribution and its patternings has made it possible by now to talk about the place of one pattern relative to others, and about the way these fit into a whole structure. With more work of this type we may be able to say wherein and to what extent two languages differ from each other, and thus approach a structural classificatory principle.

Descriptive Function. This structural limitation did not affect the general linguistic approach that was made possible by recognition of patterning. Sapir's patterning is an observable (distributional) fact which he can discover in his data and from which he can draw those methodological and psychological considerations which he cannot observe directly, such as function and relevance, or perception and individual participation. He can the more readily do this because his patterning is established not directly on distributional classification but on an analysis in depth of the way in which the various elements are used in the language. The 'way the elements are used' is equivalent to their distribution; but talking about such use gives a depth which is lacking in direct classification of environments.

Thus Sapir uses the patterning of elements in order to express their function (their functional position within the language): 'to say that a given phoneme is not sufficiently defined in articulatory acoustic terms but needs to be fitted into the total system of sound relations peculiar to the language is, at bottom, no more mysterious than to say that a club is not defined for us when it is said to be made of wood and to have such and such a shape and such and such dimensions. We must understand why a roughly similar object, not so different to the eye, is no club at all ... To the naive speaker and hearer, sounds (i.e. phonemes)[11] do not differ as five-inch or six-inch entities differ, but as clubs and poles differ. If the phonetician discovers in the flow of actual speech something that is neither "club" nor "pole", he, as phonetician, has the right to set up a "halfway between club and pole" entity. Functionally, however, such

---

[11] Sapir means: sounds as phonemically heard (perceived, structured) by the naive speaker and hearer.

an entity is a fiction, and the naive speaker or hearer is not only driven by its relational behavior to classify it as a "club" or a "pole," but actually hears and feels it as such' (46–7).[12]

Perception. In a related way, patterning is used as a basis for the structuring of perception. Sapir reports that English-speaking students often mistakenly hear *p, t,* or *k* instead of a final glottal stop; and after learning to recognize a glottal stop, they often mistakenly hear a glottal stop at the end of words ending in an accented short vowel (they write *smɛ'* for *smɛ*). He then points out (59–60) that the second type of error is simply a more sophisticated form of the first. Since words ending in accented short vowel do not occur in English, the students who fail to recognize the glottal stop in *smɛ'* cannot perceive the words as *smɛ* (since such words are out of their pattern) and therefore (selecting a consonant nearest ') hear it as *smɛk* or the like. Later, when they know about glottal stops and hear *smɛ*, they can still perceive only a word ending in a consonant and (selecting a consonant nearest zero) hear it as *smɛ'*.

This effect upon perception is claimed not only for such phonemic hearing, but also for the structuring of experience in terms of the morphological and vocabulary patterns of the language: 'Even comparatively simple acts of perception are very much more at the mercy of the social [more exactly: linguistic] patterns called words than we might suppose. If one draws some dozen lines, for instance, of different shapes, one perceives them as divisible into such categories as "straight," "crooked," "curved," "zigzag" because of the classificatory suggestiveness of the linguistic terms themselves' (162).

System. Sapir goes on to recognize patterning as one of the basic characteristics of language: 'Of all forms of culture, it seems that language is that one which develops fundamental patterns with relatively the most complete detachment from other types of cultural patterning' (164). Had he used the descriptive word 'consists of' instead of the process word 'develops', he might have gone beyond this to add that we can even use this linguistic patterning to determine what is to be included in 'language'. There are scattered bits of speech-like noises—coughing, crying, shrieking, laughing, clucking—which may or may not be considered part of 'language' on one basis or another, but which we count out of language because they do not fit into its detached patterning.

Out of all this Sapir was able to make important generalizations about language as a system. Recognition of the detachment of linguistic patterning leads to the statement that 'the patterning of language is to a very appreciable extent self-contained and not significantly at the mercy of intercrossing patterns of a non-linguistic type' (165). This explicit talk about the fact of patterning makes possible the distinction between the grammar (specific pattern) and grammaticalness (degree of patterning) of language: 'In spite of endless differences of detail, it may justly be said that all grammars have the same degree of fixity One language may be more complex or difficult grammatically than another,

---

[12] Note 'relational behavior' for our 'distribution'. The hearer might also classify it as a 'bad pole', so that even if the difference between the halfway sound and the regular sounds is noticed and not lost, it is nevertheless referred to (i.e. structured in terms of) the functionally (distributionally) determined points of the pattern.

but there is no meaning whatever in the statement which is sometimes made that one language is more grammatical, or form bound, than another' (9–10).

From this, Sapir could go on to an interesting formulation of the adequacy of language. We all know the statement that any language can be used as the vehicle for expressing anything. Sapir removes the air of triviality from this by saying, 'New cultural experiences frequently make it necessary to enlarge the resources of a language, but such enlargement is never an arbitrary addition to the materials and forms already present; it is merely a further application of principles already in use and in many cases little more than a metaphorical extension of old terms and meanings' (10). In other words, the adequacy of language is not simply definitional, but derives from the possibilities of extension and transference within the language structure, without either disregarding or destroying the structure. 'The outstanding fact about any language is its formal completeness ... No matter what any speaker of it may desire to communicate, the language is prepared to do his work ... Formal completeness has nothing to do with the richness or the poverty of the vocabulary ... The unsophisticated natives, having no occasion to speculate on the nature of causation, have probably no word that adequately translates our philosophic term "causation," but this shortcoming is purely and simply a matter of vocabulary and of no interest whatever from the standpoint of linguistic form ... As a matter of fact, the causative relation ... is expressed only fragmentarily in our modern European languages ... [but] in Nootka ... there is no verb or verb form which has not its precise causative counterpart' (153–5). Sapir might have continued here to point out that the work of language in communication and expression can be carried out both by grammatical form and by vocabulary (though with different effect), since one can insert *to cause to* before any English verb somewhat as one can add a causative element to every Nootka verb.[13] Hence what is important is not so much the distinction between grammatical form and vocabulary, as the fact that the distribution of grammatical elements, and so the grammatical structure, can change in a continuous deformation (the structure at any one moment being virtually identical with the immediately preceding structure), and that vocabulary can be added without limit (and changed in meaning). What we have, therefore, as the basic adequacy of language is not so much the static completeness of its formal structure, but rather its completability, or more exactly its constructivity without limit.

1.3. LANGUAGE AS SOCIAL ACTIVITY. *The fact of patterning.* A person who is interested in the various kinds and relations of patternings, for their own sake, can establish pattern and structure as bland distributional arrangements, and thence move toward the mathematical investigation of the combinatorial possibilities. Sapir, however, was interested in the fact of patterning, and what

---

[13] We omit here the important difference that an English verb by itself contrasts most immediately with the small class of affix combinations (e.g. verb plus -*ed*), and only secondarily with a vast class of phrasal sequences in which that verb could be set (of which *to cause to do so-and-so* is one), while a Nootka verb by itself contrasts with a few specific combinations of verb plus affix (of which the causative affix is one), and only secondarily with the large class of phrasal sequences.

could be derived from the discovery that language was so patterned a bit of human behavior. This was not only because Sapir was above all an anthropologist, but also because of the particular development in linguistic science at the time.

From de Saussure to the Prague Circle and Sapir and Bloomfield, the fact of patterning was the overshadowing interest. In the later work of this period in linguistics we find attempts to analyze and classify these patterns, but the big result was still the very existence of structure. This was the big advance in several sciences at the time. In the late depression years, when neither admiration of Russia nor war preparations in America had as yet obscured the scientific and social results of Karl Marx, Leonard Bloomfield remarked to me that in studying Das Kapital he was impressed above all with the similarity between Marx's treatment of social behavior and that of linguistics. In both cases, he said, the activities which people were carrying out in terms of their own life situations (but in those ways which were socially available) turned out to constitute tight patterns that could be described independently of what people were about. In language, they communicate, or pronounce words they have heard, but with the descriptive result of maintaining a patterned contrast between various subclasses of verbs or the like. In economic behavior, they may do various things just in order to make profit, but with the descriptive result that the producing population becomes increasingly removed from control over its production. Sapir saw this fact of patterning even more clearly—in language, in culture, and later in personality. Throughout his writings one sees how impressed he was with this fact, one which was also being stressed at the time (but with less happy success) in other social sciences. In his comments about language as patterned behavior he reached the heights of his subtlety, and pioneered a form of research which few have as yet taken up.

Talking as part of behavior. About the very act of talking he says: 'While it may be looked upon as a symbolic system which reports or refers to or otherwise substitutes for direct experience, it does not as a matter of actual behavior stand apart from or run parallel to direct experience but completely interpenetrates with it ... It is this constant interplay between language and experience which removes language from the cold status of such purely and simply symbolic systems as mathematical symbolism or flag signaling ... It is because it is learned early and piecemeal, in constant association with the color and the requirements of actual contexts, that language, in spite of its quasi-mathematical form, is rarely a purely referential organization' (11–2). This understanding of the relation of language to other experience is involved also in the view that psychological suggestion (and, in extreme form, hypnotism) is in essence the same as talking. In The psychology of human conflict (174), E. T. Guthrie says: 'Suggestibility is the result of learning a language. When we acquire any language, such acquisition lies in associating the sounds of the language with action. The use of suggestion is merely the use of these acquired cues ... There is no essential difference between causing a man to perform some act by suggestion and causing him to perform that act by request.' Arthur Jenness amplifies:[14] 'In the past,

---

[14] Hypnotism 496 (where the Guthrie quotation is given in full) = Chap. 15 of J. McV. Hunt (ed.), Personality and the behavior disorders, Vol. 1.

the subject has been drowsy when the word "drowsy" has been spoken, and the state of drowsiness has thereby become conditioned to the word "drowsy". The word "drowsy" repeated later *under the proper circumstances* tends to elicit drowsiness.'

Sapir's point has the merit that instead of referring language back to an undefined and dangerously over-used 'symbolism', he presents it as a direct item of behavior, associated with other behavior: 'If language is in its analyzed form a symbolic system of reference, it is far from being merely that if we consider the psychologic part that it plays in continuous behavior' (12).[15] In order to treat of the 'symbolic' character of language, he says that symbols 'begin with situations in which a sign[16] is disassociated from its context' (566); and he adds, 'Even comparatively simple forms of behavior are far less directly functional than they seem to be, but include in their motivation unconscious and even unacknowledged impulses, for which the behavior must be looked upon as a symbol' (566-7). Language, then, is just an extreme type (and a physiologically and structurally separable portion) of the associations and dissociations that occur in all behavior.

Sapir goes on to distinguish two characteristics (and origins, and types) of symbols: the 'substitute for some more closely intermediating type of behavior', and the 'condensation of energy' (565-6). His first or 'referential' symbolism, like telegraphic ticking, is the one we all know in science and technology;[17] his second, like the washing ritual of an obsessive, is that which occurs in psychoanalysis. In ordinary behavior, and even in language, both are blended.[18]

Forms and meanings. Sapir's interest in language as patterned behavior, in some respects continuous (associated) with other behavior and in some respects

[15] This was published in 1933. The novelty of this view may be seen from the fact that in 1929 Sapir had given it a more traditional formulation: 'If I shove open a door in order to enter a house, the significance of the act lies precisely in its allowing me to make an easy entry. But if I "knock at the door," a little reflection shows that the knock itself does not open the door for me. It serves merely as a sign that somebody is to come to open it for me' (163-4). His later understanding would suggest that the knock can be viewed instead as a tool, an indirect step in the course of getting the door opened (like the stick with which Köhler's ape knocks down the banana, or the lever with which we pry up a rock). It is part of the continuous behavior which makes the person inside unlock the door for us, or which makes him ready for our intrusion. It is not a 'substitute for shoving' but rather the equivalent for shoving in a society where people are customarily apprised of a visitor's arrival. In social situations where this is not customary (as among intimates), one indeed opens the door without knocking.

[16] For 'sign' we should say: any associated behavior, such as a noise.

[17] Note Martin Joos's statement of it in the last paragraph of his paper Description of language design, Jour. Acoustic Soc. America 22.707 (1950).

[18] It is conceivable that there might have been yet another element of symbolism in language, if the noise behavior that became dissociated had had such a relation to the situation with which it was associated as would be independently arrived at by every speaker (or by every speaker in the given culture). Such associations occur in onomatopoetic elements (14), and they would have made words more a matter of individual expression than of arbitrary social learning. Sapir found some traces of such phonetic symbolism by a neat use of the methods of experimental psychology; part of this work appears in the present volume (61-72), part is as yet unpublished.

dissociated from it (symbolic), enabled him to use readily the morphological approach current at the time. Grammars were usually organized not only on the basis of the formal (distributional) relations of elements,[19] but also on the basis of the major relations between form and meaning—such as whether there are gender or tense paradigms. Sapir accepted this as a basis for grammatical description, and used it in distinguishing language types.

This kind of consideration is quite different from the purely formal one. The formal typology would note to what extent linguistic elements have positional variants (i.e. environmentally determined alternants), what kinds of combinations of classes there are to be found, at what points in the structure we find domains of varying lengths (as against unit length of operand), and the like. The form–meaning typology notes the importance of noun classification on the basis of gender, or the like; to this Sapir added the criterion of 'the expression of fundamental syntactic relations as such versus their expression in necessary combination with notions of a concrete order. In Latin, for example, the notion of the subject of a predicate is never purely expressed in a formal sense, because there is no distinctive symbol for this relation. It is impossible to render it without at the same time defining the number and gender of the subject of the sentence' (21).

The correlation of form and meaning is, however, only one side of linguistic typology. It can tell us whether certain meanings are always either explicitly included or explicitly excluded (like the plural in *book* ~ *books*), or are undefined when absent (as in Kwakiutl, where nothing is indicated about number if no explicit plural morpheme is given). It can tell whether some meanings are very frequently indicated, as any paradigmatic morpheme like the English plural would be. It can tell what meanings are expressed together, as in the Latin example cited above. But the differences are largely in degree. As Sapir recognized, even a meaning which is not paradigmatically expressed can be expressed in any given language, even though absence of the morpheme would not then mean presence of its paradigmatically contrasted meaning (as absence of -*s* indicates singular, or absence of -*ed* and the *will*-class indicates present). The fact that a particular meaning is expressed as a grammatical category (rather than, say, in a separate noun) is of interest to cultural history (443), but is not essentially different from having the meaning expressed by any morpheme, of any class (100).

Which meanings or kinds of meaning are expressed by which kinds of structural elements (paradigmatic sets, large open classes like nouns, etc.) is nevertheless of considerable interest in discussing a language as social behavior. It may affect perception, and may in part determine what can be efficiently said in that language. Sapir pointed out, for example, that the Nootka translation for *The stone falls* would be grammatically equivalent to *It stones down* (something like the difference between *Rain is falling* and *It's raining*), and commented that such differences show a 'relativity of the form of thought' (159).

---

[19] E.g. what large open classes there were (such as stems, or distinct verb and noun classes) which occurred with small closed classes (such as affixes, or distinct verb and noun affixes in various environmental subclasses).

Meanings. This line of interest led to research of a purely semantic character. Around 1930, Sapir wrote three long semantic papers as preliminary researches toward an international auxiliary language: Totality (Language Monograph No. 6); The expression of the ending-point relation in English, French, and German (in collaboration with Morris Swadesh; Language Monograph No. 10); and Grading (reprinted here on pp. 122–49). We can distinguish several problems in these investigations. First, there was some analysis of the purely semantic relations among the meanings themselves. For example, Sapir says: 'Grading as a psychological process precedes measurement and counting ... The term four means something only when it is known to refer to a number which is "less than" certain others' (122). And farther on: 'Judgments of "more than" and "less than" may be said to be based on perceptions of "envelopment" ' (i.e. of successively inclusive bounds). Such analysis could be aided by the abstract study of relations in mathematics and logic (as in the relation between order and quantity which is involved on p. 124), and perhaps also by investigations along the lines of experimental psychology into basic (not culturally determined) perception and behavior.

Second, we find analysis of the precise meanings of the relevant words of a given language. Sapir was always an artist at bringing out the complexities of meanings hidden in a particular word, or in someone's use of the word in a given situation. Here he does this in a more formal way. He shows, for example, that there are two different uses of *good, near,* and other grading terms (126–8): referred to an absolute norm (e.g. *brilliant,* or *better* in *Thanks. This one is better*); and referred to comparison (e.g. *better* in *My pen is better than yours, but I confess that both are bad*); note that one wouldn't say *A is more brilliant than B, but both are stupid.* In this second category we have *good* in the sense of *of what quality* (*How good is it? Oh, very bad*), and *near* in the sense of *at what distance* (*How near was he? Still quite far*). Similarly, he points out that many grading terms 'color the judgment with their latent affect of approval or disapproval (e.g. "as much as" smuggles in a note of satisfaction; "only" and "hardly" tend to voice disappointment)' (139).[20]

Third, from his analysis of the total meanings which are expressed in each word, Sapir isolates various factors of meaning, chiefly the following: the dis-

[20] It is always possible, of course, to overlook various environmental factors in analyzing the meanings of words. Sapir says (140): 'if a quantitative goal is to be reached by increase, say "ten pages of reading," *more than* necessarily has an approving ring (e.g., "I have *already* read *more than three pages,*" though it may actually be less than four), *less than* a disapproving ring (e.g., "I have *only* read *less than eight pages,*" though it may actually be more than seven). On the other hand, if the quantitative goal is to be reached by decrease, say "no more reading to do," *more than* has a disapproving ring (e.g., "I have *still more than three pages* to do," though actually less than four remain to be done), *less than* an approving ring (e.g., "I have *less than eight pages* to do," though more than seven pages remain to be done out of a total of ten).'—If the form of the verb were taken into consideration here, it might be possible to show that the approving ring comes from the conjunction of *more* with the past tense and *less* with *to do,* the disapproving ring from *more* plus *to do* and *less* plus the past tense. To isolate the 'affect in grading', which Sapir seeks here, we extract an element 'approval' out of *more* plus past and *less* plus future, and an element 'disapproval' out of the opposite combinations.

tinction between grading with reference to a norm and grading with reference
to terms of comparison (125–6), noted above; open and closed gamuts of grading
with one central or two end norms (127–30); reversible and irreversible sets
(132–3); direction of increase or decrease (and also goal) implied in the grading
word, as in *good* : *better* versus *good* : *less good* (134–5, exemplified in fn. 20 above);
the intrusion of affect in regard to the grade (and the goal) (139–44, and cf. fn.
20 above). Such isolating of 'elements of meaning' is not subject to the usual
criticisms directed against semantic work, because it is an empirical linguistic
investigation. It does not derive elements of meaning from some deductive system of presumed basic meanings, but discovers what elements can be separated
out from the total meaning of each word; and it discovers this by comparing the
various words of a semantic set, by seeing the linguistic environment in which
these occur, and the social situation or meaning of each use.

All these investigations involving meaning, when carried out with the kind of
approach that Sapir used, have validity and utility. The formal analysis of
language is an empirical discovery of the same kinds of relations and combinations which are devised in logic and mathematics; and their empirical discovery
in language is of value because languages contain (or suggest) more complicated
types of combination than people have invented for logic. In much the same
way, we have here an empirical discovery of elements of meaning in natural
languages, instead of the seemingly hopeless task of inventing basic elements of
meaning in speculative abstract semantics.[21] True, the particular elements we
obtain depend on the languages considered and upon the degree and type of
analysis. But it serves as a beginning, to suggest what kind of elements can be
isolated and arranged in varied patterns, which ones can be combined within a
single morpheme (with what effect), what would result from expressing some of
them in grammatical forms and others in ordinary words, and so on. We thus
obtain both a picture of how meanings are expressed in languages, and a suggestion of how other ways can be constructed.

Communication and expression. Having surveyed the relation of talking to
other behavior, and the meaning of talk, we turn now to the place that talking
occupies in the life of a person—what might be called the function of speech.

Sapir points out that talking fills various functions beside communication.
There is first the direct expressive effect to oneself of talking and of the way one
talks. To this Sapir adds the symbol of social solidarity that is expressed by
having speech forms in common—in the nicknames of a family, in professional
cant, in all sorts of small and large common-interest groups: 'No one is entitled
to say "trig" or "math" who has not gone through such familiar and painful
experiences as a high school or undergraduate student ... A self-made mathema-
tician has hardly the right to use the word "math" in referring to his own interests because the student overtones of the word do not properly apply to him'
(16). Finally, because of the dissociated character of language, there is 'the im-

---

[21] As is well known, logic and especially semantics are also based in part upon the language of their practitioners, and are limited by their linguistic experience. However, this
linguistic basis is not explicit because usually unacknowledged; narrow because usually
limited to European languages; and arbitrary because not subject to explicit empirical and
analytic techniques or to controls.

portant role which language plays as a substitute means of expression for those individuals who have a greater than normal difficulty in adjusting to the environment in terms of primary action patterns' (18). Such functions of language, though episodically mentioned by linguists, merit further study, even though these functions are often filled more adequately by other behavior—gesture, symbol, art, and the like. As a method of communicating, however, no other behavior compares with language. Writing originated as an independent method of communicating, but Sapir points out that 'true progress in the art of writing lay in the virtual abandonment of the principle with which it originally started' (13): the pictorial and direct symbolization of experience was replaced by symbolization of words; and we may add that in most systems the direct symbolization of words was replaced by signs for the sounds of speech.

Of non-verbal communication, such as railroad lights or wigwagging, he adds that 'while they are late in developing in the history of society, they are very much less complex in structure than language itself' (107). This statement holds only in certain senses. It is true that each field of mathematics, and all of them together, can deal with but a small range of subjects. And the symbols and statements (equations) and sequences of statements of mathematics may each, taken individually, be less complex than those of language. But the possibility of including the results (output) of one relational statement into the terms of another, by means of successive definitions, makes it possible for mathematical statements to carry a far greater communication load than linguistic statements on the same subjects: compare any mathematical formula but the most trivial with its translation into English. Furthermore, developments in electrical circuit systems, in electronic control instruments, and in electronic computers open the possibility of highly complicated activities equivalent to communication. The ultimate communicational operation in these instruments is simpler than in mathematics (and much simpler than the countless experiential associations of language), since it is generally reducible to yes–no (closing or opening a circuit) or to a distribution of a given current as among several branches in the circuit (depending on the resistance of each branch). Nevertheless, the innumerable possible lay-outs of paths, and the rapid and numerous occurrences of the basic operation, may enable these instruments to carry more complex communication than language can, within a limited range of subject-matter.

Sapir notes, indeed, that non-verbal communication may be more useful even when it is not more complex (or because it can be more simple); namely 'where it is desired to encourage the automatic nature of the response. Because language is extraordinarily rich in meaning, it sometimes becomes a little annoying or even dangerous to rely upon it where only a simple this or that, or yes or no, is expected to be the response' (107).

Behind the discussion of language as a method of communication lies the less important but still relevant question of just how much of language-like communication is language proper. This is largely the question of the intonations and gestures which occur with speech. Sapir says: 'The consistent message delivered by language symbolism in the narrow sense may flatly contradict the message communicated by the synchronous system of gestures, consisting of movements of the hands and head, intonations of the voice, and breathing symbolisms. The former system may be entirely conscious, the latter entirely unconscious. Linguistic, as opposed to gesture, communication tends to be the official and socially accredited one' (105).

While all this is quite true, a few cautions may be in place. Some of the intonations may be reducible to patterned sequences of a few contrasting tones (tone phonemes), and may thus be considered morphemes no less than the ordinary morphemes with which they occur: in English this may be true of the assertion or command intonations, but not of the ones for excitement or for irony.

This means that the question of which intonations are part of language and which are gestural sounds is simply the question of which of them can be described like the other elements of language—as combinations and sequences of phonemic elements (in this case phonemic tones). In turn, this means that at least some of the distinction between gesture and language is a matter of the linguist's methods of analysis. This is not to say that the distinction is not important. The fact that ordinary morphemes and some intonations can be described as fixed combinations of fixed phonemic elements, while other intonations and all gestures cannot be so described, reflects a difference in the explicitness and type of use of these two groups of communicational (and expressive) activities.

For the linguist, one group is language, the other is not. For the hearer and the speaker the difference may be one of degree, with decreasing awareness and explicitness as we go from morpheme to morpheme-like intonations to other intonations and gestures. But there is still considerable awareness of gesture and intonation, which most people can understand with nicety. And there is often great unawareness of the 'accredited' linguistic communication and expression, as when a person reveals his attitudes or wishes by what we call his 'natural choice of words' (with or without the hearer's understanding of what lies behind this choice).

The decision of what to include in the linguistic structure rests with the linguist, who has to work out that structure, and is simply a matter of what can be fitted into a structure of the linguistic type. The question of what activities constitute what kind of communication is largely an independent one, and is answered by observing the kind of use people make of the various communicational and expressive activities.

Constructed language. So far the description and analysis. It is fine to do this for its own sake. It is fine to obtain from this work generalizations and predictions about language, or interconnections with more general problems about the patterning of behavior. However, the linguist who has all these results in his hands is also able to construct something with it, to synthesize something by means of his knowledge. He can carry out critiques of people's language and communication activities, showing what is being effected by them, or how they fall short by one standard or another. He can use his particular analytic experience in devising combinatorial techniques, not only of linguistic material. He can try to construct a communication system (and perhaps a representation system) more efficient and free than existing languages.

This last is always an attractive task to any linguist who is interested in the productive potentialities of his work. It is little wonder that Jespersen and Sapir, two linguists who were avidly interested in life and in their work, were each concerned with the construction of a superior language.

The most obvious source of interest lay in the need for international communication. Because Sapir's anthropological horizons were naturally wider than Jespersen's, the problem was more complicated for him because 'international' meant for him more than just the western world: 'As the Oriental peoples become of more and more importance in the modern world, the air of sanctity that attaches to English or German or French is likely to seem less and less a thing to be taken for granted, and it is not at all unlikely that the triumph of the international language movement will owe much to the Chinaman's and the Indian's indifference to the vested interests of Europe' (119). Furthermore, an international language meant more than a pidgin auxiliary: 'It is perfectly true that for untold generations to come an international language must be auxiliary, must not attempt to set itself up against the many languages of the folk, but it must for all that be a free powerful expression of its own, capable of all work that may reasonably be expected of language' (113). Special audiences for it already exist, as in the 'social unity' of the scattered scientific world (108); but Sapir recognized the social blocks: 'Any consciously constructed international language has to deal with the great difficulty of not being felt to represent a distinctive people or culture. Hence the learning of it is of very little symbolic significance for the average person' (31). Under possible future political circumstances, however, such a language might conversely be 'protected by the powerful negative fact that it cannot be interpreted as the symbol of any localism or nationality' (113). And Sapir's comment quoted above about the possible effect of the Asiatics on the establishment of an international language is an example of the kind of social need which alone would bring such a language into currency.

The need for a language of international communication arises not only from the fact that communication without it may be impossible (where people do not know each other's language), but also from the fact that it may be inefficient (where one depends on translation, interpreters, or one's limited knowledge of a foreign tongue). We are here dealing with the question of information loss in translation. On this subject Sapir says: 'To pass from one language to another is psychologically parallel to passing from one geometrical system of reference to another. The environing world which is referred to is the same for either language; the world of points is the same in either frame of reference. But the formal method of approach to the expressed item of experience, as to the given point of space, is so different that the resulting feeling of orientation can be the same neither in the two languages nor in the two frames of reference' (153).

There is however a difference between the two cases. One might claim that what is said in one geometric frame (or language) is different from what is said in another, or that the relation of the given information to its universe (or to other bits of information) is different in one from its translation in the other. Still, any identification of a point or relation in, say, Cartesian coordinates can be given completely in, say, polar coordinates, and conversely (though the 'translation' may be more complicated than the original statement). This does not in general hold for language translation. Except for relatively simple parts of the physical world (like the smaller numbers), or very explicitly described parts of it (like the set-up of a scientific experiment), we cannot get a description of the physical world except as variously perceived by the speakers of one language or another.[22] It is therefore not in general possible to see how two language systems depart from their common physical world, but only how they depart from each other. The question of translation is the question of correcting for the difference between the two systems. But neither system can be referred to an absolute physical system (as is possible in the case of scientific terminology), nor is there at present any general method for establishing equivalence relations among them (as can be done among geometric frames of reference). Therefore it does not seem possible to establish a general method for determining the information loss in translating from one language to another, as Wiener would do on the basis of his measure of 'amount of information'.[23]

These two types of difficulty in international communication may have been the major stimulus to the many attempts at forming auxiliary languages. To Sapir, however, as to some linguists and logicians, there was also the incentive of fashioning a superior language system. He was well aware of the limitations of our language, which both narrows our perception and prevents us from expressing adequately some of the things we have perceived: 'As our scientific experience grows we must learn to fight the implications of language ... No matter how sophisticated our modes of interpretation become, we never really get beyond the projection and continuous transfer of relations suggested by the forms of our speech. After all, to say "Friction causes such and such a result" is not very different from saying "The grass waves in the wind" ' (10–1). He was also able to show that linguistic systems are much less satisfactory than might appear: 'The fact that a beginner in English has not many paradigms to learn gives him a feeling of absence of difficulty ... [but] behind a superficial appearance of simplicity there is concealed a perfect hornet's nest of bizarre and arbitrary usages ... We can "give a person a shove" or "a push", but we cannot "give him a move" ... We can "give one help", but we "give obedience", not "obey" ... "To put out of danger" is formally analogous to "to put out of school",

---

[22] See E. Sapir and M. Swadesh, American Indian grammatical categories, Word 2.103–12 (1946)—an item not included in the bibliography. On p. 111 Swadesh quotes a perfectly valid note of Sapir's: 'Naiveté of imagining that any analysis of experience is dependent on pattern expressed in language. Lack of case or other category no indication of lack functionally ... In any given context involving use of language, lang. response is not to be split up into its elements grammatically nor sensorimotorly but kept as unit in contextual pattern.' Elsewhere, however, Sapir says: 'The "real world" is to a large extent unconsciously built up on the language habits of the group ... The worlds in which different societies live are distinct worlds, not merely the same world with different labels attached' (162). There is no contradiction here, since the 'environing world' is the physical world, whereas the 'real world', in quotes, is also called 'social reality' (162) and constitutes the physical world as socially perceived: 'Even the simplest environmental influence is either supported or transformed by social forces' (89); 'The physical environment is reflected in language only insofar as it has been influenced by social forces' (90).

[23] Norbert Wiener, Cybernetics, Chap. 3, esp. 75–9.

but here too the analogy is utterly misleading, unless, indeed, one defines school as a form of danger' (114-5).

Because of his sensitivity to these limitations, Sapir had in mind 'an engine of expression which is logically defensible at every point and which tends to correspond to the rigorous spirit of modern science' (112). He pointed out that the inadequacies of language systems have led to the development of separate systems of symbolism in mathematics and symbolic logic (118). The problem was therefore one of constructing a language system which by its structure would avoid ambiguities and inefficiencies, would be a conformable vehicle for our present scientific understandings, and would be able to change with growth of our understanding. However, there may well be a distinction between the construction of an international language for flexible use in ordinary life, and that of a scientific language which would not only express in its structure the various types of relations, of operations and operands, known to science, but would also have the truth-value retention of a logical system.[24]

The program called for a language that would be easy to learn for people coming with the background of the existing languages, and that would be as simple as possible in its structure, while selecting the kind of structure that would fit the scientific understanding of the world. Because these were his interests, Sapir did not try to construct a language, like Jespersen's Novial, but tried rather to find out what should go into the construction of such a language. Even his investigation of phonetic symbolism is relevant here, as showing what meanings might be less arbitrarily expressed by particular sounds. The investigations which he made specifically for the International Auxiliary Language Association were the semantic papers mentioned above, which would show how useful or harmful it was to have certain meanings expressed together within a morpheme, and what component factors of meaning could be extracted from given words by seeing how they are used. The questions of what meanings could be conveniently expressed by what kinds of structural elements, and of what patternings and formal structures were possible, were not touched by Sapir.

1.4. CHANGE IN LANGUAGE. Sapir's tendency toward analysis in depth, which he could express within descriptive linguistics by means of the process type of formulation, led also to the historical investigation of patterned features. In the process formulation, time was not involved, and depth was a matter of various analytic layers of the system. We now consider investigations in which depth was a matter of historical time, of various successive forms of the system through time.

A descriptive pattern can of course be viewed as being just an interesting arrangement of the data. However, since Sapir saw it as the result of various distributional processes (such as protective mechanisms) among the elements,

---

[24] For an example of how particular logical relations can be built into a constructed language, consider the 'newspeak' of George Orwell's novel Nineteen eighty-four. One of the distributional features which is only lightly suggested in his system is the technique (not unknown in our real languages) of letting opposites equal or replace each other in certain environments, with the result that no distinction between opposites (say between *war* and *peace*) can be made in the language.

he could readily see it also as the result of various historical processes affecting the elements. An instance is the historical addition of a glottal stop between morpheme-final vowel and morpheme-initial vowel in the example cited earlier: in terms of descriptive process, the ? in -V + V- was based on a descriptively prior absence of -VV-; in terms of history the ? in -V + V- may actually have been a late development, due analogically to the absence of -VV-.

A detailed example of this is the discussion of glottalized continuants in certain west-coast languages. After making it clear that all or most of the types ẏ, ẃ, ṁ, and ṅ are distinct phonemes in the languages under consideration, Sapir points out that they are 'so singular that it is tempting to seek evidence accounting for their origin' (226–7). Their singularity is partly distributional (in Navaho, these alone of all consonants do not occur as word-initial), partly morphophonemic (in Navaho, these occur in morphemic environments which can be otherwise shown to have once contained a d morpheme, 228–9). For Wakashan (Nootka and Kwakiutl), he shows that these consonants go back to coalescences of ? or h with neighboring continuants (244); the argument is far too involved and detailed to be summarized here (230–44). In the course of his analysis, Sapir shows that additional glottalized continuants probably existed once in Wakashan (231), and that Boas' 'hardening' process is not the opposite of his 'softening' but is simply a glottalized softening (233). The whole reconstruction, based on comparative evidence, is then used to suggest that when phonetically 'weak' consonants drop they may leave influences in neighboring phonemes, i.e. that they are absorbed rather than dropped (244). With this background, Sapir than reconstructs Indo-European laryngeal bases out of various sets of irregular cognates (245–50), by explaining the various consonantal irregularities as regular reflexes of the effect of lost laryngeals (i.e. of their absorption).

The same methods of investigation are apparent in the famous series of articles on word cognates and word borrowings in Indo-European, Semitic, and other Mediterranean languages, which began to appear in 1934. Two of these are reprinted here (285–8, 294–302); all are of course listed in the bibliography. Studies of loanwords were prominent in this series, because they made it possible to consider the effect of each language system on the form of the word, and to explain otherwise unexplained forms. These papers, together with that on glottalized continuants, are masterpieces of brilliant association, bringing together all sorts of apparently unrelated data, and of meticulous responsibility to every possibly relevant consideration or counter-argument. To discuss what Sapir does in them would take as much space as the original articles; only a careful reading can reveal their remarkable craftsmanship. Some aspects of the method of work used in them, however, will be discussed in Part 4 below.

Much of this brilliance and craftsmanship went into Sapir's painstaking work on Tocharian, which was one of his main projects during those years, and most of which is as yet unpublished.

In addition to all this work, which was of a unique character and bore the stamp of his personality, Sapir also carried out standard work in comparative linguistics, as for example in the Encyclopaedia Britannica article on Philology, or in The concept of phonetic law as tested in primitive languages by Leonard Bloomfield (73–82), in which he presented Bloomfield's Algonkian reconstructions and his own Athabascan ones.

Sapir being what he was, he not only carried out historical linguistic investigations but also made historical linguistic interpretations. In his book Language (Chapter 7), he suggested that similarities among genetically related languages which were too late for their common ancestry, but which could not easily be explained as diffusion, might be explained by a 'drift' which occurs in each of these languages independently of the other but along parallel lines of development. This view has been generally questioned and disregarded by linguists, although data that may support it are not lacking.[25] Sapir granted that such drift could be explained only on the basis of what he sometimes called 'configurational pressure' in the structure with which each of the sister languages started. That is to say, the parent structure may have contained certain imbalances or irregularities, or may otherwise have favored the occurrence of certain changes rather than others; and as this structure developed in various separate places (in what became the various daughter languages) it underwent some of these structurally favored changes in several places independently of each other. Elsewhere, Sapir uses the concept of drift, i.e. of structural favoring as a source of change, to explain the bulk of changes—differentiating ones as well as parallel ones (23). Little, however, can be done with this concept until we can say what kind of structure favors what kind of change in it, i.e. until we can specify 'configurational pressure' and then test to see if it operates.

In addition to this tentative suggestion about the direction of linguistic change, Sapir commented on the even more general problem of the rate of change. There have been various conditional suggestions, as for example that languages with tightly knit structures (e.g. Semitic) change more slowly than those with looser structures (e.g., in comparison, Indo-European). To this Sapir added the general statement that all languages change much more slowly than culture (26–7) and at a more even rate (433),[26] although he thought that changes in both rates might be interconnected: 'The rapid development of culture in western Europe during the last 2000 years has been synchronous with what seems to be unusually rapid changes in language' (102). He then used this statement for a possible explanation of why there is no structural correlation between the patterning of language and the patterning of culture: even if there was once a 'more definite association between cultural and linguistic form, 'the different character and rate of change in linguistic cultural phenomena ... would in the long run very materially disturb and ultimately entirely eliminate such an association' (101, also 26 and 102).

2. CULTURE

Sapir's primary standing was as an anthropologist; but since the bulk of his technical work was in linguistics, his understanding of culture was affected by

[25] Cf. Zellig S. Harris, Development of the Canaanite dialects 99–100 (New Haven, 1939).
[26] An echo of this appears in the work of Sapir's student Morris Swadesh on rate of vocabulary change. Cf. in particular his Salish investigations, carried out under the auspices of the Boas Collection in the American Philosophical Society Library, and published in Salish internal relationships, IJAL 16.157–67 (1950).

the experience gained from analyzing language. It was quite natural to transfer this experience, because he dealt with language as an item of culture (166). There are other though less central ways of treating linguistic material: as a separate set of physiological actions (in experimental or articulatory phonetics), as a problem in hearing and in acoustic engineering (in acoustic linguistics), as an example of combinatorial relations (and other problems of mathematical logic). Sapir did not deal with these. He did not even deal with the technical analogs between the structure of language and the structure of music, though he was deeply interested and proficient in music, and though it is very natural to think of analyzing thematic patterning, phrasing, and the like in music with the techniques developed for language.[27]

The central aspects of language with which he dealt involved basically the same problems as culture: the behavior of individuals along lines that are patterned for the whole social group (see his 'psychology' in Part 3 below); the patterned relations that can be seen among items of language, and among items of culture (e.g. phonemics); the way linguistic forms are used (linguistic usage as an example of custom, 366; the modification of words as a mocking technique in the article Abnormal types of speech in Nootka, 179–96); diffusion (as in the loanword articles); historical change, where not only is the process of change closely related for language and for culture, but also specific changes in one may be related to changes in the other and may throw light upon them (as in the monograph on time perspective, cf. 432–3).

In addition, cultural and speech behavior simply occur together, and are distinguished from each other by the linguist and the ethnologist more than by the people whose actions are being studied. 'Some day the attempt to master a primitive culture without the help of the language of its society will seem as amateurish as the labors of a historian who cannot handle the original documents of the civilization which he is describing' (162).

2.1. CULTURAL PATTERNING. This argument—that conditions and actions are to be treated in culture only in terms of their relation to other items of the culture—runs closely parallel to the argument made in the article Sound patterns in language. This applies even to the question of what environmental items are included in the culture: 'The mere existence of a certain type of animal in the physical environment of a people does not suffice to give rise to a linguistic symbol referring to it. It is necessary that the animal be known by the members of the group in common and that they have some interest, however slight, in it' (90). And it applies to the question of what actions are cultural: 'Ordinarily the characteristic rhythm of breathing of a given individual is looked upon as a matter for strictly individual definition. But if the emphasis shifts to the consideration of a certain manner of breathing as due to good form or social tradition or some other principle that is usually given a social context, then the whole subject of breathing at once ceases to be a merely individual concern and takes on the appearance of a social pattern' (546). Compare the argument in the article on

---

[27] His writings on music dealt with its relation to poetry rather than to linguistic structure. See for example his article The musical foundations of verse, JEGP 20.213–28 (1921).

sound patterns, that the sound of blowing out a candle is not speech whereas the rather similar *wh* sound is speech (33-4).

Similarly, a distinction is drawn between innovation (non-cultural) and fashion (cultural): 'If there is a shortage of silk and it becomes customary to substitute cotton for silk ... such an enforced change of material, however important economically or aesthetically, does not constitute a true change of fashion ... If people persist in using the cotton material even after silk has once more become available, a new fashion has arisen' (374). Just as a sound in one language may have quite a different phonemic place from a similar sound in another language, so 'Gothic type is a nationalistic token in Germany, while in Anglo-Saxon culture the practically identical type known as Old English has entirely different connotations' (376).

The actual patterns within culture are far less easily describable in terms of intricate combinatorial relations than is the case for linguistic patterns. Sapir described cultural patterns, as for example in The social organization of the West Coast tribes (468-87), where, in discussing their groupings according to rank, he shows that various privileges are as characteristic of rank as is authority (473-4), and that these perquisites of rank are handed down from holder to heir (475-6), and finally connects it all into a social pattern: 'The idea of a definite patrimony of standing and associated rights which, if possible, should be kept intact or nearly so. Despite the emphasis placed on rank ... the individual as such is of very much less importance than the tradition that for the time being he happens to represent' (476). This is the kind of patterning that Sapir worked out for culture—specific, and achieved by interrelating variegated data into a single whole. He had too much experience with the intricate and demonstrable patterns of linguistics, and with the great difference between a pattern within a language and the structure of a whole language, to speak of a whole culture as constituting a unified pattern. He did not call one society 'Dionysian', or another 'oral-sadistic'—even though (or rather because) he had an early and deep understanding of psychoanalytic theories, as is evidenced by his reviews of Freud and Freudian writers (522-32).

Function of Patterns. His picture of cultural patterns was quite different from the views of the functionalists. He argued specifically that cultural patterns do not correlate readily with social function (339-40) and that 'it is more than doubtful if the gradual unfolding of social patterns tends indefinitely to be controlled by function' (341). He was sensitive to the relevance of each behavioral item, and noted when the pattern of an activity revealed that something beyond its social function was involved. Concerning fashion, for example, he shows that the same role is played by all fashions, no matter what their cultural content—namely giving people an opportunity to express themselves without exceeding the bounds of custom, i.e. 'to legitimize their personal deviation'. Therefore fashions are not relevant to function, where function is understood as the avowed social content of a behavior: 'Functional irrelevance as contrasted with symbolic significance for the expressionism of the ego is implicit in all fashion' (381).

Because of his interest in bringing such points home, Sapir failed to mention the more indirect and subtle functions which these patterns could still be shown to have. He did this, indeed, in showing the personality function of the fashion pattern; but in the example of Gothic and Old English type he could have pointed out that while the pattern point of this type face is quite different in Germany and in England, still there is some functional similarity: in both areas the type face represented a symbolism with some national (or national-historical) aura, as contrasted with an efficient search for clear printing. Similarly, in a very early paper (1919) we find: 'A magic ritual which, when considered psychologically, seems to liberate and give form to powerful emotional aesthetic elements of our nature, is nearly always put in harness to some humdrum utilitarian end—the catching of rabbits or the curing of disease' (319; the next sentence has it 'functionally or pseudo-functionally interwoven with the immediate ends'). But the magic ritual often has another function, the maintenance of certain social rankings, or of the privileges of a particular occupational group; and the ritual is useful for this function precisely because it can serve it indirectly. Hence we see that while the ritual has undoubted expressive value, it also has some intrinsic social function aside from its pseudo-function—which last is merely the function (or social correlate) of its outcome rather than the function of the specific behavior peculiar to it.

A similar question of remoter social effect may be raised at another point in the same paper: '[A genuine culture is one] in which no important part of the general functioning brings with it a sense of frustration, of misdirected or unsympathetic effort ... If the culture necessitates slavery, it frankly admits it ... It does not make a great show in its ethical ideals of an uncompromising opposition to slavery, only to introduce what amounts to a slave system into certain portions of its industrial mechanism' (315). But one cannot have an arrangement like slavery in a society without having certain effects that are excluded from the 'genuine culture'. Where there is any exercise of power by one group over another, the ruled will have cause enough for 'a sense of frustration'. If the power is overt, the ruling group presumably has to justify its actions to itself (and will often insist that the ruled accept that justification), with all sorts of resultant effects upon the ideology, the rationalizations, and the social forms at least of the rulers. If the power is covert, the ruling group has to conceal the actual social relations from the ruled (and often also from itself), with the result that there are many social forms whose indirect social function is not recognized, that the ideal culture differs widely from the real, and that there are many other features which are precisely excluded from the picture of the 'genuine' culture.

From all these examples, it follows that a greater (though indirect and remote) functional character can be shown for social patterns. Sapir did not miss all this, as would be obvious to anyone who knew him. But he did not use this material in his generalizations, whether because of his desire to correct for the superficial functionalism that was often espoused, or because his linguistic interests made him favor intra-cultural explanations as against those involving social organization or economics. In a few places he refers to culture instead of social and economic organization (although, of course, the former could be understood to include the latter): 'As a result of cultural reasons of one kind or another a local dialect gets accepted as the favored or desirable form of speech within a linguistic community that is cut up into a large number of dialects' (85). Or consider: 'In custom bound cultures, such as are characteristic of the primitive world, there are slow non-reversible changes of style rather than the often reversible forms of fashion found in modern cultures ... It is not until modern Europe is reached that the familiar merry-go-round of fashion with its rapid alternations of season occurs' (377). Sapir did not work into his generalization here the factor which he mentions on the next page, and without which this modern change appears strange: 'The extraordinarily high initial profits to be derived from fashion and the relatively rapid tapering off of profits make it inevitable that the natural tendency to change in fashion is helped along by commercial suggestion' (378). Similarly, Sapir speaks of 'the nuclei of consciousness from which all science, all art, all history, all culture, have flowed as symbolic by-products in the humble but intensely urgent business of establishing meaningful relationships between actual human beings' (581)—failing to add 'and the business of obtaining food and making a living'. Yet further on in the same article he points out brilliantly that 'personalities live in tangible environments and that the business of making a living is one of the bed-rock factors in their environmental adjustment ... For all practical purposes a too low income is at least as significant a datum in the causation of mental ill-health as a buried Oedipus complex or sex trauma' (588).

In all these cases we seem to see an understanding come clear in the specific analysis, but not used in the generalization. This was not like Sapir, who used to create powerful new generalizations by extracting every bit of implication out of his subtle analyses of specific points. We can only assume that he failed to follow up his own analyses here because they were too far from the main directions of his cultural interests, which were in linguistics and in personality.

Inertia of Patterns. Certainly his linguistic experience may have influenced him to give more weight to cultural inertia (or lag) than is its due. In language, of course, this seems an unquestionable fact. Not only is there the barely changing persistence of grammatical structure, but there is also the 'adaptive persistence' of vocabulary, 'which tends to remain fairly true to set form but which is constantly undergoing reinterpretation ... For example, the word robin refers in the United States to a very different bird from the English bird that was originally meant. The word could linger on with a modified meaning because it is a symbol and therefore capable of indefinite reinterpretation' (368). In one or two places comparable statements are made for culture and social organization: 'the universal tendency for groups which have a well defined function to lose their original function but to linger on as symbolically reinterpreted groups. Thus a political club may lose its significance in the realistic world of politics but may nevertheless survive significantly as a social club in which membership is eagerly sought by those who wish to acquire a valuable symbol of status' (362). And more generally: 'Old culture forms, habitual types of reaction, tend to persist through the force of inertia' (317). Now it is of course true that forms often persist; but instead of saying merely that they may persist, we can specify some of the conditions which make them persist: for example, if the political club is an organ of a ruling group which no longer operates through politics but still maintains a social ruling position. Such formulations make it unnecessary to appeal to a principle of inertia, since persistence like anything else will then appear to have causes (or, at least, particular antecedents). One can then see that the word *robin* was used for the new bird if the settlers had no name for it and at the same time had little occasion to use the old word *robin* in their new homes (and if the birds had some sufficient similarities). And the political club became a prestige club because status was still a functioning part of the social organization, and this club was available for a status-symbol since it was losing its political function and was associated with a socially powerful class.

2.2. CULTURAL CHANGE. Just as Sapir dealt not only with the patterns of language but also with their historical depth, so he dealt both with culture patterns and with their sources in culture history. In The social organization of the West Coast tribes (468–87) he analyzes their clan and crest organization, and from a distributional description of the crests—where they occur, which occur together, which represents a subdivision of the other—he works out a time perspective for them, showing which can be presumed to be earlier, reconstructing the earlier relations of the crests, and buttressing all this by the kind of names the clans have, and the like (480–7). All this is very similar to the kind of work he did in historical linguistics based on distributional descriptive analysis. In addition, Sapir did the standard type of investigation, making historical linguistic analyses in order to derive historical interpretations of social and cultural contact—for example in his Tocharian work (e.g. Tibetan influences on Tocharian, 273–84).

The whole of such historical analysis, both for culture and for language, was organized by Sapir in his famous 1916 monograph Time perspective in aboriginal American culture: A study in method (reprinted 389–462). This monumental work shows how one can judge the age of cultural elements from their relation to various other cultural and linguistic items, and thus place the present cultural elements into a chronological perspective in respect to each other. Not only is half the material here linguistic, but the method used in reconstructing the purely cultural chronology is closely related to the methods of historical linguistics. Thus, 'inferential evidence for time perspective' is divided into two main parts, one dealing with the evidence from ethnology (400–32), the other with the evidence from linguistics (432–60). The ethnologic evidence is divided into evidence from cultural seriation (400–2), cultural associations (402–10), geographical distribution (subdivided into diffusion, 410–25, and cultural areas and strata, 425–32). The linguistic evidence is listed under language and culture (432–4), inferences from analysis of words and grammatical elements (434–44), and geographical distribution of culture words (444–51), of linguistic stocks (452–8), and of grammatical features (458–60).

Suspicion of greater age attaches to the simpler forms of a cultural element (e.g. the single-figure Nootka totem pole as against the more elaborate poles to the north, 401);[28] the logically prior forms (e.g. realistic designs as against the

---

[28] Comparison of the page references in this paragraph with those in the preceding one will indicate which point is included in which category. Thus, simplicity of form is discussed under the seriation of culture elements from the simple or primary to the derived.

geometric ones derived from them, 401);[29] the elements which are presupposed by others (the art of dressing skins must be older than the tipi, 402–3);[30] the more stereotyped forms and those frequently referred to in ceremonies and the like (404); forms with widely ramified associations in the culture (407) and with elaboration of detail (408); isolated elements which seem out of context (409, though these may be borrowings rather than survivals); elements which are distributed over a larger area (412–3) and occur in those tribes which are nearer the center of the area of distribution (412);[31] and elements whose area of distribution is a broken one (their diffusion having preceded the break, 423–4). Various cautions have to be observed throughout, such as the possibility of parallel or convergent developments in various tribes, which may account (instead of diffusion) for the distribution of an element (420). Also, the age of a cultural element need not be the age of the complex in which it is set in one or more tribes (413–4). One can then reconstruct the culture of an area by eliminating all the late-coming elements, and may find that it then forms a continuous culture area with its neighbors, or that it reveals an earlier areal cleavage, or the like (426). Sapir goes on to argue against the notion of a culture stratum, i.e. a group of elements which go back to a common period and which move together though not technically related to each other (427–30).

Linguistic evidence suggestive of antiquity of culture elements is of several kinds: non-descriptive terms for the element, as against terms which analysis (whether obvious or not) shows to be descriptive (e.g. English *king* from OE *cyning*, derivative of *cynn* 'kin', 435);[32] meaningless place names (435); the meanings of the component elements in descriptive (i.e. morphologically derivative) words whose later meaning is not the sum of its parts (e.g. *spinster* is composed of elements meaning 'one who spins', whence certain cultural inferences may be drawn, 439); culture complexes having more ramified vocabulary (440–1); words of cultural interest having survival features in their grammar (e.g. *oxen*, 441; but words with regular grammar may be equally old, 442);[33] cultural elements expressed by affixes (which are of more certain antiquity than stems, 443); elements whose names are diffused widely (444–5);[34] any words shown to be from the parent stage of a language family by the fact that the daughter languages contain cognates of it (449); borrowed words shown to be subject to (hence older than) the operation of some phonetic change in the

---

[29] But one must guard against such other factors as simplification of a form in the course of borrowing (402).

[30] But a cultural element (e.g. ritual use of tobacco) may be borrowed without its chronological antecedent (cultivation of the tobacco plant; 403).

[31] Larger areas will often not mean greater age, since some elements diffuse faster than others (e.g. elements which are not secret, or are detachable from their context, 414–5), and some environments favor quicker diffusion (e.g. areas covered by related languages, or lines of easy communication, 416–9).

[32] But some languages favor descriptive word formations (437); and old non-descriptive words may have been changed in meaning to apply to a later culture element (438).

[33] And languages differ in their hospitality to analogic regularization of grammar (442).

[34] In language, unlike culture, borrowed material can often be readily recognized by its phonetic structure, morphological unanalyzability, length, or the like, and can be traced to its language of origin (445–9).

borrowing language (450); widely spread, and in particular heavily diversified, language families (452; 'A tribe may overrun a large territory at a very much more rapid rate than a language splits up into two divergent dialects').[35]

In somewhat later work, Sapir dealt more generally and interpretatively with cultural change. Thus, he shows how technical innovations which are not in themselves changes of custom can become changes of custom because of their relation to other culture items: 'The introduction of the automobile, for instance, was not at first felt as necessarily disturbing custom, but in the long run all those customs appertaining to visiting and other modes of disposing of one's leisure time have come to be seriously modified by the automobile as a power contrivance' (367). This is quite similar to phonologization in linguistics, the process whereby a non-phonemic sound change comes to alter the phonemic pattern of the language. Elsewhere, Sapir also suggested a cultural drift, somewhat like the drift he proposed in linguistics: 'Wherever the human mind has worked collectively and unconsciously, it has striven for and often attained unique form. The important point is that the evolution of form has a drift in one direction, that is seeks poise, and that it rests, relatively speaking, when it has found this poise' (382).

By far his most interesting and valuable remarks about culture change came out of his interrelating of cultural form and individual activity. He saw culture change as stemming from the reactions of individuals, and culture itself as the deposit and growing framework of interpersonal behavior. A full discussion of this, however, is possible only after his treatment of the individual is surveyed, and the subject will therefore be taken up in the next section.

3. PERSONALITY

From the early thirties on, Sapir's great new interest was the interrelation of personality and culture. To the study of personality he brought two special backgrounds. His linguistic experience gave him rigor in the treatment of behavior. His ethnologic background contributed relativism and emphasized the place of social forms in the growth of a personality. Although he is considered by many to be the chief figure in this field, his formulations have hardly been understood or used by any professionals, because they are so incisive and lead so readily to social criticism.

Before we consider the personality-and-culture formulations, we will survey Sapir's statements on psychology and personality in general.

3.1. PERSONALITY AS A SYSTEM. Sapir saw personality as he saw language and also culture—as a systemic result of interrelated processes. He defined the psychiatric view of personality as 'an essentially invariant reactive system' (560).

---

[35] In discussing what can be learned historically from the way a language family is spread and diversified (453-8), Sapir says that the fact that both Aleut and Eskimo are spoken in Alaska, while only Eskimo is spoken in Canada, supports Alaska as the center of dispersion Eskimo. But such considerations will not hold if there are successive waves of emigration from a center, which pile up at coast-lines or other boundaries, thus making the periphery more differentiated in language than the center (cf. the diversified Semitic periphery as against the Arabian center).

Because of this there is little wonder that he was so impressed with the depth analysis and the coherent systematization of personality that marked the Freudian schools as against the older trait psychology (513).

After arguing that psychiatry cannot deal with the individual except in terms of his social (interpersonal) relations (512), and that cultural anthropology cannot deal with culture except in terms of individual behavior (512, 515, 569), Sapir asks what he calls the social-psychological question: 'What is the meaning of culture in terms of individual behavior?' (513). His answer is that individual behavior is the individual's selection and personal systemization of what we can observe in the gross as social behavior (when we disregard the personality selection but use social correlates instead). 'We have thus defined the difference between individual and social behavior, not in terms of kind or essence, but in terms of organization. To say that the human being behaves individually at one moment and socially at another is as absurd as to declare that matter follows the laws of chemistry at a certain time and succumbs to the supposedly different laws of atomic physics at another' (545).

Whatever is the character of particular social forms, then, is also the character of the individual behavior which carries out those social forms. The individual who carries out the forms cannot say, 'This is not me; it is a social form.' It is his behavior, and Sapir speaks of 'the world of meanings which each one of these individuals may unconsciously abstract for himself from his participation in these interactions' (515).

From this it follows that what the anthropologist and linguist describe as social and linguistic patterns are at the same time patterns of individual behavior.[36] With the prime example of language patterning at his hand, Sapir shows how the speaker of a particular language uses the particular pattern of that language no matter what he is saying (550-3). He then proceeds to the important point that this patterning is 'unconscious' for the individual (549). When these patterns are described impersonally, for the language or the culture as an abstraction or an aggregate, the question of whether they are 'conscious' is meaningless. But once we take into consideration that the individual's behavior is patterned along much the same lines, we have to recognize that it is not a 'conscious' arrangement of behavior for him. 'Not all forms of cultural behavior so well illustrate the mechanics of unconscious patterning as does linguistic behavior, but there are few, if any, types of cultural behavior which do not illustrate it ... There is not only an unconscious patterning of types of endeavor that are classed as economic, there is even such a thing as a characteristic patterning of economic motive. Thus, the acquirement of wealth is not to be lightly taken for granted as one of the basic drives of human beings. One accumulates property, one defers the immediate enjoyment of wealth, only in so far as society sets the pace for these activities and inhibitions' (556-7).

---

[36] In some cases, as in social organization or linguistic usage and vocabulary, the individual carries out only a part of the socially observed pattern (516), and we cannot say that his selection of behavior is the same as the social pattern. In other cases, as in grammatical structure, the individual's behavior is virtually the same as that which is described for the society as a whole.

One might ask what is the importance of recognizing the unconscious status of these patterns in the individual who carries them out. The answer: it is of interest to our understanding of the personality because it points out a major set of activities which never rises up into awareness. And it gives a clear parallel to the better-known cases, of the more personally clouded behavior which has not entered into awareness. Writing before his close association with Harry Stack Sullivan, Sapir discussed unconscious behavior in a way which fits in closely with Sullivan's picture of awareness: the unconscious is not always something suppressed, but includes the individual's patterning of his behavior along the lines of the cultural patterns (549).

3.2. Sapir's 'psychology': individual participation in social patterns. At this point it becomes possible to explain Sapir's use of the word 'psychology' in his linguistic and ethnographic discussions, something which has disturbed many of his readers. He did not use it to explain linguistic forms, as many linguists had done in the past; he would never say, for example, that a language contained three genders because people 'needed' to distinguish male, female, and neuter objects. Quite the contrary, he was a master at the craft of stating one linguistic occurrence in terms of other, partially similar, linguistic occurrences;[37] and his work and explicit statements were major factors in raising linguistics above the level of the circular and ad-hoc psychological explanations which had been the order of the day. In culture and in personality, as in language, he argued for formal explanations as against 'psychology'. In his article on Group, he says: 'In the discussion of the fundamental psychology of the group such terms as gregariousness, consciousness of kind and group mind do little more than give names to problems to which they are in no sense a solution. The psychology of the group cannot be fruitfully discussed except on the basis of a profounder understanding of the ways in which different sorts of personalities enter into significant relations with each other' (363).[38] And in the article on Fashion: 'A specific fashion is utterly unintelligible if lifted out of its sequence of forms. It is exceedingly dangerous to rationalize or in any other way psychologize a particular fashion on the basis of general principles which might be considered applicable to the class of forms of which it seems to be an example' (375–6).

A detailed examination of Sapir's use of *psychology* and kindred words shows they refer not to some new forces within the individual which can affect his language, culture, or personality, but simply to the fact that the individual participates in linguistic, cultural, and personality patterns. This is the meaning—i.e. the use—of the word; and it is quite different from what many thought it meant. Characteristically, the sentences containing *psychology* or its equivalents have two parts, the first in terms of formal pattern and the second in terms of the 'psychological' participation in the pattern. An example: 'In other lan-

---

[37] E.g. of 'explaining' an unusual suffix by analyzing it as a combination of two suffixes which are members of classes whose sequence would indeed occur precisely in the position occupied by the strange suffix.

[38] In linguistics, the analog to 'the way personalities enter into relations with each other' is the distributional interrelation of elements.

guages, with different phonologic and morphologic understandings ... 'm and 'p would have a significantly different psychologic weighting' (57–8).

The meaning 'individual participation in a pattern' comes out clearly: 'the formal procedures which are intuitively employed by the speakers of a language' (9); 'the psychological difference between a sound and a phoneme' (54); 'In Sarcee ... there is a true middle tone and a pseudo-middle [i.e. morphophonemic] tone which results from the lowering of a high tone to the middle position because of certain mechanical rules of tone sandhi. I doubt very much if the intuitive psychology of these two middle tones is the same' (40). This is also the use of the word *feel*: 'Since no word can begin with a cluster of consonants, both 'p and 'm [which occur initially] are felt by Nootka speakers to be unanalyzable phonologic units [i.e. not clusters]' (57); 'the English theory of syllabification feels the point of syllabic division to lie in the following consonant' (59); 'se battre gives the Frenchman the same formal feeling as se tuer' (116).[39]

This individual participation in patterns is then said to be unconscious: 'unconscious linguistic forms which in their totality give us regular phonetic change' (161; elsewhere, in discussing drift, linguistic change is attributed to the patterning of the language); 'unconscious phonologic pattern' (58); 'the subconscious character of grammatical classification' (101). It was easier for a linguist than for anyone else to recognize that the 'patterns of social behavior are very incompletely, if at all, known by the normal naïve individual' (549), and Sapir used language as his main example of this (552–5). He says that the development of an individual's participation in a pattern is unconscious: 'in each case an unconscious control of very complicated configurations or formal sets is individually acquired' (555); 'the language-learning process, particularly the acquisition of a feeling for the formal set of a language, is very largely unconscious and involves mechanisms that are quite distinct in character from either sensation or reflection' (156). 'The unconscious nature of this patterning consists not in some mysterious function of a racial or social mind ... but merely in a typical unawareness on the part of the individual of outlines and demarcations and significances of conduct which he is all the time implicitly following' (548). Since the socially patterned behavior figures in the life of each participating individual, the effect of the pattern is observable not only in the linguist's or anthropologist's analysis but also in the individuals themselves. This is the meaning of Sapir's phrase 'configurational pressure': 'Owing to ... the lack of obvious paradigmatic relationship of ʔi·ńiʔ and dińí to di-....-nt, it is safe to assume that the [historical] analyses that we have given, however clear to the dissecting linguist, have not the "configurative pressure" that would justify our considering the phoneme ń as merely a resultant of d + n. If such an interpretation was at one time possible, it is probably no longer the case from a purely descriptive point of view' (227).[40]

---

[39] Note also the 'feeling' due to the range of occurrences of the morpheme -kʃ·h in Navaho (220–2).

[40] A descriptive pattern would have been the same as a configurational pressure on the individual speakers; a historical reconstruction would not.

Then cofigurational pressure would be what makes the speakers change their speech in such pattern-favored directions as analogic levelling. The static equivalent of it is simply the individual's patterned perception. His participation in patterned behavior determines his perception of that behavior. His perception of one utterance, for example, is structured by his knowledge of partially similar other utterances. A case in point is phonemic hearing: 'it was this underlying phonologic configuration that made Alex [Sapir's Nootka informant] hear *'m* as sufficiently similar to *p̌* to justify its being written in an analogous fashion' (57). Or mishearing: 'Owing to the compelling, but mainly unconscious, nature of the forms of social behavior, it becomes almost impossible for the normal individual to observe or to conceive of functionally similar types of behavior in other societies than his own, or in other cultural contexts than those he has experienced, without projecting into them the forms that he is familiar with' (549). 'Thus, the naïve Frenchman confounds the two sounds "s" of "sick" and "th" of "thick" in a single pattern point—not because he is really unable to hear the difference, but because the setting up of such a difference disturbs his feeling for the necessary configuration of linguistic sounds' (555-6).

We can now understand why Sapir had to stress the fact that the individual's participation in these patterns is unconscious. It is precisely because the individual is not aware of the way his behavior is patterned that he cannot explicitly compare his patterning with that of others, and so has his perception of others' behavior determined in advance. His awareness is restricted to certain aspects of his behavior, to the particular use he is making of his patterned actions, but does not extend to the resulting pattern. Thus Sapir points out that an unending cycle of fashion is the pattern for a society organized as ours is; but it results from the interplay of people bridging the gap to the next class above them, while the class above expresses its status by creating fashions that distinguish it from the one below; the result is an unending cycle (375).

It is important to understand how Sapir used these terms, both because it removes any hint of psychologizing, and also because it nets us two results: the reminder, first, that each person's behavior is patterned by his participation in these social forms (§3.1 above); second, that the structuring of perception is related to the individual's lack of awareness of how his behavior is patterned. Nevertheless, the vocabulary available to Sapir leaves certain unclarities which will have to be eliminated in future work. For the generation of linguists which has learned, from Sapir and Bloomfield, to avoid psychological explanations, the use of such words as *feel* and *intuitive* is uncomfortable. In contexts dealing with culture and personality the words may slip by unnoticed. For example, Sapir analyzes the West Coast Indians' system of ranking to be not an individual ranking (as it appears in the immediately observable behavior) but a method of preserving sets of privileges down through the generations. He then summarizes this analysis and attributes some of this to the individual participating Indian: ' "For men may come and men may go," says the line of descent with its distinctive privileges, "but I go on forever." This is the Indian theory as implied in their general attitude' (477). At the same time Sapir recognizes that this is an 'unconscious patterning' descriptive of the society, rather than an explicit attitude of the individual: 'One accumulates property ... only insofar as society sets the pace' (557).

It would be more rigorous if in all these fields we only recognized, first, the analytically discovered social pattern which results from the behavior of the individuals, and second (following Sapir), the unaware participation of the individuals in this pattern—i.e. the fact that the individual's behavior follows along the patterned lines. Whether, and in what sense or to what degree, the individual feels his participation, is a matter for separate investigation, though there are many reasons to think (as Sapir did) that the individual may somehow do so.

Another reason for being careful about this formulation is that it seems to make the individual merely a creature of the social pattern, someone who 'actualizes' it by participating in it. Sapir himself was quite sensitive to this danger, and used the pattern to detect variation as well as conformity: 'To one who is not accustomed to the pattern, [the individual] variations would appear so slight as to be all but unobserved. Yet they are of maximum importance to us as individuals; so much so that we are liable to forget that there is a general social pattern to vary from' (534). Perhaps the relation of the individual behavior to the social pattern could be more generally expressed by saying that the social pattern (i.e. the behavior of the other individuals in society) provides experience and a model which is available to each individual when he acts.[41] Just how he will use this available material depends on his history and situation: often enough he will simply imitate it, but not always. This formulation does not say that the individual participates in the social pattern (and sometimes varies from it), or that he feels it; it says that he uses it as available material when he acts. It will appear below that this formulation fits Sapir's own view of the position of the individual in society.

3.3. THE RELATION OF THE INDIVIDUAL TO THE CULTURE. The crux of Sapir's happy and fruitful understanding of the relation between individual and culture is that it is a reactive relation. The culture is seen not as a matrix in which the individual is stamped, but in the best tradition of the Enlightenment as part of the environing situation (together with the physical conditions) within which the individual operates: 'The social forces which thus transform the purely environmental influences may themselves be looked upon as environmental in character insofar as a given individual is placed in, and therefore reacts to, a set of social factors' (89).[42]

[41] Sapir seems to say that the native 'grasps' the social pattern, while the outside observer just sees the resultant behavior (547). But by observing enough of the behavior, the observer can see as much as the native has grasped. The native himself has grasped it only by observing a great deal of behavior; he is a 'participant observer' of his own society. Hence the social patterns are really not 'felt' by him, but observed; the observations are experiences upon which he can draw when he acts.

[42] Gordon Childe, What happened in history 8: 'In practice ideas form as effective an element in the environment of any human society as do mountains, trees, animals, the weather and the rest of external nature. Societies, that is, behave as if they were reacting to a spiritual environment as well as to a material environment.'

Sapir makes the implications explicit: 'Culture is not something given but something to be gradually and gropingly discovered' (596). '[Society] is only apparently a static sum of social institutions; actually it is being reanimated or creatively reaffirmed from day to day by particular acts of a communicative nature which obtain among individuals participating in it' (104).[41] This recognition of the difference between the social patterns or channels and people's behavior or interrelations gave Sapir insight into the relation of social form to individual life. He was thus able to distinguish the efficiency of technology from the efficiency of the human use of it: 'The telephone girl who lends her capacities, during the greater part of the living day, to the manipulation of a technical routine that has an eventually high efficiency value but that answers to no spiritual needs of her own is an appalling sacrifice to civilization. As a solution to the problem of culture she is a failure—the more dismal the greater her natural endowment ... The American Indian who solves the economic problem with salmon-spear and rabbit-snare operates on a relatively low level of civilization, but he represents an incomparably higher solution than our telephone girl of the questions that culture has to ask of economics' (316).[42]

Sapir was further able to distinguish between social function and personal function: 'The increasing ease of communication is purchased at a price, for it is becoming increasingly difficult to keep an intended communication within the desired bounds. A humble example of this new problem is the inadvisability of making certain kinds of statements on the telephone' (108). Sapir could hardly have had wire-tapping in mind as an example in this remark (which was published in 1931), but the intrusion upon privacy which has developed since he wrote these lines shows how much perspicacity can result from the understanding with which one approached a problem. Sapir was interested in how such social techniques as communication relate to the individual's life, and was therefore able to recognize the general fact that privacy can be lost and controls can be exercised.

Sapir's final conclusion was: the observables are people and patternable behavior. Society is just the 'state in which people find themselves', and culture is the abstracted pattern of their behavior (576). 'The true locus of culture is

[41] The siren of literary effect, which is not always identical with meticulous statement, sometimes led Sapir into such sentences as this (106): 'It is largely the function of the artist to make articulate these more subtle intentions of society.' Some writers really mean it when they refer to the 'subtle intentions of society'; Sapir obviously did not.

[42] The 'higher solution' lies in the fact that the Indian makes fuller use of available technical knowledge, and has more opportunity to participate in the arranging of his own work, and to make any changes in it. If he fails to carry out any developments in his own work, it is because he lacks the immediate need or the means to make such changes, not so much because he is restricted as to his own activities (as he would be in our society) by orders from others and by a tight organizational structure into which he fits as a cog. One might argue that not only our society has such restrictions, and that the problem is not so much whether primitive societies are freer of them but rather how in our society the people who work can become more free of such limitations. But Sapir's comment is more important as a critique of his own culture than as a commendation of the Indian's—which is natural, since Sapir knew the detailed difficulties of his own culture better, and since these touched him more closely.

in the interactions of specific individuals' (515). The continuity and permanence of culture is provided for in a way that explains both its permanence and its changeability: 'We shall have to operate as though we knew nothing about culture but were interested in analyzing as well as we could what a given number of human beings accustomed to live with each other actually think and do in their day to day relationships. We shall then find that we are driven, willy-nilly, to the recognition of certain permanencies, in a relative sense, in these interrelationships, permanencies which can reasonably be counted on to perdure but which must also be recognized to be eternally subject to serious modification of form and meaning with the lapse of time and with those changes of personnel which are unavoidable in the history of any group of human beings' (574).

This formulation is strongly supported by the fact that the culture of the individual is not the same as the whole culture of a society but is rather a selection and subsection within it. Sapir pointed this out, and used it productively: 'It is impossible to think of any cultural pattern or set of cultural patterns which can, in the literal sense of the word, be referred to society as such. There are no facts of political organization or family life or religious belief or magical procedure or technology or aesthetic endeavor which are coterminous with society or with any mechanically or sociologically defined segment of society. The fact that John Doe is registered in some municipal office as a member of such and such a ward only vaguely defines him with reference to ... "municipal administration" ... If John Doe is paying taxes on a house ... and if he also happens to be in personal contact with a number of municipal offices, ward classification may easily become a symbol of his orientation ... But there is sure to be another John Doe ... who does not even know that the town is divided into wards and that he is, by definition, enrolled in one of them' (515–6).[46]

Viewed in terms of the society, the fact that no cultural item extends over

---

[46] In two somewhat earlier articles, Sapir talked in a more standard anthropological manner without recognizing the limitations of cultural uniformity that were stressed in the excerpt quoted above: '[A Haida Indian] cannot be born, become of age, be married, give feasts, be invited to a feast, take or give a name, decorate his belongings, or die as a mere individual, but always as one who shares in the traditions and usages that go with the Killer-whale or associated crests' (345). 'If we leave the more sophisticated peoples and study the social habits of primitive and barbaric folk, we shall find that it is very difficult to discover religious institutions that are as highly formalized as those that go under the name of the Roman Catholic Church or of Judaism. Yet religion in some sense is everywhere present. It seems to be as universal as speech itself and the use of material tools' (346). Sapir's own argument above leaves little room for doubt that we could find many actions by Haida individuals which would manage to keep clear of any crest identification, just as the second John Doe avoided involvement in the ward system; and that many primitive individuals are free of any religious identification, just as are many moderns. It is quite understandable that Sapir should have noticed the individual differences in his own society and missed them—or simply not had the data—in other societies which he necessarily knew in far less detail. When anthropologists have turned to write about their own society, they have customarily found conformity and acceptable conditions, in contrast with the class controls and major cultural inadequacies which they found in enemy or primitive societies. It is to Sapir's credit that he used his critical powers where they might do most good: in remarks about his own society. He might omit some individual variation or some cultural critique of a primitive society, but he would be sure to fight it out at home. (See §2.3, end, and Part 4 below.)

the whole population means that the 'whole' culture is a composite of varying and overlapping subcultures. Viewed in terms of the individual, it means that persons within a society may differ from each other in various cultural respects: 'If we make the test of imputing the contents of an ethnological monograph to a known individual in the community which it describes, we would inevitably be led to discover that, while every single statement in it may, in the favorable case, be recognized as holding true in some sense, the complex of patterns as described cannot, without considerable absurdity, be interpreted as a significant configuration of experience, both actual and potential, in the life of the person appealed to' (593). More than that, all this means that only particular items of culture (i.e. of patterned interpersonal experience) and not others are inter-related within particular personalities: '[Personality is not] a mysterious entity resisting the historically given culture but rather a distinctive configuration of experience which tends always to form a psychologically significant unit and which ... creates finally that cultural microcosm of which official "culture" is little more than a metaphorically and mechanically expanded copy' (595).

The implication is that society and culture do not determine and control people as fully as the social scientists suppose or would like to suppose. The social scientists may be led to their beliefs by the supra-individual composite arrangement of their data, or by their occupational position in schools and administrative offices. But their statements represent an occupational ideology rather than a relativistic understanding. It is true, of course, that each person is considerably affected by the patterned behavior, demands and expectations, of those around him. 'Some modes of behavior and attitude are pervasive and compelling beyond the power of even the most isolated individual to withstand or reject. Such patterns would be, for example, the symbolisms of affection or hostility ... and many details of the economic order' (517). However, even here it may be possible to view the acquiescent response of the individual not as submission to control, or as being stamped by a matrix, but as participation in ways (ways of recognizing affection, ways of functioning economically) which are available to him—the compelling character being due precisely to their pervasiveness, i.e. to the fact that the person has at the time no alternative way for recognizing people's affection or for interrelating with them in production.

For Sapir, then, the individual's relation to the culture is that he acts and in particular interrelates with others, and that in developing his ways of acting he makes use of his particular experience as to the behavior of others. This differs from the naive formulations of perception, which would make the individual merely a reflection of the culture, perceiving everything in terms set by the culture.[46] Sapir supports his position by pointing to cultural individuality:

[46] Sapir sometimes spoke of language as determining people's perception: 'The "real world" is to a large extent unconsciously built up on the language habits of the group' (162). In later work he says rather that a particular language can 'help and retard us in our exploration of experience' (11)—i.e. retard us but not stamp us irrevocably; that mathematics has gone on to develop its own alternative system (118), rather than remaining blocked by perceptions based on language; and that 'as our scientific experience grows we must learn to fight the implications of language' (10), rather than accept it as inevitable that we can do no more than reflect the existing linguistic structure.

'Vast reaches of culture, far from being in any real sense "carried" by a community or a group as such, are discoverable only as the peculiar property of certain individuals, who cannot but give these cultural goods the impress of their own personality' (594–5).

3.4. THE RELATION OF THE INDIVIDUAL TO SOCIETY. The discussion hitherto has dealt with the behavior of others which an individual observes and with which he interacts. The anthropologist, as also the linguist, organizes his description of this behavior into a culture pattern. The individual observes the behavior, imitating it or varying upon it or whatever, but without explicitly recognizing the various behaviors as interrelated points in some pattern. Nor does the individual recognize the effect (the 'function') of the pattern if the pattern has some other effect than its component behaviors. This is the meaning of Sapir's statement that the patterning is unconscious (549). One can say that the individual pronounces *met* with a certain tongue position and *mat* with another, simply because he has learned to pronounce each word so, and not because the difference in tongue position is needed in order to preserve the phonemic patterning of /e/ and /æ/. And when the child's mispronunciation is corrected, he is told simply to say it more like the person who is doing the correcting; he is not told to speak in such a way as to keep *met* and *mat* (and certainly not /e/ and /æ/) apart. Similarly, when Sapir analyzes West Coast rankings, he obtains a pattern which could hardly be present in the Indians' awareness (474–5).

The importance of recognizing the purely analytic status of the pattern lies in this: it means that the individual's participation in culture patterns is something quite different from the conformity that keeps a person from 'deviating from the norm'. When a 'deviant' is corrected, it is not in the name of the pattern or of its function—since these are not generally explicit—but in the name of the individual behaviors and their functions.[47] The relation of the individual to culture patterns is therefore something quite different from the relation of the individual to social demands for conformity. Culturally patterned behaviors vary in the degree of social demands associated with them. Some are sought out by the individual, e.g. the ways of scientific investigation which the student learns—though even here there are subpatterns that are imposed rather than sought out: Russian students must not accept Morgan's genetics; American students find (far less violently, to be sure) that they had better not accept Lamarck. Other culturally patterned behaviors are not so much imitated (learned) for their own sake as imposed upon individuals by demands for conformity.

Sapir's great preoccupation with the relation of the individual to culture patterns and to conformity (the 'givenness' of culture and so on) is due to a growing awareness of the distinction between these two. The cultural environment which 'the individual is placed in, and therefore reacts to' is the culture pattern itself (as 'exemplified' in the patterned behaviors); the only pressure that these pat-

---

[47] What the anthropologist constructs are cultural patterns. What members of the society observe, or impose upon others, are culturally patterned behaviors.

terns may exert upon the individual is their own 'configurational pressure'. In contrast, the pressure to imitate the culturally patterned behaviors, i.e. to conform, is not a matter of the patterns at all but simply of social control.

Where Sapir had argued for the validity of patterns as describing or 'explaining' behavior, he argued against the idea that these patterns involve conformity. 'Cultural anthropology, if properly understood, has the healthiest of all scepticisms about the validity of the concept "normal behavior" ... Personalities are not conditioned by a generalized process of adjusting to "the normal" but by the necessity of adjusting to the greatest possible variety of idea patterns and action patterns according to the accidents of birth and biography' (514–5). From this, and from the statement that almost no cultural item covers the whole population, it follows that individuals conform much less than is supposed. The administrative social scientist expects the conformity of the 'coordinated man'. He considers any person who doesn't conform to a particular cultural item to be a 'deviant'—an invidious word which came to be used after the term 'abnormal' could no longer be defended. (More recently, the term has been 'maladjusted', to indicate that the experts should adjust the person.) But that person is merely trying to do what everyone else does: to use his experience in meeting the problems of living. If he does the identical things that others in his society do, it is because he meets similar problems and has had similar experiences upon which to draw—not primarily because he is the creature of the culture pattern. If he does different things, it is because he has had somewhat different experiences or has integrated them into different values (or into a different level of understanding within the basic common values).

The many indisputable cases of conformity are therefore seen not as 'human nature' but as the result of specific pressures by specific people to make people conform. It was because of this whole chain of understandings, no less than because of his personal humanistic values, that Sapir was so alert to all cases of control and so subtle in analyzing them. He recognized submission to cultural control even when the submission was clouded in apparent independence: '[Followers of fashion] are not fundamentally in revolt from custom but they wish somehow to legitimize their personal deviation without laying themselves open to the charge of insensitiveness to good taste or good manners. Fashion is the discreet solution of the subtle conflict' (374). He recognized the effect of control even in social requirements which the controllers claim to be innocent, as in the following remark about the acquiescence involved in communication: 'Imitation, while not communicative in intent, has always the retroactive value of a communication, for in the process of falling in with the ways of society one in effect acquiesces in the meanings that inhere in these ways. When one learns to go to church, for instance, because other members of the community set the pace for this kind of activity, it is as though a communication had been received and acted upon' (105–6).[48] And to take an example of joint cultural and social

---

[48] Princeton University official register 1941 §33.3 (257): 'Freshmen and sophomores are required to attend at least one-half of the Sunday services in the University Chapel in each quarter of the academic year ... To be appreciated, the service of public worship must be experienced and this is the basis of the requirement for chapel.' One can imagine what com-

control: when Sapir says, 'Human beings do not wish to be modest; they want to be as expressive—that is, as immodest—as fear allows' (380), he is defining the cultural expectation called 'modest' as a contradiction of human expressiveness, and points to the social situation (fear) which gives the victory to the cultural demand.

Looking at all this from the point of view of the individual, Sapir not only saw fearful submission where social scientists often see natural conformity, and independent expression where they see deviation, but also resistance of the individual where they see failure of cultural conditioning: 'In spite of all these standardizing influences, local dialects have persisted with a vitality that is little short of amazing. Obviously the question of the conservation of dialect is not altogether a negative matter of the inertia of speech and of the failure of overriding cultural influences to permeate into all corners of a given territory. It is, to a very significant degree, a positive matter of the resistance of the local dialects to something which is vaguely felt as hostile' (86).

The resistance of individuals or subgroups consists in their use of particular ways in spite of the demands of others that they change to other ways. Sapir sees the ways of the individual or the subgroup as constituting a subculture in themselves (515, 519), so that the individual is never 'wrong' while the majority culture is 'right'. Speaking of an Indian who denies a cultural form which others accept, he says: 'If we think long enough about Two Crows and his persistent denials, we shall have to admit that in some sense Two Crows is never wrong ... The fact that this rebel, Two Crows, can in turn bend others to his own view of fact or theory or to his own preference in action shows that his divergence from custom had, from the very beginning, the essential possibility of culturalized behavior' (572).[49]

Sapir's question of the relation of individual to society is, then, not the administrator's problem of 'the extreme limits within which human behavior is culturally modifiable', but the human being's problem of making his way through life. Hence, Sapir does not assume that the individual should adjust to society, but asks how valid or adequate the cultural ways are for the individual who has to make do with them (513). His deep criticisms of our own culture (especially in Psychiatric and cultural pitfalls in the business of getting a living, 578-89, and Culture, genuine and spurious, 308-31) shows how important these inadequacies were to him.

3.5. THE INDIVIDUAL AND CULTURAL CHANGE. Control and the adequacy of cultural forms are important not only in themselves, but also for their relation

munication Sapir would have recognized when the regents of the university whose press published this volume of his selected writings demanded oaths of its faculty and fired the non-submissive.

[49] Sapir adds: 'We have said nothing so far that is not utterly commonplace. What is strange is that the ultimate importance of these commonplaces seems not to be thoroughly grasped by social scientists at the present time.' The strangeness disappears, of course, when one remembers that the social scientists are not catering to the rebels. As John F. Embree says (American anthropologist NS 52.431 [1950]), 'The applied anthropologist ... advises managers how to manage their workers; he has been little concerned to advise the managed how to maintain their own social interests vis-a-vis the managers.'

to cultural change. Since Sapir saw culture in general as being the continuing interrelation of people, he naturally saw cultural change as stemming from changes made by individuals (425). The problem then becomes one of investigating under what circumstances changes appear in the individual behavior. This would include, among others, the fact that the act of change can itself be a personality expression, the differences in what each person learns from his experiences with others, the possible operation of a tendency for formal configuration (Sapir's 'drift' in language and in culture), and the reaction to controls and cultural inadequacies. Cultural inadequacies lead to attempts at change, as Sapir implies in saying that mathematics had to develop its own language and that people have to fight the trammels of their own language (cf. fn. 45 above). 'It is sometimes necessary to become conscious of the forms of social behavior in order to bring about a more serviceable adaptation to changed conditions' (558). The direction is toward liberation: 'The attitude of independence toward a constructed language which all national speakers must adopt is really a great advantage, because it tends to make man see himself as the master of language instead of its obedient servant' (119). To this extent an observer who is unaware of the cost to the individuals of their participation in particular social forms—costs due to the inadequacy of the forms, or due to their control effect—would not be able to understand the changes that arise from people's attempts to escape these costs, from the tendency to take up or develop other forms that do not involve such costs whenever these become available to the people.

The changes which the individual attempts in his own life, whether for any of the reasons mentioned above or for other reasons, can become the changes of culture. Sapir illustrates this by having his maverick Indian, Two Crows, interchange A and Z in the alphabet order. 'No matter how many Two Crows deny that two and two make four, the actual history of mathematics, however retarded by such perversity, cannot be seriously modified by it. But if we get enough Two Crows to agree on the interchange of A and Z, we have what we call a new tradition' (571). The change may be made by making new use of existing social patterns which are available to the individuals in question, but that does not make it any less a change: 'Thus, the particular method of revolting against the habit of church-going in a given society, while contradictory, on the surface, of the conventional meanings of that society, may nevertheless receive all its social significance from hundreds of existing prior communications that belong to the culture of the group as a whole' (106).

The importance, then, of seeing the origins of these changes in the individual lives is that the changes make sense in terms of the individual lives in which they originated. 'We cannot thoroughly understand the dynamics of culture, of society, of history, without sooner or later taking account of the actual interrelationships of human beings' (575). 'That culture is a superorganic, impersonal whole is a useful enough methodological principle to begin with but becomes a serious deterrent in the long run to the more dynamic study of the genesis and development of cultural patterns because these cannot be realistically disconnected from those organizations of ideas and feelings which constitute the individual' (512). In his famous rationalistic criticism of supra-human social 'forces' as accounting for history (or as manifesting themselves in history), Do we need a 'Superorganic'?, Sapir wrote: 'The social is but a name for those reactions or types of reaction that depend for their perpetuation on a cumulative technique of transference, that known as social inheritance. This technique, however, does not depend for its operation on any significantly new "force" ... Social science is not psychology, not because it studies the resultants of a superpsychic or superorganic force, but because its terms are differently demarcated.'[50]

It is possible of course to find long-range correlations and regularities in the time-sequence of cultural patterns and social conditions. These can be described as social or cultural causes of historical change. Sapir's formulation does not deny this. The particular material and social conditions in which people find themselves at any particular time and place determine to a large extent the kind of problems they encounter, problems which are dealt with in biologically favored directions. The cultural patterns that are available to people at any particular time and place favor particular kinds of patterned behavior: the obedient conformists will all be doing much the same thing; those who tend more toward personal variation and expression will be using essentially the same underlying patterns as a base upon which to vary or express; those who react more actively against the costs of controls and of cultural inadequacies all find much the same controls and inadequacies to overcome; and those changes which are elicited by response to the formalism of the patterning (the drift) are in a direction suggested by the existing configuration.[51] Changes which are attempted at any one time will therefore be intimately connected with the cultural patterns existing at that time, and will lead to patterns which differ in certain directions rather than in others, and which are not entirely different and unrelated to the previous patterns. A more or less continuous and directional shift, with observable regularities, is therefore often discernible in the history of cultural patterns taken by themselves, even though the agency of change is the reaction of the individual.

3.6. CULTURE IN THE STRUCTURE OF THE PERSONALITY. Sapir approached the problems of personality from his analysis of culture, and his contributions lay in showing relationships between culture and the development of the personality. Like Sullivan, he found that 'the locus of psychiatry turns out not to be the human organism at all in any fruitful sense of the word but the more intangible, yet more intelligible, world of human relationships and ideas that such relationships bring forth' (512).[52] Since he also said much the same of culture (515), he

---

[50] Sapir, Do we need a 'Superorganic'?, American anthropologist NS 19.444 (1917). This article is not included in the present volume.

[51] This effect of the formal configuration may be seen most readily in limited well-structured fields, such as music or some particular science. Aside from the more generally social factors that lead to particular developments and tendencies in each field, it seems probable that the existing pattern at any one time (the kind of scales used, the type of composition potentialities which have been well investigated) favor certain directions of change, rather than others, by those who try out changes.

[52] The effect of culturally patterned interpersonal relations is treated by Harry Stack Sullivan, Conceptions of modern psychiatry.

denies 'the conventional contrast of the individual and his society' (519). His statement that each individual or group constitutes a subculture (519), which he connects with the fact that each culture pattern reaches only some part of the population, enabled him to see structural parallels between personality and culture. An individual's mental breakdown 'invites a study of his system of ideas as a more or less distinct cultural entity which has been vainly struggling to maintain itself in a discouraging environment' (520).

This formulation, which at first may seem to be just a manner of speaking, leads to interesting results when taken seriously. For it means that the individual's ways of relating to people constitute a complete system which can do for him all the work done by a national culture. The psychiatric problem is then one of clearing up sources of difficulty within the individual's existing system of understandings and behaviors, rather than of getting the person to become a part (or participant) of the supra-individual culture. 'Psychiatrists who are tolerant only in the sense that they refrain from criticizing anybody who is subjected to their care and who do their best to guide him back to the renewed performance of society's rituals may be good practical surgeons of the psyche. They are not necessarily the profoundly sympathetic students of the mind who respect the fundamental intent and direction of every personality organization' (521).

This structural similarity between personality and culture led Sapir to see cultural items as factors in the development of the personality. He speaks of the confusion between the personal and cultural implications of experience in childhood, 'when the significant personality is interpreted as an institution and every cultural pattern is merely a memory of what this or that person has actually done' (590). 'The more obvious conflicts of cultures with which we are familiar in the modern world create an uneasiness which forms a fruitful soil for the eventual development, in particular cases, of neurotic symptoms and mental breakdowns but they can hardly be considered sufficient to account for serious psychological derangements. These arise not on the basis of a generalized cultural conflict but out of specific conflicts of a more intimate sort, in which systems of ideas get attached to particular persons, or images of such persons, who play a decisive role in the life of the individual as representative of cultural values' (510–1). Hence 'it is a dangerous thing for the individual to give up his identification with such cultural patterns as have come to symbolize for him his own personality integration' (519–20).

The difficulties which are intrinsic to the culture patterns thus have a direct relation to difficulties in persons who participate in these patterns: 'Mechanisms which are unconsciously evolved by the neurotic or psychotic are by no means closed systems imprisoned within the biological walls of isolated individuals. They are tacit commentaries on the validity or invalidity of some of the more intimate implications of culture' (513). The same relation appears in more chronic but milder forms, forms that no one would think of treating because almost everybody in the society is affected in one way or another. A 'social' example: 'The endless rediscovery of the self in a series of petty truancies from the official socialized self becomes a mild obsession of the normal individual in any society in which the individual has ceased to be a measure of the society itself' (375).

An 'economic' example: 'For all practical purposes a too low income is at least as significant a datum in the causation of mental ill-health as a buried Oedipus complex or sex trauma' (588). A 'cultural' example (speaking of an impoverished overworked farmer): 'It is only when the sober, inevitable, corroding impoverishment of the farmer's personality is lit up by some spectacular morbidity of sex or religion that the psychiatrist or novelist or poet is attracted to him. The far more important dullness of daily routine, of futile striving, of ceaseless mental thwarting, does not seem to clamor for the psychiatrist's analysis' (588).

In view of all this, it is not surprising that Sapir opposes all ideas of 'adjusting' individuals to society. His critique of our society and of its effects upon personality comes as groundwork for considering how a society and culture could be more satisfactorily structured, just as his critique of the form-meaning relation in existing languages was offered as groundwork for considering how a more satisfactory language could be constructed. The question can be one of adjusting cultural patterns to the individual (which is one of the types of cultural change, as has been seen), rather than adjusting individual to culture. In his article The unconscious patterning of behavior in society, Sapir ends by saying: 'Complete analysis and the conscious control that comes with a complete analysis are at best but the medicine of society, not its food' (559). Which means: Don't take it as food; but also: Do take it as medicine.

4. CONCLUSION

Sapir's methods of work were essentially the same in language, in culture, and in personality. He was outstanding not only for his contributions but also for his methods and his presentation. His writing was often an artistic expression, as in the article Psychiatric and cultural pitfalls in the business of getting a living; or a masterpiece of getting the point across, as in Why cultural anthropology needs the psychiatrist. He could make very subtle definitions of words, as in some of his encyclopedia articles (365, 373), and very perceptive formulations, as in his summary of Jung (530-1).

Three major work methods of his were so impressive that everyone sensed them, even if only vaguely: his ability to extract results out of elusive data; the dramatic way in which his conclusions came out of his data; the sensitivity and critical independence with which he approached his problems.

His handling of elusive data was related to a very clear sense of the structure of the line of scientific argument. Data that were too uncertain in the light of a loosely constructed argument become relevant when the argument is built up more carefully. For example, when Sapir argued that Wakashan glottalized continuants developed out of glottal stop plus continuant, he showed that there were reasons to analyze initial $\mathring{y}$ as reduced from earlier $ʔ$ + vowel + y—something which would not have been thought of if he had not needed it in his chain of argument. Of course, this is what happens in all use of data for scientific conclusions, except that Sapir carried it out with greater detail and finesse. Many of his tours de force came simply out of scientific and artistic integrity: he would not be satisfied with a minimally sufficient chain of argument, but would cast about to see if there were any possible counter-arguments to discuss,

any data that could be elucidated in the light of the new conclusions (and elucidation which would in turn lend further support to the conclusion). Thus, after
showing the development of $?$ + continuant, he remarked that there are a
number of words in *ha-* which look like irregular reduplications, and that this
reduplicated *ha-* occurs more frequently before glottalized continuants than one
would expect; from this he proceeded to show that another source of glottalized
continuants is h + continuant (240; and note the more complicated point about
IE y-, 247). He never dismissed weak data, but analyzed it for what it was worth.
In the monograph on time perspective he showed that though density of population in an area would normally not be considered in any discussion of the antiquity of settlement in that area, since it could be due to geographic conditions,
nevertheless consideration of the density can be useful in conjunction with other
data (399–400; cf. also 381, 214).

The dramatic structure of his argument resulted both from the many inter-
weaving details and the disposing of counter-arguments, and also from his habit
of using his straightforward data to build up a working hypothesis, then bringing
in large-scale considerations to show it as a reasonable and expectable conclusion,
and finally explaining complicated data in the light of all this, in a way that
both proves the hypothesis and shows how much work it can do. He did this
at many points, characteristically in explaining Navaho forms (e.g. 216–7, 218–9),
Indo-European laryngeals (e.g. 248–9, 296–7), and the way in which Yana
expresses in a single word what English gives in a fairly complicated sentence
(552). These things have to be read to appreciate their construction.

Sapir's sensitivity and something of his critical approach may be seen in many
of the quotations cited above. His critical independence is perhaps best seen
in his treatment of his own society. He did not at all mind making searching and
incisive comments about modern society, both in his anthropological papers and
in various popular articles; and if these comments often had the effect of ex-
claiming 'But the emperor has no clothes on', this was due to the situation he
was describing rather than to a prior intention on his part. A few examples will
suffice.

About the ideal of the 'cultured person' current in this society he says: 'It
is an attitude of perhaps even more radical aloofness than snobbishness outright ... Another of its indispensable requisites is intimate contact with the past
... But perhaps the most extraordinary thing about the cultured ideal is its selection of the particular treasures of the past which it deems worthiest of worship
... [This] selection of treasures has proceeded chiefly according to the accidents
of history' (309–10). About the actual 'ethnologist's' culture he says: 'in the
case of America ... a chronic state of cultural maladjustment has for so long a
period reduced much of our higher life to sterile externality ... the present world
wide labor unrest has as one of its deepest roots some sort of perception of the
cultural fallacy of the present form of industrialism' (318).

In a discussion of 'economic factors in personal adjustment', Sapir gives a
poignant novelistic sketch, written with sad irony, of the interlace of economic
and social and personal problems in the tragedy of a typical low-paid professional (586–7). With this he contrasts the position of Banker C, asking what

are the services for which he receives his income: 'Should any impertinent, thoroughly unscientific, snooper whisper to the economist that, so far as he can see, C's $500,000.00 income (in virtue of his vice-presidency of the X bank plus shareholdership in the Y company plus investment in the Z oil-fields of Mexico plus a long list of other services rendered his fellowmen) seems to be strangely unaffected by the tissue of physical and psychological performances of the psycho-physical entity or organism called C, it making apparently little difference whether C is on hand to instruct one of his secretaries to cut his coupons or is resting up in the Riviera, the economist loses patience' (583). Sapir sums up the economic factor in personal adjustment by asking, in regard to the underpaid professional's breakdown, 'Why should not the psychiatrist be frank enough to call attention to the great evils of unemployment or lack of economic security?' (588). And he adds: 'As to C, the interest of the psychiatrist in his moods, conflicts, and aspirations is perennial ... Perhaps C too inclines to suffer from an economic ill—that obscure, perverse, guilt feeling which, the psychiatrist tells us, so often festers in one's heart of hearts when one tries to balance one's usefulness to society with the size of one's income ... Is it conceivable that good mental hygiene, even expert psychiatry, may find it proper to recommend some share of income reduction ...?' (589).

Although most of Sapir's comments refer to the position of the individual, he also touched on more typically sociological matters, often with an ironic note. Speaking of how a Frenchman fails to see the difference between our *s* and *th*, since the difference lies primarily in our structuring of these sounds, he adds: 'It is as though an observer from Mars, knowing nothing of the custom we call war, were intuitively led to confound a punishable murder with a thoroughly legal and noble act of killing in the course of battle' (556). Speaking of the dependence of fashion on social factors, he says: 'In a democratic society, for instance, if there is an unacknowledged drift toward class distinctions fashion will discover endless ways of giving it visible form. Criticism can always be met by the insincere defense that fashion is merely fashion and need not be taken seriously' (376). And in respect to acculturation from above, a matter in which anthropologists today are unavoidably interested, he remarks: 'A culture may well be quickened from without, but its supersession by another, whether superior or not, is no cultural gain. Whether or not it is attended by a political gain does not concern us here. That is why the deliberate attempt to impose a culture directly and speedily, no matter how backed by good will, is an affront to the human spirit. When such an attempt is backed, not by good will, but by military ruthlessness, it is the greatest conceivable crime against the human spirit, it is the very denial of culture' (328).

So refreshing is this freeness and criticalness, that we are brought to a sharp realization of how such writing has disappeared from the scene. In part, this was the writing of pre-administrative anthropology. We have seen that Sapir was against the very idea that culture is 'given': 'This metaphor is always persuading us that culture is a neatly packed up assemblage of forms of behavior handed over piecemeal, but without serious breakage, to the passively inquiring child. I have come to feel that it is precisely the supposed "givenness" of culture that is the most serious obstacle to our real understanding of the nature of culture and cultural change and of their relationship to individual personality' (596). It is to be expected that the present situation, in which anthropology finds itself helping to make it 'given',[53] would affect the current picture of culture and the way of writing about it: 'Canned culture is so much easier to administer' (330). However, important as this development in anthropology may be in explaining why Sapir's writing is so different, it is not the only source of Sapir's way of writing. In part, too, this source was the difference between the atmosphere of a depression period and the atmosphere of the continuous war period which replaced it. And in part it was Sapir.

[53] Cf. John F. Embree, A note on ethnocentrism in anthropology, American anthropologist NS 52.430-2 (1950).

SAPIR AND THE TRAINING OF ANTHROPOLOGICAL LINGUISTS*

MARY R. HAAS

In Voegelin and Harris's recent article, "Training in Anthropological Linguistics," a point of history is brought up which is deserving of some further clarification. In particular I have reference to the following statement:

"While at Chicago, Sapir's graduate students, though engaged in descriptive linguistics, worked in the anthropology department, and this with Sapir's full blessing. At Yale Sapir seemed to reverse himself; he recommended that all work in linguistics be done in the linguistics department, and this despite the fact that he himself was chairman of the Yale department of anthropology." (1952: 324)

Since the authors then attempt to seek the reason for what they call "this seeming reversal in attitude" on the part of Sapir, I should like to point out that, as I remember it, there was no real reversal in Sapir's attitude. What may appear on the surface to have been a change in attitude was brought about by a change in circumstances. In other words, what Sapir did at Yale he would have done at Chicago had circumstances permitted. But in order to clarify this, I should like to summarize what I can remember in the way of pertinent information during the period immediately before and immediately after Sapir's transfer from Chicago to Yale.

During Sapir's sojourn at Chicago, all anthropology students were expected to study some linguistics, a plan which was reflected in Cole's remarks: " . . . when Sapir and I were developing plans for graduate work at Chicago, we were both insistent on training in all branches of the subject" (1952: 162). Students who intended to specialize in ethnology, archeology, or some other non-linguistic branch of anthropology, took most, if not all of their linguistic work under Sapir, and their course work thus remained entirely in the Department of Anthropology. Students who expected to specialize in linguistics, on the other hand, were required to take additional linguistics courses in some other department, e.g., such courses as Sanskrit and Comparative Indo-European in the Department of Comparative Philology, as well as Gothic and frequently also Old High German in the Department of German. Thus a considerable amount of cross-departmental training was insisted upon. This cross-departmental training did not all work in one direction, either, for students in the Department of Comparative Philology were expected to do some work under Sapir, in particular to take his course in phonetics. This requirement, however, met with some opposition, as I recall it, because some students in comparative philology were disposed to feel

* Reprinted, with permission of the American Anthropological Association, Washington, D.C., and the author, from *American Anthropologist* 55.447-50 (1953).

that the study of nonliterary languages was too bizarre to be taken very seriously.

In the case of an occasional student who might wish to specialize in linguistics to the exclusion of other branches of anthropology, Sapir would have been willing, even while still at Chicago, to permit such a student to take his degree in some department other than anthropology provided the dissertation could still be written on the subject of a primitive, i.e., nonliterary language. However, it was not feasible at Chicago at that time to work out such an arrangement with any other department. The Department of Comparative Philology was exactly and quite properly that, and not a department of linguistics. Therefore the only department in which a doctoral dissertation in primitive linguistics could be appropriately considered was in the Department of Anthropology. This, then, is the reason why, "While at Chicago, Sapir's graduate students, though engaged in descriptive linguistics, worked in the anthropology department." In this connection it is also important to note that Sapir's title at Chicago (as well as, later, at Yale) was Professor of Anthropology and Linguistics.

Sapir's earlier training was in Germanics and he entered the field of anthropology after being inspired by Boas' unique knowledge of primitive languages. Boas, however, insisted that Sapir study all branches of anthropology, including physical anthropology which he disliked. According to Cole, "this nearly sent Sapir to Indo-Germanic" (1952: 162).

Just as Sapir came to study under Boas after having acquired his interest in linguistics in another department, so an occasional student came to Sapir after having begun linguistic studies in some other department. Sapir, remembering his own dislike of physical anthropology in his student days, no doubt sympathized with such a student's lack of interest in other branches of anthropology. He would therefore have been willing to work out an arrangement of the sort I have mentioned here had it been possible. He remained true to the Boas tradition, however, in that he had no wish to alter the broadly-conceived requirements for a degree in anthropology.

The situation at Yale, on the other hand, was quite different from that which obtained at Chicago. In the year that Sapir went to Yale (1931), the Department of Linguistics was set up, consisting of Sapir himself, and three eminent linguists already at Yale, namely, Professor Franklin Edgerton and the late Professors Eduard Prokosch and Edgar H. Sturtevant, the last-named of whom was the chairman. Sapir was also, of course, the chairman of the Department of Anthropology. Within this framework, then, it was possible for a student interested in working on nonliterary languages to take a degree in either the Department of Anthropology or the Department of Linguistics. And this is exactly what happened. For example, during the early part of Sapir's Yale career, there were four students working towards degrees with the expectation of writing grammars of American Indian languages. Of these, two were enrolled in the Department of Anthropology and two in the Department of Linguistics. The distinction was made, not on the basis of the subject matter of the dissertation, but on the nature of other phases of the students' training. Those whose training was in the field of general anthropology took their degrees in anthropology, while those whose training was in the field of general and historical linguistics took their degrees in linguistics.

The above facts are submitted as a matter of history. The most interesting point is the fact that Sapir would have been willing to institute a disciplinary distinction between linguists and anthropologists *even earlier* than he was able to institute it. And this, I think, is an important point which changes in part the interpretation that Voegelin and Harris have put upon it.

According to their interpretation (pp. 324–325), the change was brought about by the new developments in descriptive linguistics which took a definite upswing in the 1930's. There can be no doubt that Sapir fully appreciated the importance of these developments, since he himself had of course made important contributions to them. But I doubt very much that this was the only reason, or even the chief reason why Sapir wanted to encourage some (not all) of his linguistics students to study more linguistics rather than more anthropology. The principal reason, as I see it, was that Sapir still held to his conviction that since the problems of the historical relationships of American Indian languages were going to have to be solved by Americanists, such linguists should have sound training in the methods of Indo-European comparative linguistics. After all, training in descriptive linguistics as a part of anthropology was in the Boas tradition; it was training in Indo-European comparative methodology that had to be sought outside anthropology.

There is also another important motivation, which should by no means be overlooked. Sapir was very unhappy about the indifference and even antagonism he encountered among many historical linguists toward the study of nonliterary languages. This antagonism is still to be encountered in some quarters, but it is less virile than it was during his lifetime; and the fact that it is less virile is due in no small measure to his efforts. In the early 1930's, when a group of us were planning a book which was to contain concise but complete grammatical sketches of a wide variety of American Indian languages (Hoijer and others, 1946), he often expressed the feeling that he hoped such a volume would serve to show that the grammatical structures of nonliterary languages are every bit as deserving of serious study as are those of literary languages. He even named a few prominent historical linguists whom he hoped to influence by means of such a volume. This, however, is but one aspect of the battle he waged unceasingly throughout his life against closed frontiers wherever he saw them, whether in linguistics or in anthropology. And in view of this, I cannot help but suspect that one of the reasons why he wanted some of his students to take their degrees in linguistics was that he hoped to "infiltrate," if I may be permitted to use the term in this connection, the ranks of linguists with some who were trained in the techniques and methods of working on nonliterary languages. Therefore it was not that "Sapir felt that linguists were non-anthropological beings who had to work in a frame of reference of their own, and in a department of their own," (p. 324), as Voegelin and Harris surmise. It was not anthropologists who had to be convinced of the value of the study of primitive peoples—in those days it was their bread and butter, but many linguists did have to be convinced. After all, there were linguists before there were "anthropological" linguists. Sapir was not trying to bring about a break between anthropological linguists and other anthropologists—he was trying to promote a better understanding between anthropological linguists and other linguists.

In their concluding paragraph, Voegelin and Harris describe the goal of present day linguistic training in the following terms:

"The goal includes a structural description of the languages of the world. . . . It includes also the study of the relationship of languages of the world to cultures of the world. For both descriptive and ethnolinguistic work, training is needed that will bring about sophistication in phonemics and in combinatorial linguistics." (p. 327)

This goal is admirably stated as far as it goes. But it includes no mention of historical linguistics, and to this I should like to voice my objection, as I believe Sapir would also voice an objection. To the historically minded linguist, descriptive analyses are necessary before historical studies can be begun. In the field of nonliterary languages they are in fact a *sine qua non*. However, these analyses are not an end in themselves, but a very necessary means to another and more far-reaching end, namely the discovery and validation of broad historical relationships.

BIBLIOGRAPHY

COLE, FAY-COOPER 1952 Eminent Personalities of the Half Century. American Anthropologist 54: 157–167.

HOIJER, HARRY and OTHERS 1946 Linguistic Structures of Native America. Viking Fund Publications in Anthropology 6. New York.

VOEGELIN, C. F. and Z. S. HARRIS 1952 Training in Anthropological Linguistics. American Anthropologist 54: 322–327.

PART III

Appraisals of Sapir's Life and Work, 1956 - 1980

*Thomas T. Waterman, Paul Radin, Ishi, Robert H. Lowie, and Edward Sapir
(Berkeley, Calif., August 1915).*

*Paul S. Martin departing for a field-trip to the Southwest, with Fay-Cooper
Cole and Edward Sapir (Chicago, 1926).*

COMMENTS ON EDWARD SAPIR,
HIS PERSONALITY AND SCHOLARSHIP*

ROBERT H. LOWIE

Edward Sapir left so deep an impress upon linguistics and ethnology that documents illuminating his personality and his intellectual development may claim historical interest. The letters herewith presented are all those still in my possession;* my part of the correspondence has been irretrievably lost, because Sapir burned all his letters before he died. For the sake of the record I have been chary of eliminations, merely excising a few paragraphs of strictly personal nature, such as inquiries about my mother or sister. Since there are many references to people and circumstances not generally known nowadays, I am appending a series of Notes. I have, however, refrained from explaining what is already adequately elucidated by the context, and I have not identified such well-known anthropological figures as Boas, Wissler, or Kroeber.

There are obvious limitations in the value of the materials here offered. The letters are to be read in terms of the period and place of their composition and of the relationship then existing between the writer and the recipient. As for time and place, the most revealing letters date from Sapir's long residence in Canada (1910-1925), where he was working for the Geological Survey in

---

* [This essay was composed in 1956, one year before the death of its author, Robert Harry Lowie (1883-1957), as an introducion to his projected edition of Sapir's letters to him written between 6 September 1908, while he was on a field trip in Utah, and 17 January 1938, while he was on leave from Yale in New York City. It was posthumously typed up by his widow, Luella Cole Lowie, and privately published in 1965, in Berkeley, Calif. The author's original intent remains obvious in his introduction, but it appeared to me that what he has to say about Sapir's personality and about certain aspects of his work is of a broader appeal, so that its separate publication in the present volume may be justified. No doubt, the *Letters from Edward Sapir to Robert H. Lowie* deserve to be more widely known and should be republished as well, together with Lowie's Introduction, but as Lowie himself would have preferred, together with other letters from (and, wherever possible, to) Edward Sapir. – On the 1965 publication of the Sapir letters, cf. the reviews by Dell Hymes in *Journal of the History of the Behavioral Sciences* 5:1.87-88 (1969) and by the late A. Irwing Hallowell in *American Anthropologist* 68:3.774-75 (1966). – *Ed.*]

Ottawa. Judged purely on its potentialities for scientific research, his position was ideal, but repeated complaints amply demonstrate that it soon ceased to satisfy him. For one thing, in a city without a university[1] he found no chance to lecture on a higher level or to mingle with colleagues from the several humanistic disciplines. What was more, he felt isolated from contemporary trends in the arts. How important aesthetic creativeness was for him appears from the beautiful, moving letter of 27 September 1916. New York was the musical center of America; and both in New York and Chicago new literary journals were sprouting, with the guiding spirits of which he craved communion. His interests and mine by no means coincided, but they did overlap; and during eleven years of what he considered his Canadian exile I was a resident of New York and in potential, and to some degree, in actual touch with the avant-garde. I had joined the·Liberal Club under the presidency of the Rev. Percy Stickney Grant and had remained faithful to it in its less fashionable quarters in McDougall Street. In either setting one met a motley crew of poets, authors journalists, editors, publishers, reformers, and radicals — some of them members, many of them guests. Dr. Grant introduced Carl [Gustav] Jung on the latter's first American visit, and we heard an enthralling talk on folklore from a psycho-analyst's point of view. Robert Henri enlightened us about the first American exhibition of modernist painting and sculpture. Edna St. Vincent Millay and Amy Lowell read from their poems. Jacques Loeb expounded the latest advances in physical science. The notorious Frank Harris thrilled an audience with a two-hour lecture on Shakespeare. In the basement restaurant of the Greenwich Village headquarters one might dine at the same table with Bill Hayward of the Industrial Workers of the World or with Jim Larkin, the Irish labor leader. Upstairs during the dance craze of the period members even learned the latest tango steps to the tune of "Maurice Irrésistible".

It was, of course, the literary contacts in New York that prompted the correspondence with Sapir. The New Republic had accepted an article of mine in 1914 and had subsequently asked me to do some reviewing. I became slightly acquainted with several of the editors, such as Walter Lippman and Francis Hackett, and suggested Sapir as a collaborator. With The Freeman, published by B. W. Huebsch and edited by Albert Jay Nock, I had closer ties, and according to my recollection, in that quarter also I called attention to Sapir. It was certainly on my recommendation that Mr. Alfred Harcourt, to whom I had been introduced by Walter Lippmann, accepted the manuscript of [Sapir's] Language. After Sapir had moved to Chicago, he no longer needed an intermediary, hence one stimulus of our rather intensive exchange of letters dropped out. Moreover, he was extremely busy when obliged for the first time to plan an ambitious program of new courses at Chicago. We remained on thoroughly friendly terms, but my documentation for Sapir's development began to thin out.

More important no doubt was the second source of deficiency in my records. Cordial as our relations were, I was never as close to Sapir as I was, at one time or another, to Alexander A. Goldenweiser, Paul Radin, Ruth Benedict, Leslie Spier, and of course, Edward Gifford and Alfred Kroeber.

It follows that for a *complete* picture of Sapir the correspondence with me should be supplemented by letters to his closest friends and by both such letters and the reminiscences of his assistants and associates at the peak of his career, when he had gained a following of devoted disciples, had assumed a dominant role in learned societies, and was hobnobbing with the heads of great foundations — a period during which he and I did meet ossasionally at gatherings of the American Anthropological Association but were for the most part separated by a distance of three thousand miles.

Frankly admitting the lacunae in my materials. I nevertheless consider them valuable both in form and in content. Sapir's literary style has been greatly admired, and deservedly so, for the lucidity of his exposition and the remarkable facility of phrase that distinguished his writing. But his diction suffered from mannerisms and at times from a cavalier disdain for established usage. Thus, within a short essay he uses 'impute' over and over again — never in its more customary, pejorative sense. 'Nuance', an overworked noun of his, he converted into a verb with participial derivatives connived at by some dictionaries, but hardly in the best of taste. In *Time Perspective*, 'differentia' repeatedly figures as a plural form;[2] and elsewhere the reader unexpectedly faces monstrously involved sentences.[3] By contrast, the letters are free from serious flaws, showing only at times the pardonable slovenliness of informal discourse.

What is more, their spirit is admirable, marked as they are by an engaging candor and a willingness to accept objective criticism. The substance is often significant in foreshadowing the writer's mature thought in its most characteristic aspects. The affinity of Yurok with Algonkian, the reduction of the traditional North American stocks to six major divisions, the application of the pattern principle to linguistic phenomena, the emphasis on the individual psyche in relation to culture — all these basic concepts are broached at one time or another of this correspondence.

Something should be said to explain certain acrid judgments to be found here and there in the letters. Sapir was keenly sensitive in both senses of the word. Personalities are many-faceted, and he was quick to seize elusive phases of an acquaintance's character, responding so strongly to a particular trait that he temporarily overlooked others. Hence resulted discrepancies in his views of the same person at different times. In other words, any one pronouncement of his should not be taken as a definitive all-round verdict. The caustic comments of an essentially kindly spirit are accordingly to be regarded with charity. Yearning for a complete understanding of his moods and aspirations, he was deeply grateful for it, but proportionately hurt if his expectations were disappointed; and then he might strike out savagely.

Though a change in mutual relations is a common enough phenomenon, it may surprise anthropologists of the younger generations that during his first Californian stay Sapir developed a warm attachment to Goddard,[4] the older man entertaining then and for years afterward an unbounded admiration for his junior's gifts. But later on Sapir noted certain limitations in Goddard's abilities and became scornful of him. However, it is not profitable to expatiate upon such personal relationships except the historically significant attitudes that developed between him and Boas.

Intellectually Boas did for Sapir what Hume did for Kant: he roused him from dogmatic slumbers. In the obituary written after Sapir's death his student, Dr. Swadesh tells us: "He [Sapir] has told us how he came away from a conference with Boas impressed that he had everything to learn about language. For every generalization he had before believed was certain and exceptionless, Boas could summon indubitable contrary examples from the American Indian languages he knew" (Swadesh 1939:132). I have heard Boas describe this same interview in much the same terms. It was, of course, through Boas that Sapir gained access to the world of anthropology and secured the exceptionally favorable position in Ottawa. At an informal luncheon in honor of Boas on his sixtieth birthday [in 1918] I remember that Sapir feelingly recounted an episode on one of his first field trips — how he had run into a financial difficulty, which our teacher had relieved out of his own pocket.

Yet, given the disparity of personalities, this parental-filial bond was intrinsically a tenuous one. A hostile critic once described Boas as a Prussian drill-sergeant, and a friendly commentator called Sapir something of a prima donna. Neither of these casual utterances is acceptable, yet it is significant that they could be made at all; no would ever refer to Boas as a prima donna or to Sapir as a martinet. When a dominant personality exacting in matters of loyalty clashed with an independent younger spirit on scientific questions, periods of mutual irritation and estrangement became inevitable.

More suo, Sapir would sometimes express himself violently on the subject, yet the totality of his comments offsets the belittling references. Thus, in August 1918, he concludes some uncomplimentary statements with the revealing confessions that: "I find that through speaking with him [Boas] that the essential strength and bigness of his personality breaks through every time. I suppose that it is fineness that is lacking rather than bigness".[5] In October 1920, after lamenting the deficiencies of Americanist students of language, he writes: "Boas is about the only decent one I can point to". In February 1921, he says: "I would not for the world run afoul of him — I like him too well personally". Finally, in January 1923, when for a change I had voiced a longforgotten grievance against our old teacher, Sapir was in no mood to share my irritation, considering Boas 'magnificient generosity' during Mrs. Sapir's illness.[6]

So far as I know, Sapir's scholarly achievements as a whole have been assessed in print by only one contemporary, A. A. Goldenweiser (1933:162ff.; 1941: 158-59). Although adequately appreciative, his estimates are indiscriminating; hence I offer the following summary, considering in turn Sapir's work in linguistics, in theoretical ethnology (including culture and personality), and ethnography.

That Sapir was an outstanding linguist is beyond question. Our foremost Sanscritist, Professor Edgerton (1940:461): considered him "one of the greatest linguistic scholars of the world", and Boas (1939:58) regardless of all differences in interpretation, calls him "one of the most brilliant scholars in linguistics and anthropology", who "with a phenomenal knowledge of a wide field of facts" combined "a rare intuition" (p.59). He was no less highly regarded abroad. In 1924 Father Schmidt told me how disappointed he was at Sapir's absence from the Congress of Americanists in Gothenburg, where he had hoped to discuss basic problems with him. As the letters demonstrate, whenever I consulted him on linguistic matters he replied with an amplitude of specific knowledge at the same time indicating that he had pondered all sorts of relevant issues. As Professor Edgerton (1940:461) notes, "he was able ... to produce at a moment's notice, vast stores of detailed facts about an unbelievable number of languages in many parts of the earth". To illustrate his rapid mastery of new linguistic fields, I should like to refer to his virtually unnoticed but masterly critique of Meinhof's Hamitic theory, in which he anticipated some later findings (Sapir 1913a; cf. Greenberg 1950:63).

Before turning to the theoretical writings we had better recall the basis of his linguistic distinction — a specific gift coupled with unique knowledge. He had been thoroughly trained in Indo-Euopean philology and had supplemented his knowledge with an avid assimilation of aboriginal languages. For theoretical ethnology there is no such specific talent and here the value of Sapir's work was directly proportional to the depth of his information. Now, in the field of 'culture and personality' there simply was not yet the store of facts to be absorbed that existed in linguistics. To quote from one of Sapir's last essays: "we do not for a moment mean to assert that any psychiatry that has yet been evolved is in a position to do much more than to ask intelligent questions" (Sapir 1938:12). Accordingly, while acknowledging the open-mindedness he showed in the face of dimly visioned potentialities, I cannot share the enthusiasm of some colleagues over the papers that Sapir devoted to this subject. I fail to find a formulation of clearly defined problems, let alone their solution. I find only a crusader's summons to arms, but no conquest of new domains.

I must also demur to the panegyrics on the articles concerning "Culture, Genuine and Spurious" (Sapir 1924). According to Goldenweiser (1933:162) they opened "vistas of psychological analysis on a much higher level of insight and refinement than has hitherto been customary in anthropological literature". As a matter of fact, they have nothing to do with anthropology, for Sapir explicitly sets aside the technical meaning of 'culture', thus dealing with something beyond the sphere of the science altogether. As for psychological analysis, he employs no principles known to scientific psychology. What he presents are charming literary compositions, valuable in shedding light on their author's frame of mind in 1920 or thereabouts.

That Sapir had not digested thoroughly and remolded creatively the facts cited is clear from his re-echoing the hackneyed characterization of French national character (1949[1924]:312-13). Surely it is nothing new that the French ethos is predominantly formalistic. What one would expect from an original mind is an explanation of how Rabelais, Hugo, and Balzac – not wholly negligible figures, surely – fit into this threadbare scheme.

It was when Sapir combined a control of facts with his rare intelligence and intuition that he achieved noteworthy results. I shall single out his interpretation of the levirate to exemplify his treatment of concrete data, and his discussion of culture areas as a sample of his dealing with concepts (Sapir 1916b).

The former paper should be viewed in historical perspective. I challenged its thesis at the time, and Professor Murdock (1949:176-77) more recently rejected it peremptorily. Irrespective of its correctness, however, the hypothesis rested on empirical data and could be tested; it directed attention to the nomenclatural significance of step-relationships and to the systems of clanless groups. It was 'suggestive' in the only permissible sense of that greatly abused term, for it suggested further exploration of the subject by Kirchhoff (1932:53-54) and myself (Lowie 1917:144-50; 1919). Finally, it should be noted that Sapir expressly stated his belief that his explanation might not hold generally. In my judgment the subject might well be re-examined on the widest basis with reference to *loosely* organized societies. Parenthetically, one might add that Sapir's concern with kinship terminology antedated the revival of interest that stemmed from W.H.R. Rivers' *Kinship and Social Organization* (1914), though Sapir naturally enough stressed the linguistic aspects of the topic. Subsequently he produced a telling instance of diffusion in this field (Sapir 1913b; 1921b).

To turn to the problem of culture areas, one finds Sapir's discussion of the matter in *Time Perspective* (originally printed in 1916). On this treatise as a whole I must make a reservation. Like all similar attempts, it is rather a contribution to the logic of ethnological research than to ethnology itself. Just as Aristotle's *Poetics* cannot teach a playwright to become a great tragedian, so neither Sapir nor Gräbner nor Schmidt can ensure sound historical reconstruction by their readers. Precisely because Sapir is so eminently sane, he is obliged to qualify every principle of procedure beyond the point of practical utility. Thus, he does not reject the reality of survivals, but at once admonishes us that "great caution is needed in the utlilization of them". What an investigator wants, of course, is a fool-proof method of detecting survivals, not the barren assurance that they could be of great importance "if we can only be sure we really have them" (Sapir 1949[1916a]:410).

Nevertheless, the paper is full of helpful asides — witness the reminder that the differentiation of American linguistic stocks may have antedated the peopling of the New World. But the most significant point for me is bound up with the main argument and consists in the elucidation of the concept of culture areas. Sapir knew the pertinent facts and had pondered them. He thus got ahead of most of his contemporaries in recognizing that the conventional areas were primarily classificatory, hence of unequal historical importance; that accordingly a quite different grouping into a few major divisions was permissible and indicated (Sapir 1949[1916a]:409-410).

If Sapir's work in theoretical ethnology is of unequal value, his distinction as an ethnographer is beyond cavil and has perhaps not been adequately appreciated. I do not mean that his knowledge of aborginial cultures, though certainly adequate, was exceptional. It would have been superhuman to have added such familiarity to his amazing grasp of linguistic data. But as a collector of facts he ranks with our very best observers — with Boas, Kroeber, Radin, Spier — showing the same capacity for immersing himself in the phenomena under scrutiny and plumbing them to their depths, and then presenting them to his readers or students with 'deftness and incisiveness' (Leslie Spier [1939:237]). What he has published, moreover, forms but a small part of what he gathered, especially among the Nootka (Sapir & Swadesh 1955). His resourcefulness in the field is illustrated by his technique for eliciting the Yahi kinship terminology from a native barely conversant with English. To quote his own account, the authencity of his material was

> due to the fact that terms were collected very slowly and with the utmost care and circumspection, with repeated checking-up whenever opportunity was offered; further to the fact that data already obtained from the Southern Yana helped me to follow the informant. The many agreements in nomenclature between the Yahi and the Northern Yana are in no case due to suggestion on my part. The work was rendered possible by the use of counters, differing in appearance for males and females arranged in the form of a geneological tree; this device put the whole investigation on a directly visible footing. (Sapir 1916b:329-30)

Here, as in other instances, the ethnographer derived unique aid from his linguistic competence.

It is a great pity that Sapir was not fated to give us a full synthetic account of the Nootka, a task for which his talents eminently fitted him.

I have already skimmed the subject of Sapir's relation to the arts. At times he went so far as to belittle scholarly effort in comparison with the creative urge of the composer or poet and to avow a relative indifference to 'scientific' problems, but the ardor with which he planned and pursued his major linguistic projects belies his professions as being more than strong expressions of fleeting moods. In the more congenial environment of Chicago and New Haven scientific work assumed its rightful place in his total orientation. This adjustment seems eminently proper; for though his numerous poems found favor with contemporary magazines, I am not aware that they have found a place in modern anthologies. And to his musical compositions Goldenweiser, a fervent admirer and competent judge in this field, did not attach great significance.

Nevertheless, as Mandelbaum (1949:vi) has said, the aesthetic element in Sapir's make-up was of the utmost importance. From it stems the finish of his linguistic argumentation and of his ethnographic reporting; it made him the eminent humanist that Professor Edgerton described in his obituary. Sapir was indeed a civilized human being, and he spread a civilizing influence about him. He left his distinctive mark upon his students and upon all with whom he came in close contact.

EDITOR'S NOTES

1ʼ Lowie is in error when he says that there was no university in Ottawa at the time Sapir lived in the Canadian capital; as a matter of fact, the French-speaking Université d'Ottawa had been established by Oblate fathers back in 1848. But it may reflect on the *envergure* of this church-run institution that it did not seem to have had any impact on Sapir, since, while he was trying unsuccessfully to establish courses on anthropology at McGill University in Montreal and at the University of Toronto, no mention appears to have been made by him of this local institution (which only in 1965 became a bilingual state university).

2) See Sapir (1916a) in the References and cf. Lowie's review of the monograph in *American Anthropologist* N.S. 21.75-77 (1919); repr. in this volume, pp. 39-42.

3) In a footnote to his Introduction (on page 5 of the 1965 text), Lowie refers to the following places in *Language* (Sapir 1921a): 48, 103, 180, and 208, and also in *Selected Writings* (Sapir 1949): 426, 427, and 431 (from Sapir 1916a), 540, 544, 545, 546, 547, and 558 (all from 1927 publications), and 588 (dating from 1938).

4) The reference is to Pliny Earle Goddard (1869-1928); cf. the following of his papers, "The Present Condition of our Knowledge of North American Languages", *American Anthropologist* N.S. 16.555-601 (1914).

5) These quotations and the following are taken from letters by Sapir addressed to Lowie.

6) Sapir's (first) wife Florence, née Delson, died in 1924.

REFERENCES

Boas, Franz. 1939. "Edward Sapir". *International Journal of American Linguistics* 10.58-63. (This volume, pp. 3-4, reprints the text without Sapir's Bibliography.)

Edgerton, Franklin. 1940. "Edward Sapir". *Yearbook of the American Philosophical Society* 1939.460-64. (Reprinted in this volume, pp. 5-7, minus post-1937 publications by Sapir.)

Goldenweiser, Alexander Alexandrovitch. 1933. *History, Psychology, and Culture.* New York: A. A. Knopf; London: K. Paul, Trench & Trübner, xii, 475, xii pp.

—————. 1941. "Recent Trends in American Anthropology". *American Anthropologist* N.S. 43.151-63.

Greenberg, Joseph Harold. 1950. "Studies in African Linguistic Classification: IV. Hamito-Semitic". *Southwestern Journal of Anthropology* 6.47-63.

Kirchhoff, Paul. 1932. "Verwandtschaftsbezeichnungen und Verwandtenheirat". *Zeitschrift für Ethnologie* 46.41-71.

Lowie, Robert Harry. 1917. *Culture and Ethnology.* New York: D. C. McMurtie, 189 pp.

—————. 1919. "Family and Sib". *American Anthropologist* N.S. 21.28-40.

Mandelbaum, David Goodman. 1949. "Introduction". Sapir (1949), v-xii.

Murdock, George Peter. 1949. *Social Structure.* New York: Macmillan.

Rivers, William Halse Rivers. 1914. *Kinship and Social Organization.* London: Constable & Co., vii, 96 pp.

Sapir, Edward. 1913. Review of Carl Meinhof, *Die Sprachen der Hamiten* (Hamburg: L. Friedrichsen, 1912). *Current Anthropological Literature* 2. 21-27.

—————. 1916a. *Time Perspective in Aboriginal American Culture: A study in method.* (= Department of Mines, Geological Survey of Canada, Memoir 90, *Anthropological Series*, 4.) Ottawa: Government Printing Bureau, 87 pp. (Repr. in Sapir 1949.389-462.)

—————. 1916b. "Terms of Relationship and the Levirate". *American Anthropologist* N.S. 18.327-37.

—————. 1921a. *Language: An introduction to the study of speech.* New York: Harcourt, Brace & Co., vii, 258 pp.

—————. 1921b. "A Haida Kinship Term among Tsimshian". *American Anthropologist* N.S. 23.233-34.

—————. 1924. "Culture, Genuine and Spurious". *American Journal of Sociology* 29.401-429. (Repr. in Sapir 1949.308-331.)

—————. 1938. "Why Cultural Anthropology Needs the Psychiatrist?". *Psychiatry: Journal of the biology and the pathology of interpersonal relations* 1.7-12. (Repr. in Sapir 1949.569-77.)

—————. 1949. *Selected Writings of Edward Sapir in Language, Culture and Personality.* Ed. by David G. Mandelbaum. Berkeley & Los Angeles: Univ. of California Press, xv, 617 pp.

—————, and Morris Swadesh. 1955. "Native Accounts of Nootka Ethnography". *International Journal of American Linguistics* 21:4 (Oct. 1955).

Spier, Leslie. 1939. "Edward Sapir". *Science* 89.237-38 (17 March 1939). (See excerpt in this volume, pp.13-14.)

REFLECTIONS ON EDWARD SAPIR, SCHOLAR AND MAN*

ALFRED LOUIS KROEBER

[. . .] I will begin with a comparison, but a comparison, instead of being with a pure linguist as Bloomfield was, would be with another man who is both linguist and anthropologist, namely Franz Boas. I have always felt that Boas was an extraordinary person for his dynamism, for the energy, intellectual and ethical, which he could and did develop for the output of his work, his range of interests, and so on. But, I asked myself when I was doing one of the obituaries on him, whether he was by the ordinary understanding of the term, a genius or not. And I came to the conclusion that while he was a great man, he lacked the quality of genius of the sort that Sapir did exemplify.

Edward Sapir, I should say, is the only man that I have known at all well, in my life, whom I would unreservedly class as a genius. I did not know enough about the inner developments of linguistics and the outer developments [. . .], to have a feeling that within another year or so a revival of interest in Sapir would be manifest. But I have been wondering whether something of the sort was not due. It is now a little over thwenty years since he died, and there has been really very little assessment or attempt at reappraisal of Sapir. Boas has provoked that several times on a smaller scale, and as you probably all know there is a monograph on him about to come out which reviews him from all angles, again.

I would say that Sapir was more of a linguist than an anthropologist, but more than he was either or both together, he was a humanist. And that, both in

---

* [This text derives from a presentation made by Alfred Louis Kroeber (1876-1960) on 11 May 1959, twenty years after Sapir's death, at the University of California, Berkeley. The presentation was taped by David M. Schneider of Chicago and transcribed by Richard J. Preston of McMaster University, Hamilton, Ontario, who kindly consented to its publication. Permission to publish the text was also obtained from the late Alfred Kroeber's son Karl of Columbia University, New York. Kroeber's informal, yet quite informative paper was preceded by a paper given by Yakov Malkiel on "The Prospects for a Sapir Renaissance in Linguistics", to which Kroeber is referring in his own presentation. The published version follows the oral presentation fairly closely, with few omissions. (Malkiel's paper, revised by the author for publication, has now been published in *Historiographia Linguistica* 11:3.389-396 [1984]). —*Ed.*]

what is ordinarily called a creative, directly immediately creative, way, and also as a humanistic scholar. I think Malkiel is entirely right when he says that Sapir was always thinking of a wider and general intellectual audience, rather than a professional one. I think he was at his best when he was writing in an Encyclopedia of Social Sciences, for which reading audience a systematic study of language scarcely exists,[1] or when he's writing for "The Mercury" or for "The Dial", or "The Nation". He spared his readers nothing except technicalities and pedantry, but on the other hand, having before him this sort of a wide intellectual audience which was not professionalized, he could release certain things in him that got weighted down and perhaps cramped a little, when in his mind he faced a professional audience.

I think one thing we need about Sapir is a reappraisal of his verse. It's very much scattered, he published over 150 poems, in a great variety of sources. And, well, his poetry might be good, or it might be excellent, or it might be mediocre, without affecting his scholarship. But it has the side that, to him, meant something. It meant a good deal, for a number of years at least. And I think when we reappraise him we shall have to reappraise that side, as well as what he did in scholarship.

The most important, best known, most cited work of Sapir so far [. . .], which is dealing with cultural anthropology, is perhaps his *Time Perspective*, and that was reprinted without abridgement in the collected volume that David Mandelbaum edited.[2] That was done when he was only 32 years old, in 1916. To me that seems more dated than most of his other things, precisely because [. . .] it is essentially a professional monograph. As a matter of fact at the time this came out, archaeology in North America was not doing the work which it should have been doing. It had not then developed a time element, which seems to us now in hindsight almost incredible. But it was not until the twenties that the first serious gropings appeared in print by American archaeologists to make archaeology a diachronic instead of an essentially synchronic or timeless discipline. And at that time, 1916, really the effort to get back into the past of the native cultures of this continent was being carried on, at any rate in north of Mexico, through ethnographic studies and the analysis and resynthesis of those [. . .] various efforts. Wissler spoke in the same theme,[3] I made efforts and so on. I think the *Time Perspective* is the most finished, the most complete, most important book. But we have so many other devices, we have a mass of archeological data, we have in addition to that Carbon 14 and so on, that there will never be any more situations such as we had then, when we had to use the indirect and necessarily fragmentary, and partly speculative evidence of current contemporary ethnology in order to try to walk back into the past. That's what I mean when I say that — it is dated, and still as an example of method, a beautiful piece of work and it is as important as ever, but it does not have the practical bearings that it did at that time, when we literally had nothing for the many peoples north of Mexico, to use except the method which he exemplifies there. A contrast with that is afforded by an *American Anthropologist* article which he published 20 years later about four Navajo words which he analyzed and compared with other Athabascan words, and comes to the conclusion that from these four words we can infer that the Navajo came from the North.[4] It is a matter of virtuosity. But I think he proves his case with these four words. The sample may be small but the fineness of the analysis is remarkable as well as the range of knowledge of the whole of Athabascan which essentially he carried in his head. We haven't *yet* got a comparitive Athabascan grammar. We have very few Athabascan grammars of individual languages, and Sapir just took out of his head or from scattered literature the particular little bits that he needed and wore them together into this masterpiece.

When I said a moment ago that he was more of a linguist than a cultural anthropologist, I had in mind that he never did any major descriptive piece of ethnography. The Wishram ethnology, published in Seattle, is in a sense an exception, but Spier and Sapir were co-authors,[5] both had done field work among the Wishram. And glancing the volume over again this afternoon, I feel assured in saying that the majority of the material and the majority of the paragraphs of text, paragraphs of writing, are the work of Leslie Spier, and Sapir threw in what he had; essentially Spier worked the book over.

In language, Sapir's contribution was manifold. He did learn — it's hard to say how many languages he wrote in. He worked in Tocharian, he knew Indo-European, he knew Semitic, he made contributions in both of those fields. He did write a full-length grammar of Takelma, and another one of Southern Paiute. He almost had finished — he was up to the last stage of work in doing a grammar of Yana. He knew Athabascan as nobody else knew it, at the time. Just by way of comparison, to illustrate the point I made in reference to Boas before, the number of what you might call full-length dramas that Boas is responsible for is about ten, instead of more or less three.

A very influential part of Sapir's linguistic work has been his classification of the languages. He took the modest beginnings that were made by Dixon[6] and myself and others of about that same period, and carried them infinitely farther. There are reasons of course why classification of that sort would be used to a certain extent even if it wasn't very good. The ethnologists need the grouping:

the archaeologists always wanted a classification of that sort that they can tie up with the archaeology. But his is not just an ad hoc piece of guesswork, but it tried to present Sapir's following out certain cues or clues to which he was exceedingly sensitive. And when he really cut fine, it was almost incredible how fine he could really cut and get an entering wedge and then follow that up or not follow it up. The modern tendencies, since there's been a renewed interest on account of glottochronology – all we have to do apparently now is to be able to have a method which enables us to put a date on something, and everybody gets excited. Just as up to forty years ago you could not get American scholars, let alone the American public, to think that dates were anything but impediments – something unfortunate that perhaps now and then – something like 1776, we were happy in a timeless, in an ahistorical world. And we are coming to maturity, because now, again with characteristic American impetuosity, dating things is important even if we don't know exactly what we're dating. Well, I'm by nature very much more conservative in linguistic grouping than Sapir, and some of the groups which he lumped together, Penuntian, Tsimshian, and Chinookan, and so on, I have not been able to see for myself. But the younger linguists of today are accepting all of his classification and going beyond it and transcending it. I sometimes wonder what he would say if he could come back.

Then of course he had a number of technical papers which were meant for a professional audience, and he was very fond of writing papers which were sort of philological or general humanistic – reflection turned loose upon a small point [. . .], he would start out, and proceed and really philosophize widely. Some of his happiest work is of that sort both in and out on linguistics. I was very much interested in Malkiel's account of how professional linguists as a class, as a group, felt about Sapir's book *Language* which was done in 1921. I get more echoes, and reactions from anthropologists, the majority of whom are not linguists, of course, and I would say that the two chapters that I have heard most discussed in that book *Language*, are first the chapter of 'drift'. I think that has an appeal for a lot of people because they feel something imminent in 'drift', some unknown force. I don't know what I myself quite believe about the matter. It has always seemed to me quite possible that what Sapir called 'drift' was something like 'momentum in language', in which a group of languages gets going in a certain direction because it has a certain kind of structure, and that basic structure dissipates or gets altered, superceded very slowly and the result is even after languages are split apart, the more or less parallel momentum in which they are running, parallel in direction, may explain it. But other people have sensed more in it, and the word that usually comes out is the somewhat mystically tinged word 'immanent'. I think that's what the excitement there by non-linguists has been about.

The other chapter is typology, and here Sapir made a very definitely risky contribution. The typing of languages began with von Humboldt and other people of 100 years or even more ago, and it was carried on mostly by Germans and I think finally crystallized about in the 1880s, about the time Sapir was born. And it was very bad work of scholarship. It was really completely ethnocentric, it was completely arbitrary and dogmatic. It picked out features which were evaluative as to intrinsic excellence, and it distorted the evidence too — even scattered evidence which it brought to bear was distorted or ultra-selective in order to make any sort of a case. I think the sounder linguists simply ordered no more traffic in that sort of thing. They avoided the subject and did nothing in it, Sapir wrote his book in two months, essentially, say eight weeks, [7] and I suppose that more than one of those eight weeks went into the writings of the chapter on classification of languages by type. This also attracted some attention among people who were primarily cultural anthropologists rather than linguists. Lowie was very much intrigued by that chapter and discussed it in seminars. I think so far as I know he did not discuss the chapter on drift. Lowie had a healthy aversion to anything that might be 'mystic'. And the typological chapter, Lowie was so much intrigued by it; it got to be one of the standard examination questions for graduates' work. And I don't know whether students of then, when he was active, got onto this foible of interest. I think if they did they could have boned up on that and have been almost sure to get a question on Sapir's classification of languages. It had however no follow-up by the linguists until a few years ago. Joseph Greenberg [. . .] did not take Sapir's scheme of classification outright, but he took some of his criteria, added others, and gave the thing what, it seems to me, is a workable shape, and I think we may be on the way to getting typological classification which is broad enough, which is unselected and sound. Sapir himself never carried the matter any farther. I don't know why he lost interest. He may have been interested only for the fortnight or so in which he developed this chapter.

A third feature in the linguistic world which has had wide influence is the so-called Sapir-Whorf hypothesis. And I looked over his collected works to see how he really felt about that; the residue of the impression I had was that he did not go very far. I know he did not go as far as Whorf did.[8] He did make some statements which say there must be an influence. It was in general terms, however; there must be an influence of the categories of speech on our thinking, on the whole of culture. But there are other passages in which he shows how autonomous, in the main, language must be. And I think we should stop talking about a Sapir-Whorf hypothesis. It's a Whorfian hypothesis, and I think the point there is to concentrate on what evidence Whorf really had or produced for his hypothesis. That the basic idea, the germ of the idea, that Whorf took and developed is to be found in Sapir — that he got it from Sapir, I don't doubt in the least. But it remained a suggestion with Sapir, and it was a suggestion which, if he approached the subject from this side or that side, he said rather conflicting things about. Not that he didn't know his own mind, but things *do* look different from different angles.

Sapir liked [. . .] open-ended problems and, if you will read his more generally literary articles (I mean these are belles-lettristic rather than professional), you will see how he liked to speculate and throw out another suggestion, and with that sprawl in a new direction. I think that's what he did in these various statements he made about the influence of linguistic form on thought. In fact you might say he liked opening up problems, and that would mean in many cases prematurely opened before other people were ready to push through; perhaps *he* wasn't ready to push through. But he often only hinted at possible answers.

Sapir's role in regard to psychology I want to touch on only very briefly. I think the factor that is very important there is his intense interest in people and seeing what made their wheels go around. That had nothing to do with whether he liked them or not. But he was likely to take a close friend and watch him, dissect him, try to draw him out in conversation, just from sheer interest in individuals, in personalities. And what was involved was that he gets some contact with the person, and he was rather skillful in getting a certain degree of warmth. When he wanted to find out what X really was like, he could bring a lot of resources to bear to get an understanding of X, which would make *him* feel comfortable, and people would talk with him and reveal themselves and Sapir would be fascinated. Just around a campfire, a person with a temperament — you would think the two would have very little in common. The campfire would burn down, and finally they would go off, both of them got so cold they couldn't carry the conversation any longer. The next morning he would say, "Well I had a fine talk with so and so". That, of course, was nothing. It merely indicated the way he was oriented in general.

Some of the statements he made about formal psychology, psychology as a discipline, ought to make psychologists wince. If he didn't say more it's because he had such a low opinion of psychology as a discipline that he really didn't bother to consider it. And the term 'personality' that he did use, rather than psychological — and 'psychiatry', or 'psychiatric' he also employed. I reread in the last few days his papers on personality and on psychiatry and I felt that there was an overbalance, that he was really trying to resolve culture and society and language, almost, into a kind of a personality psychology. I decided, finally, what he was really doing, was to envisage an entirely future condition. Nowadays, of course, psychiatry or personality psychology is far from being able to do this. It's too feeble. It hasn't got the instruments or the resources to undertake this, but what he envisioned was psychological study which completely embraced society, culture and individual psychology in some entirety — its hard to conceive —, but he was seeing something that took shape in his mind.

His early essay "Culture, Genuine and Spurious"[9] was along this line and that had particular interest to me because I feel that Sapir was influenced by the fact that he was born abroad, he was born not only Jewish but the son of a Cantor, he must have been raised orthodox Jewish. He was a poor boy who went though college because he got fellowships. He was not only so brilliant but so precocious and he grew into a larger world; but I think he always felt somewhat foreign, and sometimes deliberately he tried to correct that. He made conscious efforts to be more American and to be as established tastes would have dictated. A number of years after his death I felt that some of his psychiatric or personality papers of the last years —, and I say this in print, in 1950 — contain evidence of wish-fulfillment, the expression of wish-fulfillment against the backdrop of a partly regretted career. Now it may have been that Sapir's final illness was stealing upon him. I don't know how much he may have known about it or not, I'm not sure that I will say that today, but on the other hand I'm not sure that I would withdraw it. I feel that Sapir's career reached it's intrinsic culmination, at any rate in so far as the happiness of himself as a person is concerned, in the Chicago days from 1925 to 1931. He went then to bigger things, to bigger professorships. Cued off, he was sought after by the foundations, and by the larger world. His ego was blown up by people. He had remarkably little ego previously. And at the same time it brought him strain and situations and activities which fundamentally he did not like. He liked the contemplative life with freedom to speculate but not make decisions about people, or about affairs.

All this is not the fault of Yale, but it was the fault of the position into which he was suddenly thrust for which the Yale appointment merely gave him the opportunity, that brought about this change. I saw him several times. I saw him in his home, I stayed in his house in the New Haven days, and had a sense of things just piling up. I don't know what the weight of these impingements may have had — something that may have had a good deal to do — with his dying at the early age of 55. 1933 [...] is the year that Bloomfield's second book came out; [it] came right about the time of the turning point. The first year or two at Yale of course were very stimulating. There were large opportunities, many people sought him, new contacts and so on, but I should say from about 1933 on, quite apart from Bloomfield's book, the negative elements more and more clouded over a career that had been essentially sunny beforehand. I am not talking against what you said,[10] but I think it's a coincidence; I think two sets of factors seem to come together then. I think some of the finest things Sapir did are first that article on 'Language' you spoke of.[11] He had another little one on 'Dialect', all in the *Encyclopedia*.[12] That whole series of encyclopedia articles are simply extraordinary.[13] He was not talking for linguists when he wrote that article. He was talking for the whole of social science. And the other things, his articles on fashion, on custom. His things on custom and culture, and other matters of that sort. It's almost incredible felicity. And I also like very much Malkiel's comparison of Mozart and prodigality. It's the same natural flow, the welling up of ideas, sentiments, and they are almost inexhaustable.

EDITOR'S NOTES

1) Kroeber is referring to Sapir's contributions on subjects such as "Communication", "Dialect", "Group", "Language", "Symbolism" in the *Encyclopaedia of the Social Sciences* (New York: Macmillan 1931-34); cf. Sapir's bibliography, for details.

2) *Time Perspective in Aboriginal American Culture: A study of method* (= Canada, Department of Mines, Geological Survey, Memoir 90; *Anthropoological Series*, 13.) Ottawa: Government Printing Bureau, 1916, 87 pp.; repr. in *Selected Writings of Edward Sapir in Lanuage, Culture, and Personality* ed. by David. G. Mandelbaum (Berkeley & Los Angeles: Univ. of California Press, 1949), 389-462.

3) See Clark Wissler's (1870-1947) successful book, *The American Indian: An introduction to the anthropology of the New World* (New York: D. C. McMurtie, 1917; 2nd ed., ibid. & Oxford Univ. Press, 1922; 3rd ed., 1938; repr., 1950).

4) E. Sapir, "Internal Linguistic Evidence Suggestive of the Northern Origin of the Navaho", *American Anthropologist* N.S. 38.224-35 (1936); repr. in *Selected Writings* (1949), 213-24.

5) *Wishram Ethnography* by Leslie Spier (1893-1961) & Edward Sapir (= *University of Washington Publications in Anthropology* 3.151-300), Seattle, Wash.: Univ. of Washington, 1930.

6) Roland Burrage Dixon (1875-1934) & Alfred Louis Kroeber (1876-1960), "Linguistic Families of California", *University of California Publications in American Archaeology and Ethnology* 16:3.47-118 (Berkeley: Univ. of California Press, 1919).

7) From what may be gathered from Sapir's letters to Robert Harry Lowie (1883-1957), it is clear that it took Sapir much longer than two months to write the book, and certainly much more than 'just a few weeks', as Yakov Malkiel suggested in his 1959 paper (cf. introductory note to this paper). Thus, by 25 May 1920 (cf. *Letters from Edward Sapir to Robert H. Lowie* published posthumously by Luella Cole Lowie, Berkeley: privately printed, 1965, p.37) Sapir had not yet a definite offer from Harcourt in New York and was reluctant to invest time and energy on the project until it was received. On 9 September 1920, he notes (p.39): "I am in the 5th chapter now. Slow work!". On 26 Ocotober (p.42), he reports: "My book on language has been neglected rather of late". And on 8 April 1921, he writes: "I am finishing my last chapter to-day" (p.46). (Further references to the MS and the book can be found in the same publication on pp.47-49.)

8) From the vast literature on the so-called (Sapir-) Whorf Hypothesis only the following may be mentioned here: Harry Hoijer's paper, "Sapir-Whorf Hypothesis", *Language and Culture: Conference on the interrelationship between language and other aspects of culture* — in fact the entire conference was inspired by this theme (Berkeley & Los Angeles: California Univ. Press, 1954; repr., 1967), pp.92-105. Another conference on this subject was held in Europe some twenty years later; cf. *Universalism versus Relativism in Language and Thought: Proceedings of a colloquium on the Sapir-Whorf Hypothesis* ed. by Rik Pixten (The Hague: Mouton, 1976), xiv, 310 pp. See also, inter alia, Jack L. Davis, "The Whorf Hypothesis and Native American Literature", *South Dakota Review* 14:2.59-72 (1976); Russ A. Rueger, *Toward a Unified Theory of Language: Transformational grammar, the Sapir-Whorf hypothesis and ethnomethodology*, Ph.D. diss., Univ. of California at Irvine, 1975, 104 pp.; Danny K. H. Alford, "The Demise of the Whorf Hypothesis: A major revision in the history of linguistics", *Proceedings of the [annual meeting of the] Berkeley Linguistics Society* 4.485-99 (1978).

9) First published in full in *American Journal of Sociology* 29.401-429 (1924); repr. in *Selected Writings* (1949), 308-331.

10) Kroeber is referring to Malkiel's paper (cf. editorial note at the beginning of this paper), in which Malkiel asserts that Leonard Bloomfield's (1887-1949) *Language* (New York, 1933) effectively eclipsed Sapir's book of 1921 by the same title and reduced Sapir's post-1933 impact on American structural linguistics to a considerable degree.

11) The reference is to Sapir's contribution "Language" to the *Encyclopaedia of the Social Sciences* 9.153-69 (New York: Macmillan, 1933); repr. in *Selected Writings* (1949), 7-32.

12) Sapir, "Dialect", *Encyclopaedia* [...] 5.123-26 (1931); repr. in *Selected Writings* (1949), 83-103.

13) Cf. note 1 (above) for details.

DISCUSSION AND CORRESPONDENCE

A BIRD'S-EYE VIEW OF AMERICAN LANGUAGES NORTH OF MEXICO

It is clear that the orthodox "Powell" classification of American languages, useful as it has proved itself to be, needs to be superseded by a more inclusive grouping based on an intensive comparative study of morphological features and lexical elements. The recognition of 50 to 60 genetically independent "stocks" north of Mexico alone is tantamount to a historical absurdity. Many serious difficulties lie in the way of the task of reduction, among which may be mentioned the fact that our knowledge of many, indeed of most, American languages is still sadly fragmentary; that frequent allowance must be made for linguistic borrowing and for the convergent development of features that are only descriptively, not historically, comparable; and that our persistently, and rather fruitlessly, "psychological" approach to the study of American languages has tended to dull our sense of underlying drift, of basic linguistic forms, and of lines of historical reconstruction. Any genetic reconstruction that can be offered now is necessarily but an exceedingly rough approximation to the truth at best. It is certain to require the most serious revision as our study progresses. Nevertheless I consider a tentative scheme as possessed of real value. It should act as a stimulus to more profound investigations and

as a first attempt to shape the historical problem. On the basis of both morphological and, in part, lexical evidence, the following six great groups, presumably genetic, may be recognized:

I. Eskimo-Aleut

II. Algonkin-Wakashan
- Algonkin-Wiyot-Yurok
- Kootenay
- Wakashan-Salish

III. Na-dene (Haida; Tlingit-Athabaskan)

IV. Penutian
- CalifornianPenutian
- Oregon Penutian
- Tsimshian

V. Hokan-Siouan
- Yuki
- Hokan
- Coahuiltecan group
- Keres
- Tunica group
- Siouan-Yuchi-Muskogian
- Iroquois-Caddoan

VI. Aztec-Tanoan
- Uto-Aztekan
- Tanoan-Kiowa

This leaves the Waiilatpuan-Lutuami-Sahaptin group, Zuñi, and Beothuk as yet unplaced. The lines of cleavage seem greatest between IV. and V., and between III., on the one hand, and I. and II., on the other. Group V is probably the nearest to the generalized "typical American" type that is visualized by linguistic students at large.

E. Sapir

Canadian Geological Survey,
Ottawa

Edward Sapir's 1921 statement concerning the classification
of North American Indian Languages

THE CULTURE HISTORIC IMPLICATIONS OF
SAPIR'S LINGUISTIC CLASSIFICATION*

MORRIS SWADESH

Time Perspective

Culture prehistorians using Sapir's synthesis of North American language classification (1929) need to exercise one essential precaution: to bear in mind the approximate scale and implicit time depth of each connection. Lackner and Rowe (1955) seem to think that the problem is one of fact versus fancy—that is, whether the languages are actually related or merely asserted to be so without foundation—but this can be shown to be a misapprehension.

While it was not customary in his day for scholars to commit themselves on the actual time depth of linguistic groupings, Sapir gave this matter more than passing attention. The following remarks (1916, pp. 77–78, and 1929) are particularly interesting:

> There can be no doubt that a very great lapse of time (probably several millennia) must be assumed to account for the geographical distribution and dialectic differentiation of the Algonkin languages proper. . . . The morphological and lexical differences that obtain between even the most divergent Algonkin languages, say Cheyenne and Micmac, while by no means inconsiderable, are of comparatively little moment when set by the side of analogical differences obtaining between two such Penutian languages as Yokuts and Miwok. There can be no doubt, then, that the distribution of Penutian-speaking tribes antedates, as a whole, the scattering of Algonkin peoples from a comparatively restricted center. If under the term "Algonkin" we include the remotely related Yurok and Wiyot of California, a comparison with the California Penutian group as to relative age of linguistic differentiation might well favor the former.
> . . . One corollary of great historical interest follows from our argument

---

* Reprinted, with permission of the Summer Institute of Linguistics, Dallas, Texas, from *To William Cameron Townsend on the Twenty-fifth Anniversary of the Summer Institute of Linguistics* (México, D.F.: Instituto Nacional de Antropología e Historia, 1961), pp. 663-71.

as to the chronological significance of linguistic differentiation. . . . We must allow a tremendous lapse of time for the development of such divergences, a lapse of time undoubtedly several times as great as the period that the more conservative archaeologists and palaeontologists are willing to allow as necessary for the interpretation of the earliest remains of man in America. . . . While it is absurd to juggle with specific figures, it may be interesting to note that at a recent scientific meeting a well-known palaeontologist, who is at the same time conversant with the problem of early man in America, expressed himself as believing ten thousand years an ample, indeed a maximum, period for the human occupation of this continent. . . . This would make it practically imperative to assume that the peopling of America was not a single historical process but a series of movements of linguistically unrelated peoples, possibly from different directions and certainly at very different times. This view strikes me as intrinsically highly probable. As the latest linguistic arrivals in North America would probably have to be considered the Eskimo-Aleut and the Nadene (Haida, Tlingit, and Athapaskan).

. . . The more deep-lying resemblances, such as can be demonstrated, for instance, for Shoshonean, Piman, and Nahuatl (Mexico) or for Athapaskan and Tlingit, must be due to a common origin now greatly obscured by the operation of phonetic laws, grammatical developments and losses, analogical disturbances, and borrowing of elements from alien sources.

While the last citation does not speak of time periods as such, it helps to round out the other remarks. From all of them together and from the arrangement of groupings by headings and subheadings, we find the following time judgments to be stated or implied by Sapir: *(a)* Algonkin proper, several thousand years; *(b)* California Penutian, more than several thousand years; *(c)* Algonkin-Ritwan, more than *b*; *(d)* Penutian as a whole, more than *b* and probably more than *c*; *(e)* Uto Aztecan, enough to account for considerable differences and possibly similar to *a*; *(f)* Aztec-Tanoan, more than *e*; *(g)* Athapaskan-Tlingit, approximately like *e*; *(h)* Nadene, more than *g* but definitely less than the maximum; *(i)* Eskimo-Aleut, definitely less than the maximum. On the basis of the older estimates of the antiquity of man in America, Sapir considered the maximum time depth of any phylum developed in America to be ten thousand years, but this figure has been extended in recent years.

To the extent that the above-listed groupings have been tested by the recently developed lexicostatistic method (Swadesh, 1954a), Sapir's judgment has proved to be consistently sound.

Sapir did not achieve correct estimates of time depth by magic, but by a definite method, the basis of which is simply: "The greater the degree of linguistic differentiation within a stock, the greater is the period of time that must be assumed for the development of such differentiation" (1916, p. 76). He made time estimates by comparing the differentiation within a given language group with that found in some other family or stock of more or less known history, such as English-German or Indo-European. The successful practice of the method called for the ability to see complicated linguistic details in the perspective of their relative historical importance, and to heed objective facts rather than preconceptions. It was a kind of mental arithmetic, based on external facts, even when the weighting procedure was not written out.

The new lexicostatistic method represents an externalization of one part of Sapir's procedure, in that the data are always written out in the form of a standard vocabulary of noncultural words, constituting the diagnostic word list. It furthermore involves a simplification, in that Sapir's multiple lexical-morphological criteria are reduced to one, which has been found to be a reliable and easily determined index of the passage of time. The calculation (Swadesh, 1955) is based on the percentage of cognates (C) found in the diagnostic vocabularies of two related languages, considered in the light of a standard retention rate (r) or, in other words, the normal percentage of elements retained after a given unit of time as determined in a series of control languages. Divergence is determined in separation-time units (st), which is equal to minimum time (min t) of nonunity. Actual time (t) can be known once one establishes which cases within a language grouping involve complete separation (max s = 1 by definition). Time (t) is usually given in centuries. Once one has found t, one can then obtain a numerical index of the average degree of separation (s) for every pair of languages during the entire period since complete unity was first broken. Thus we learn not only the time depth but the degree of contact between two languages during their period of separate development. The equation and its derivatives are:

$$st = \log C \div \log r^2$$
$$\min t = \log C \div \log r^2$$
$$t = \log C \div s \log r^2$$
$$s = \log C \div t \log r^2$$

Sapir's indications of time depth for American linguistic groupings are not complete, as one may well understand in view of the difficulty of estimating them by his procedure. By the aid of lexicostatistic techniques the problem has become much simpler. What is needed is a collection of diagnostic word lists at least for all the key languages. I now have about three hundred from different parts of the New World,[1] about a third of these being from North America, which have made possible the evaluation of Sapir's estimates as already indicated.

1. A large fraction of these were supplied by linguists of the Summer Institute of Linguistics, particularly because of the cooperation of its founder, William C. Townsend. This is one of many ways in which we see fulfilled the scientific promise of Townsend's dream, applauded and encouraged by Sapir at its inception, of an institution to train linguistic workers and place them among the many tribes of America.

Proof of Common Origin

Lackner and Rowe (1955) have the impression that Sapir "proposed to classify languages primarily by similarities of morphology." They term this "Sapir's classificatory principle" and argue that it "remains a shaky basis on which to erect a genetic classification of languages." They are no doubt correct in suggesting that Sapir made use of morphological criteria "in setting up his famous classification of all North American languages into only six superstocks," but they are surely wrong in believing that this was his primary criterion of relationship. The best proof of their misconception is to be found precisely in the only article Sapir ever wrote dealing primarily with a purely structural feature of one of his linguistic phyla, the paper entitled "A Characteristic Penutian Form of Stem" (1921). While the bulk of this article is devoted to a structural matter, it also contains a full explanation of why he recognized a Penutian phylum at all. Morphological traits are found to be secondary.

Sapir starts by citing and quoting from Frachtenberg's *Comparative Studies in Takelman, Kalapuyan, and Chinookan Lexicography*, and goes on to say (emphasis added):

> . . . All this is very interesting to me, as it chimes with conclusions or hypotheses I had arrived at independently. On the appearance of Frachtenberg's Coos grammar, it soon became clear to me that the morphological and *lexical resemblances* between Takelma and Coos were too numerous and fundamental to be explained away by accident or plausibly accounted for by borrowing. This *in spite of the very great differences of phonetics and structure* that separate the two languages. . . . Meanwhile comparison of Takelma, Coos, and Siuslaw with Dixon and Kroeber's Penutian of California (Costanoan, Miwok, Yokuts, Wintun, and Maidu) disclosed an astonishing number of *both lexical and morphological* correspondences, correspondences which were first dimly brought to my consciousness years ago by certain morphological resemblances between Takelma and Yokuts, later and more vividly by the decided Penutian "feel" of Coos grammar. After hesitating for a long while to take up seriously the

possibility of affiliating Chinook, one of the most isolated and morphologically specialized languages in America, with the Penutian languages of Oregon, I now find myself forced by the evidence to admit
such an affiliation as not only possible but decidedly probable. In view of
the clear points of *lexical contacts* and of the phonetic shifts that Frachtenberg has established . . . between Takelma and Kalapuyan, his further
hypothesis of a fundamental connection between Kalapuya and Chinook
was, for me, to be looked for *a priori.* I believe it only fair to add that the
manuscript evidence that I possess of the relation between Chinook and
various languages to the south is much stronger than the comparatively
scanty *lexical data* presented by Frachtenberg. . . .

The greatest surprise was still awaiting me: Tsimshian. . . . A tentative
comparison with the Penutian . . . languages of Oregon revealed a considerable number of correspondences both *in the lexical material* and in
some of the more intimate and fundamental features of morphology. . . .

The data for the various assertions I have made in this paper I expect
to present *in extenso* in the future. . . .

It is seen here that morphological resemblances led Sapir to *look for*
lexical correspondences, but are nowhere considered in themselves sufficient
to prove relationship. In fact, Sapir at times finds reason to infer common
origin "in spite of great differences of structure." While recognizing great
stability in certain fundamental areas of morphology, he is equally aware
that any of it is subject to change, given sufficient time and the continued
exposure to diffusional and other influences. There is, then, no contradiction
when he observes (1929) that "Chinook seems to have developed a secondary
'polysynthetic' form on the basis of a broken-down form of Penutian; while
Tsimshian and Maidu have probably been considerably influenced by contact with Mosan and with Shoshonean and Hokan respectively."

That Sapir was not alone in attaching considerable importance to
morphology may be seen from the following remark by Truman Michelson
(1921):"When there are far-reaching structural resemblances between two
or more supposedly distinct (and especially contiguous) stocks, we may
legitimately infer an ancient connection which perhaps can no longer be
proved owing to very early differentiation."

Evidence

When Lackner and Rowe speak of Sapir's groupings as made "on an
impressionistic basis," they seem to be repeating Voegelin's use of the same
adjective (1941, pp. 27–29). However, Voegelin explains (p. 27) that "a

distinction is made between impressionistic classifications and classifications based on published evidence." In other words, "impressionistic" is here a special shorthand for "based on evidence not yet published," and Voegelin's usage is completely consistent throughout his paper, even though it may be confusing for any hasty reader. He has occasion to speak of undocumented connections at only four points: (*a*) the combining of Kutenai, Wakashan, and Salishan with Algonkin-Ritwan; (*b*) the inclusion of Zuñi in Aztec-Tanoan; (*c*) the inclusion of Klamath-Modoc, Molale, Sahaptin, Alsea, and Tsimshian in the Penutian phylum; (*d*) the inclusion of Yuki, Caddoan, Keresan, and Yuchi in Hokan-Siouan, and "special sub-relationships, such as Caddoan to Iroquoian." Hoijer (1946, pp. 13–23) notes the same instances, plus (*e*) the connection of Timuqua and Natchez-Muskogian.

The roster of relationships supported by published evidence is, of course, expanded from time to time. If one takes into account new works published since the Voegelin and Hoijer papers, plus unpublished manuscripts, plus research material now being assembled (see references under Sapir, Sapir and Swadesh, Haas, Jacobs, Greenberg and Swadesh, and Granberry), very few of the relationships in Sapir's synthesis remain undocumented.

Were any of Sapir's groupings literally impressionistic or purely speculative? Apparently not. The indications are that Sapir had actually examined material for every language or language family in his scheme, and made no groupings without having found specific evidence to support them. He frequently penciled comparisons in the margins of works in his library (see e.g. Sapir 1952) or wrote out lists of cognates, and his students know that he could cite cognates in support of many relationships from memory. Of course, he was also thoroughly familiar with the published literature on comparative linguistics. The Sapir classification is a synthesis of his own findings and those of his predecessors and contemporaries, but in no case did he cite published findings without having verified the evidence on which they were based.

Standard of Proof

In Voegelin's review of Sapir's synthesis, the only point at which he suggests possibly inadequate standards of proof is in connection with the Hokan-Siouan grouping. Thus (1941, p. 29):

> Paul Radin announced that Yuki belonged with Penutian . . . but credited the insight to Kroeber. Kroeber refused the honor. Sapir finally classified Yuki with Hokan-Siouan . . . possibly because Yuki would not fit in any other group. That is to say, this final group is loosely enough characterized to admit languages otherwise unclassifiable.

The fact that Yuki resisted the first efforts to classify it does not in itself prove that Sapir had no evidence for his placement of it. Our recent studies show that Penutian and Hokan are only different portions of a single network of linguistic groups, and that Yuki belongs with those Hokan languages which come the closest to Penutian.

Hoijer is very specific in acknowledging the rigor of Sapir's work, saying (1941, p. 8), "He achieved his revisions of the Powell classification by the strict application of the comparative method to American Indian materials." However, it happens that Hoijer sets an extraordinarily high standard of what constitutes indisputable proof of linguistic relationship, and by this yardstick Sapir's evidence of Hokan, along with that of Dixon and Kroeber, remains "far from conclusive."

Hoijer accepts modifications of Powell in only two cases, Uto-Aztecan, based on Sapir's work (1946, pp. 21–22), and Shasta-Achomawi, based on Dixon's (p. 16). He is less rigorously critical of Powell's work, saying this (p. 10):

> Though a number of far-reaching modifications of this classification have been suggested since, the groups set up by Powell still retain their validity.
>
> In no case has a stock established by Powell been discredited by later work; the modifications that have been suggested are all concerned with the establishment of larger stocks to include two or more of the Powell groupings. . . . Most of these modifications have not as yet been indisputably established. . . .

Hoijer disregards the fact that the Powell classification was published without any documentary proof, even though he otherwise refuses to accept "unsupported" claims of relationship, e.g., Sapir's broad Penutian, the documentation for which had not yet been published when Hoijer wrote his paper (Sapir and Swadesh, 1953; also Sapir, c. 1920).

It is not quite true that only fusions of Powell groups have been proposed. Hoijer himself reports the opposite case with respect to Yakonan (p. 15):

> Powell included in this group the Yakona, Alsea, Siuslaw and Lower Umpqua tribes . . . Wissler, in 1938, lists Siuslaw and Lower Umpqua together and puts Yakona and Alsea in a separate group. He gives no authority for this division of the Powell stock.

If we seek out Wissler's authority, we find it must have been Frachtenberg, in the Handbook of American Indian Languages, who tells (1922, p. 437):

> In 1884 J. Owen Dorsey spent a month at the Siletz reservation, Oregon, collecting short vocabularies of the Siuslaw and Lower Umpqua, as well as other languages. Prior to Dorsey's investigations the linguistic

position of Siuslaw and Lower Umpqua was a debated question. Some investigators believed that these two dialects belonged to the Yakonan family; while others, notably Latham and Gatschet, held them to form a distinct stock, although they observed marked agreement with some features of the Yakonan. After a superficial investigation, lasting less than a month, Dorsey came to the conclusion that Siuslaw and Lower Umpqua were dialects belonging to the Yakonan stock. This assertion was repeated by J. W. Powell in his "Indian Linguistic Families." . . . It is not at all impossible that this stock, the Yakonan, and perhaps the Kalapuyan, may eventually prove to be genetically related. Their affinities are so remote, however, that I prefer to take a conservative position, and to treat them for the time being as independent stocks.

From examination of some of the comparative material, I feel that Frachtenberg's view may be the better founded, and that at any rate the Yakonan-Siuslawan relation is distant. This case serves as a reminder that standards of accuracy need to be applied to Powell just as much as to Dixon, Kroeber, Swanton, Harrington, or Sapir. The norm should provide a good margin of safety to clearly separate agreement based on common origin from chance similarity. Any excessive standard is a wasteful luxury, which has the effect of unduly foreshortening the time depth penetrable by comparative linguistics. To get away from arbitrary subjective conceptions of proof requirements, one may make a mathematical calculation of the maximum effect of pure chance in a lexicostatistic test (see Swadesh, 1954b, pp. 312–15). The indications are that Sapir's yardstick was fully adequate.

Diffusion

Powell and most of his successors have evidently felt that in linguistics, unlike some other aspects of culture, it is usually possible to differentiate clearly between genetic and diffusional agreements. Powell's only remark bearing on the subject is (p. 26): "Neither coincidences nor borrowed material . . . can be properly regarded as evidences of cognation," evidently assuming that the cases could be recognized. Boas felt that this was ordinarily true but that occasionally an ambiguous situation might arise. The only concrete example of such a case he ever suggested was that of Tlingit-Athapaskan, but evidently even this case finally yielded to accumulated evidence, for we learn from Jacobs (1954) of:

Evidence that Tlingit constitutes a subdivision of Nadene. Such evidence was assembled by Mrs. Melville Jacobs in a manuscript prepared in 1936 following her field research on southwestern Oregon Athapaskan Nadene dialects. Her discovery of many regular sound shifts between Tlingit and Athapaskan impressed Boas and Sapir with the unexpectedly close relationship of these groups. Boas then agreed that he and P. E. Goddard had been unduly hesitant about accepting the claim of Sapir that Tlingit was affiliated genetically with Athapaskan languages.

Language is that part of culture which is, as a whole, the least subject to diffusional changes. As Sapir put it (1930, p. 220), "Language is probably the most self-contained, the most massively resistant of all social phenomena. It is easier to kill it off than to disintegrate its individual form." Moreover, insofar as language is subject to the influence of diffusion, certain aspects are much more resistant than others. Consequently it is possible to single out certain aspects of linguistic morphology, phonetics, and vocabulary which tend to change at a rate so low that many centuries will elapse before any considerable difference has occurred. In the realm of vocabulary, the hard core of resistance to change generally and to diffusional change specifically is the noncultural vocabulary. Since words from foreign sources are also often to be detected by phonetic form, it is possible to build up a very dependable linguistic methodology for separating the influences of diffusion from ancient heritage. Lexicostatistics strengthens that methodology by permitting the study of maximum rates of diffusional replacement in diagnostic lists (Swadesh, 1951). With or without this refinement, the danger that "any significant fraction of the case represents old borrowing or convergence" (Lackner and Rowe, 129) in any critically developed genetic classification is, to say the least, not great.

Limitations

In Sapir's *Britannica* article, he describes his scheme of classification as "suggestive but not demonstrable in all its features at the present time." What are the features that Sapir considered chiefly undemonstrable? A general consideration of Sapir's thinking on the problem of classification, as expressed in his writings and teaching, suggest that they have been principally matters of time scale. Is language A closer to B than to C? Should a group A-B be set up alongside of C, or should the three be set on a par? And finally, how do "wave" influences modify the hierarchical scheme of groups, subgroups, and further subdivisions?

Sapir's conception of the wave theory did not confine it to the operation of diffusion, but recognized also the common retention of like features among a series of neighboring dialects. The system of showing relationships in a sequence of headings and subheadings is not subtle enough to show these relationships. If A, B, and C are branches of the same linguistic grouping, they may be parallel and equivalent branches, so that the order in which the three are set down makes no difference. In other instances, B may be an intermediate type, with A and C further removed from each other than either from B. In this event B might be a little closer to one than to the other without actually forming a subgroup with it. These subtleties, reflecting details in the prehistory of language groupings, were important to Sapir. Where he had made a sufficient study, he could express his observations in detailed discussion, but the outline form was not adequate. To improve on his bird's-eye view of American languages would require a parallel commentary, worked out only after a great deal of study, or some new devices in the technique of outlining which could reflect the same facts.

Voegelin's suggestion that Sapir sometimes had to put languages in a given place because they would not fit anywhere else may not be literally correct, but there were related problems of relative time scale which left an area of uncertainty as to where a given linguistic entity should fall within the main divisions. Thus Zuñi fits poorly with Aztec-Tanoan, as is indeed reflected in Sapir's question mark. If Zuñi is related to this phylum, it is not on a par with the other two stocks, and it is not necessarily more closely related to them than to other phyla in Sapir's classification. I feel it may be somewhat closer to Penutian.

Sapir tried to overcome the artificial geographic limitation of "north of Mexico" which Powell had been forced by practical considerations to adopt. However, lack of data still prevented him from embracing all the languages, regardless of location, which might belong with his phyla. This limitation is now gradually being overcome.

References

Frachtenberg, Leo J.
    1922.   "Siuslawan (Lower Umpqua)." In *Handbook of American Indian Languages*, ed. Franz Boas, Bureau of American Ethnology bulletin no. 40, pt. 2, pp. 431–629. Washington, D.C.: Smithsonian Institution. P. 437.

Granberry, Julian
    1955.   "Current Research Materials on Relationship of Timuqua and Muskogian." Gainesville: Department of Social Sciences, University of Florida.

Greenberg, J. H., and Swadesh, M.
    1953.   "Jicaque as a Hokan Language." *International Journal of American Linguistics* 19:216–22.

Haas, Mary R.
    1951.   "The Proto-Gulf Word for *Water* (With Notes on Siouan-Yuchi)." *International Journal of American Linguistics* 17:71–79.
    1952.   "The Proto-Gulf Word for *Land* (With a Note on Proto-Siouan)." *International Journal of American Linguistics* 18:238–40.
    1954.   "The Proto-Hokan-Coahuiltecan Word for *Water*." In *Papers from the Symposium on American Indian Linguistics*, University of California Publications in Linguistics 10:1–68; pp. 57–62.

Hoijer, Harry
1941. "Methods in the Classification of American Indian Languages." In
Language, Culture, and Personality: Essays in Memory of Edward Sapir, ed.
Leslie Spier *et al.*, pp. 3–14. Menasha, Wisc.: Sapir Memorial Publication
Fund.
1946. *Introduction to Linguistic Structures of Native America*. Viking Fund Publications
in Anthropology no. 6, pp. 9–29.

Jacobs, Melville
c.1930. "Molale Grammar." MS in the University of Washington Library, Seattle.
1954. "The Areal Spread of Sound Features in the Languages North of California." In *Papers from the Symposium on American Indian Linguistics*, University
of California Publications in Linguistics 10:1–68; p. 47, fn. 2.

Lackner, Jerome A., and Rowe, John H.
1955. "Morphological Similarity as a Criterion of Genetic Relationship Between
Languages." *American Anthropologist* 57:126–29.

Michelson, Truman
1921. "The Classification of American Languages." *International Journal of
American Linguistics* 2:73.

Powell, John W.
1891. *Indian Linguistic Families of America North of Mexico*, Bureau of American
Ethnology seventh annual report, pp. 7–142. Washington, D.C.: Smithsonian Institution.

Sapir, Edward
1916. *Time Perspective in Aboriginal American Culture: A Study in Method*, Bureau of
Mines Geological Survey, memoir 90. Ottawa: Canadian Government
Printing Office.
c.1920. "Comparative Penutian glosses," (compiled from marginal notes in books
and offprints which had belonged to Sapir). In the Franz Boas Collection
of the American Philosophical Society Library, Philadelphia.
1921a. "A Characteristic Penutian Form of Stem." *International Journal of American
Linguistics* 2:58–67.
1921b. "A Bird's-Eye View of American Languages North of Mexico." *Science*
54:408.
1929. "Central and North American Languages." In *Encyclopaedia Britannica*,
14th ed., 5:138–41.

Sapir, Edward, and Swadesh, Morris
1953. "Coos-Takelma-Penutian Comparisons." *International Journal of American
Linguistics* 19:132–37.

Swadesh, Morris
1951. "Diffusional Cumulation and Archaic Residue as Historic Explanations."
Southwestern Journal of Anthropology 7:1–21.
1954a. "Time Depths of American Linguistic Groupings." *American Anthropologist*
56:361–64.
1954b. "Perspectives and Problems of Amerindian Comparative Linguistics."
Word 10:306–32.
1955. "Towards Greater Accuracy in Lexicostatistic Dating." *International
Journal of American Linguistics* 21, no. 2.

Voegelin, C. F.
   1941. "North American Indian Languages Still Spoken and Their Genetic
          Relationships." In *Language, Culture, and Personality: Essays in Memory of
          Edward Sapir*, ed. Leslie Spier *et al.*, pp. 15–40. Menasha, Wisc.: Sapir
          Memorial Publication Fund.

SAPIR'S PHONOLOGIC REPRESENTATION*

JAMES D. McCAWLEY

The name of Edward Sapir has been invoked many times recently as a precursor of modern generative phonology. For a typical example, note Chomsky's Current Issues in Linguistic Theory,[1] where after introducing the term 'systematic phonemic' to denote the representation which forms the input to the phonological component of a transformational grammar, Chomsky states "The level of systematic phonemics is, essentially, the "phonological orthography" of Sapir." In this paper I will examine the question of the extent to which a segment in one of Sapir's phonologic representations can be identified with a segment in the dictionary representation of a morpheme in a transformational gramar.

I first note one obvious respect in which Sapir's representations agree with those of generative phonology, namely that both are 'mentalistic', in the sense of being advanced as hypotheses as to the speaker's tacit knowledge of his language. In both cases, only two segmental representations are considered of significance: an 'underlying' or 'phcnologic' representation which represents the speaker's 'mental image' of the various morphemes, and a phonetic representation which corresponds to the actual articulations made by the vocal organs in producing utterances. No systematic significance is attached to any 'intermediate' representation[2] such as a phonemic representation in the sense of e.g. Bloch and Trager's Outline

of Linguistic Analysis,[3] although in both Sapir and transformational grammar, 'underlying' phonological representations are converted into phonetic representations through several intermediate stages, since some 'rules' apply to the output of other 'rules'. That the representations which Sapir called 'phonemic' or 'phonologic' were not 'phonemic' as the term is used in the 'Neo-Bloomfieldian' tradition of Bloch and Trager op. cit. is apparent from a perusal of almost any of Sapir's grammars; to cite an example, in his Takelma grammar,[4] Sapir gives four forms of the verb *to shoot* which he observes are all pronounced [sãk'] but have different phonologic representations.

While Sapir's phonologic representations were not bound by such constraints as the biuniqueness, linearity,[5] and invariance

[1] Mouton (the Hague), 1964.

[2] At least, not within the works of Sapir which Chomsky refers to. In very late works such as the Nootka Texts (Linguistic Society of America, Baltimore, William Dwight Whitney Series, 1939), however, the texts are written in what appears to be an 'intermediate' phonemic representation.

[3] Linguistic Society of America (Baltimore), 1942.

[4] In Boas (ed.), Handbook of American Indian Languages, vol. 2 (Government Printing Office, Washington, 1922), pp. 1–296.

[5] Sydney M. Lamb (Prolegomena to a theory of phonology, Lg. 42.536–73) argues that 'neo-Bloomfieldian' linguists did not impose a condition of linearity on phonemic transcriptions, citing as evidence the fact that they virtually all recognized phonemes of stress and pitch which occurred simultaneously with 'segmental phonemes' and did not set up phonemes of 'high-pitched primary-stressed /a/', 'high-pitched secondary-stressed /a/', etc., as would be required by adherence to strict linearity. While Lamb's observation is correct, it is incomplete. The 'neo-Bloomfieldian' linguist typically separated segmental phenomena from one or more types of suprasegmental phenomena (stress, pitch) and required his phonemicization of each of these classes of phenomena to meet some criterion of linearity, albeit often one much weaker than that which Chomsky (op. cit.) attributes to them. Deviations from strict linearity within segmental phenomena were countenanced only to the extent of allowing a single phonetic segment to be phonemicized as a sequence of phonemes which occur elsewhere in the language (e.g. by representing a phonetic nasal

* Reprinted, with permission of The University of Chicago Press, the author, and the editor, from *International Journal of American Linguistics* 33.106-111 (1967).

p	t	k
p′	t′	k′
(b)	(d)	(g)
f θ	s	x
(v) (ð)	(z)	(γ)

FIG. 1

(from p. 38 of Sapir, Sound Patterns in Language)[6]

	passive aorist	dubitative	underlying form of stem
care for	gopit	gopol	gop
swear	muṭhun	muṭal	muṭ
take in	gōbit	gōbol	gōb
steal	ʔōṭ'ut	ʔōṭ'al	ʔūṭ'

Vowel becomes rounded after rounded vowel of same height.

FIG. 2

which characterize the phonemic representations of Neo-Bloomfieldian linguists, Sapir nonetheless subjected his phonologic representations to certain other constraints which have the effect of making the set of possible analyses for Sapir radically different from the set of possible analyses in generative phonology. The most important of these constraints comes to light if one considers the diagrams which Sapir often used in his discussions of phonological systems. These diagrams are tables of the phonetic segments which occur in a language, with parentheses around certain of those segments (fig. 1). Sapir calls the unparenthesized symbols 'organic' segments and uses them in his phonologic representations; the parenthesized segments are called 'inorganic' and treated as variants of the 'organic' segments. Thus, Sapir has two inventories of segments, the full phonetic inventory and the 'organic' or 'phonologic' inventory, the latter inventory being a subset of the former. Sapir makes this fairly explicit in his Language:[7] "Back of the purely objective sys-

tem of sounds that is peculiar to a language and which can be arrived at only by a painstaking phonetic analysis, there is a MORE RESTRICTED "INNER" or "ideal" system which, while perhaps equally unconscious to the naive speaker, can far more readily be brought to his consciousness as a finished pattern, a psychological mechanism." (P. 55; emphasis added.) It should be noted that the constraint that the phonologic inventory be a subset of the phonetic inventory, a constraint which Sapir adhered to virtually without exception, would exclude a large subclass of the possible analyses of generative phonology, namely those analyses in which some underlying contrast is always neutralized phonetically. For example, Yokuts[8] has only three different long vowels phonetically: [ō, ā, ē]; however, it is necessary to regard phonetic [ō] in Yokuts as representing two different underlying vowels, /ō/ and /ū/, due to the fact that for the purposes of Yokuts vowel harmony, certain occurrences of [ō] function as high vowels but other occurrences function as low vowels (see fig. 2). The constraint under which Sapir operated would exclude the analysis just suggested for Yokuts, which would involve setting up an underlying /ū/ in a language in which no phonetic /ū/ occurs.

The only possible exception which I have been able to find to my assertion that Sapir's phonologic segment inventory is always a subset of his phonetic inventory is one extremely late work, the dictionary and gram-

flap as /nd/; cf. the passage by Bloch cited in Lamb's fn. 21). Each phoneme type appearing in the 'segmental part' of these transcriptions will correspond in at least some environments to a phonetic segment rather than to a feature of a neighboring segment. Such an element as the 'phoneme of devoicing' which Lamb introduces later in the same paper is totally foreign to the notion of 'phoneme' in the authors such as Bloch whom he cites; it may be described as a prosody in the sense of Firth which Lamb treats as if it were a sound in the sense of Firth.

[6] Lg. 1.37-51 (1925); reprinted in David G. Mandelbaum (ed.) Selected Writings of Edward Sapir (University of California Press, Berkeley and Los Angeles, 1949). All page references are to the reprinting.

[7] Harcourt, Brace (New York), 1921.

[8] See S. Y. Kuroda, Yawelmani Phonology (M.I.T. Press, Cambridge, in press).

matical sketch appended to the Nootka Texts, done in collaboration with Morris Swadesh and published in 1939, the year of Sapir's death. Sapir and Swadesh's dictionary representations of Nootka morphemes contain several symbols which do not correspond to segment types which occur phonetically in the language, for example, their symbol for a [p] which alternates with an [m] and their symbols for vowels of 'variable length', which are long except when they occur in a word where they are preceded by two or more syllables, in which case they are short. However, since these symbols serve solely to abbreviate lists of allomorphs and are not interpretable as phonetic symbols in any language, let alone in Nootka, it is not clear that Sapir would have called these dictionary representations 'phonologic'.

My conjecture that Sapir would not have applied the word 'phonologic' to such representations relates to another aspect of my assertion that Sapir's phonologic segment inventory is a subset of his phonetic segment inventory. That assertion is to be interpreted in the really literal sense that not merely does he allow no underlying contrasts which are never realized as such, but also every phonologic segment type is identified with a phonetic segment type. The concept of 'archisegment', that is, a segment which is unspecified for some feature or features of articulation, was totally foreign to Sapir. Thus, for example, in describing a language such as Haida, where obstruents are predictably voiced in intervocalic position and predictably voiceless elsewhere, Sapir treats all obstruents as being phonologically voiceless and regards the voiced obstruents as arising through a 'euphonic law' which changes voiceless articulation into voiced in intervocalic position. It should be noted that in this respect Sapir's position is diametrically opposed to that of Bloomfield's Language:[9]

[9] Holt (New York), 1933. It should be noted that the conception of 'phoneme' in Bloomfield's

Bloomfield's 'phonemes' are 'archisegments' unspecified for predictable features such as the voicing of the above example. Thus, Sapir's phonologic representations are converted into phonetic representations by changing articulations into different articulations, whereas Bloomfield's phonemic representations, with one exception which I will note, are converted into phonetic representations by the filling in of unspecified articulations. The one class of exceptions to this assertion about Bloomfield is noteworthy, namely that in cases such as vowel reduction, where a phonological rule creates a new segment type in which two or more different underlying segment types are neutralized, Bloomfield will write the underlying segment symbol in his 'phonemic' transcriptions; he thus allows the Russian phonemic symbols /a, o/[10] and the English phonemic symbols /i, e, etc./ all to be pronounced [ə] when unstressed, as in his transcriptions /'gorot/, /goro'da/, /'biznes/, /'sekretejrij/.[11] However, Bloomfield does this only in cases where the neutralization creates a new segment type; in cases such as the devoicing of final obstruents in German and Russian, where the neutralization converts one already existing segment type into another, he allows, for example, only /bunt/ as the phonemic transcription of the words for *association* and *colorful*, rather than allowing 'phonemic' transcriptions /bund/ and /bunt/ respectively. I conjecture on the basis of these observations that if Bloomfield had been presented with a dialect which was exactly like standard German except that

Language is a departure from earlier works of his such as the Tagalog Texts (Urbana, 1917), which use a conception of underlying representation like Sapir's without any additional 'phonemic' representation.

[10] I replace Bloomfield's square brackets by slashes in accordance with modern practise.

[11] Bloomfield also cites /perot/, although here I suspect that orthographic rather than linguistic reasons prompted him to represent the reduced vowel as /o/.

it had two stop series, voiced unaspirated and voiceless aspirated, which were neutralized in final position into a third phonetic type, voiceless unaspirated, Bloomfield would have allowed the distinct 'phonemic' transcriptions /bund/ and /buntʰ/ for the two homophonous words [bunt]. In cases such as the reduced vowel, Bloomfield inconsistently replaced his conception of a phoneme as an archisegment by a conception reminiscent of Sapir's charts with parentheses, which attempts to identify phonetic types as variants of other phonetic types.

In connection with the point that Sapir's phonologic segments are 'fully specified' for all articulatory features, it is worth noting the following passage from Language: "In watching my Nootka interpreter write his language, I often had the curious feeling that he was transcribing an IDEAL FLOW OF PHONETIC ELEMENTS which he heard, inadequately from a purely objective standpoint, as the intention of the actual rumble of speech." (P. 56; emphasis added.) Note also another passage where Sapir comes close to the notion 'archisegment' but then, through a terminological equivocation, replaces it by his conception of 'fully specified' 'organic' segments and variants of those segments: "the t of time is indeed noticeably different from that of sting, but the difference, to the consciousness of an English-speaking person, is quite irrelevant. It has no "value". If we compare the t-sounds of Haida, the Indian language spoken in the Queen Charlotte Islands, we find that precisely the same difference of articulation has a real value. In a word such as sting "two", the t is pronounced precisely as in English, but in st'a "from", the t is clearly "aspirated", like that of time. In other words, an objective difference that is irrelevant in English is of functional value in Haida ... The objective comparison of sounds in two or more languages is, then, of no psychological or historical significance unless those sounds are first "weighted",

unless their phonetic "values" are determined" (pp. 54-5). Sapir starts off by talking about the 'value' of the difference between two sounds, but then lapses into talking about the 'values' of the sounds themselves.

In one respect, Sapir's conception of segments in phonologic representations as 'fully specified' is reminiscent of such papers of Jakobson's as On the identification of phonemic entities,[12] where Jakobson gives segment inventories with feature specifications in terms of pluses and blanks but no minuses. Jakobson held at that time (1949) that a blank for a feature specification was equivalent to a minus and that the optimum representation was that which minimized the number of pluses in the segment inventory. But to treat blanks as equivalent to minuses implies that leaving out a plus in the representation of a segment is equivalent to representing it by the opposite value, yielding not an archisegment but a fully specified less highly marked segment, e.g. representing a voiced segment as voiceless; rules converting these representations into phonetic representations would have the effect of converting articulations into different articulations, exactly as in Sapir.

I turn next to a point which was described well by Harris in his review of Sapir's Selected Writing.[13] Harris describes a hypothetical language in which there are no vowel sequences phonetically and a glottal stop intervenes whenever a morpheme which otherwise ends in a vowel precedes a morpheme which otherwise begins with a vowel. Harris states, "Sapir would say that no two vowels could come together (within a morpheme) and that when a particular morpheme conjunction would have the effect of bringing two vowels together a glottal stop comes in as a protective mecha-

[12] Travaux du Cercle Linguistique de Copenhague 5.205-13. In the reprinting of this paper in Jakobson's Selected Writings, vol. 1 (Mouton, the Hague, 1962, pp. 418-25), Jakobson has added minus signs at various places in the table of segments.

[13] Lg. 27.288-333.

nism to keep them apart." When I first read this passage, I was amazed by Harris' total neglect of another possible analysis, namely that in which all intervocalic glottal stops, the morpheme-internal ones as well as those at morpheme boundary, are inserted by a rule. However, on reflection I am inclined to say that in neglecting that solution Harris was doing as Sapir would have done, and that the solution which Harris ascribes to Sapir, namely treating only intermorphemic glottal stops as inserted by a rule, would indeed have been Sapir's solution. Two characteristics of Sapir's work play a role here: first, that any characteristic common to all the alternants of a morpheme will appear in Sapir's phonologic representation of it, so that if a morpheme always possesses a medial glottal stop, Sapir will write that segment in his phonologic representations even if there is a phonological rule of the language which would insert it anyway, and secondly, that Sapir would conversely treat one single phenomenon as two if its effects were manifested both in the alternations of some morphemes and in the constant shapes of others. A good example of this last point is that in the Southern Paiute grammar,[14] Sapir divides stem morphemes into three types: spirantizing, nasalizing, and geminating, which he indicates by so-called process markers ˢ, ⁿ, and ᵍ. However, the 'spirantizing' process marker is totally unnecessary, due to the fact that spirantization is what happens to all intervocalic stops in Paiute: the 'spirantizing morphemes' are simply morphemes which end in a vowel, and when an affix beginning with a stop and a vowel gets added, the stop becomes spirantized by exactly the same phenomenon which spirantizes morpheme-internal intervocalic stops.[15]

[14] Southern Paiute, a Shoshonean Language, Proceedings of the American Academy of Arts and Sciences, vol. 65, nos. 1–3 (1930). This work was actually written in 1917.

[15] Robert T. Harms (Stress, Voice, and Length in Southern Paiute, IJAL 32.228–35) has shown that Sapir's other two 'process markers' are also unnecessary.

A final respect in which Sapir's phonological analyses differ from those of modern generative phonology relates to the representation of segments by features or, alternatively, to the assembling of segment types into classes. This topic is perhaps the only one where Sapir, whose writings are usually models of clarity, is guilty of unusual vagueness, inconsistency, and ex post facto rationalization. One of the reasons why Sapir encounters difficulty in this area is his rejection of any universal phonetic theory. This rejection stems from a total failure on his part to conceive of the possibility of basing a universal phonetic theory on relative rather than absolute features; indeed, he used the terms 'universal' and 'absolute' as if they were interchangeable.[16] In place of the universal phonetics which he rejects, Sapir says (Sound Patterns, p. 42) that classes are to be set up on the basis of distribution (e.g. the English segments which can occur after initial [s] would form a class) or of role in phonological alternations (e.g. English [f, θ, s] form a class since they but not other segments alternate with voiced counterparts) or of phonetic parallelism (e.g. Sapir cites the fact that English [p, t, k] have voiced counterparts as reason for their belonging together as a class). However, there are many ways in which this characterization of phonological class is unsatisfactory. First of all, the latter two criteria for class membership seem either to rely on the universal phonetics which Sapir rejects or to involve circularity: how can one refer to the voiced counterpart of something if classes such as 'voiced stop' are what he is trying to define? Secondly, there is no evidence that Sapir ever went systematically through a language and set up classes on the basis of these criteria; it is hard to imagine how they could be used to justify, for example, the class of voiceless spirants [f, θ, s, š] in English. Third, and most importantly, Sapir's notion of class is such as to imply that class relationships between segments

[16] For example, Sound Patterns in Language, p. 36.

will remain the same through a 'derivation' (if I may use such a word here). This fact is the basis of the failure of Sapir's attempt to explain historical 'drift' in his Sound Patterns paper, where he suggested that historical drift tends to be in terms of the segment classes set up by criteria such as those listed above. Recall the discussion of English and Spanish [s], [θ], and [ð] in Sound Patterns. Sapir notes that [s] and [θ] often merge in Spanish dialects but not in English and that [θ] and [ð] often merge in English but not in Spanish and states, "We do not in English feel that θ is to be found in the neighborhood, as it were, of s, but that it is very close to ð. In Spanish, θ is not far from s but not at all close to ð." Sapir cites no distributional or other facts to explain these feelings, but there is one fairly obvious fact that he might have cited to explain a difference between the role of [θ] in Spanish and English, namely that Spanish [θ] but not English [θ] alternates with velars, for example, [diɣo]/[deθir]. Thus, as far as this alternation is concerned, [θ] goes in a class with the velars. However, the fact that it counts as a velar at one point in the grammar doesn't prevent it from counting as a dental at another point in the grammar, since, contrary to Sapir's claim about [θ] and [ð], [θ] does indeed get voiced to [ð] when it is in the environment for the voicing assimilation rule, as, for example, in [huðgar]. In genera-

tive phonological terms, what is going on here is simply that [θ]'s are underlying velars which a rule of the phonology turns into dentals in a certain environment; from that point on in the grammar they are dentals and not velars and are so treated by all subsequent phonological rules. Cases such as this are extremely common; for example, Finnish [v] functions as a semivowel in the 'earlier' phonological rules but as an obstruent in the 'later' phonological rules; with Finnish [h], the situation is reversed. Sapir's notion of 'class of segments' prevents him from making such distinctions and forces him, as it were, to describe a 3-dimensional object in terms appropriate to a 2-dimensional projection of it.

I close with the observation that Sapir's own work may thus be confirmation of the Sapir-Whorf hypothesis, in that one who speaks in terms of unit 'sounds' rather than in terms of complexes of features can hardly fail to be led by this manner of speaking to introduce a notion of 'class of sounds' which does not allow a segment to change its class membership during the course of a derivation. The history of linguistics might have been vastly different if Sapir had learned to interpret the names p, t, k, etc. syntactically as common nouns (thus represented semantically as conjunctions of properties) rather than as proper nouns (represented semantically as individuals).

THE SAPIR YEARS AT THE CANADIAN
NATIONAL MUSEUM IN OTTAWA

REGNA DARNELL

The importance of the position of Edward Sapir as Chief of the Division of Anthropology within the Geological Survey of Canada during the years 1910-1925 has largely been underestimated in the history of Canadian anthropology.* Because of his association with Franz Boas at Columbia University, where he completed his doctorate in 1909, and, more importantly, because he returned to the United States to pursue a brilliant career as a university professor, first at Chicago, then at Yale, there has been a tendency in both countries to minimize not only his contribution to the development of a Canadian tradition of anthropology but also the significance of his sojourn in Ottawa to the development of his own career.

I will argue, in contrast, that Sapir encouraged the entrance of Canadian anthropologists into the mainstream of the discipline on an international scale. Professionalization was the dominant trend of early 20th century anthropology everywhere, and Sapir ensured that Canadian anthropologists would have to meet the more rigorous research standards which were emerging. Later professional anthropologists in Canada were necessarily influenced by the tradition and standards extablished by Sapir. Without his sustained effort to develop federal government research in anthropology in Canada, the discipline would have remained at a pre-professional level much longer.

* [This paper originally appeared (under the title "The Sapir Years at the National Museum, Ottawa") in the Proceedings of the Plenary Session of the Canadian Ethnology Society, *The History of Canadian Anthropology* ed. by James Freedman (Hamilton, Ont.: Can. Ethn. Soc., 1976), 98-121. It is reprinted here with slight revisions, and the permission of both the author and the Canadian Ethnology Society. – For accounts commenting on similar aspects of Sapir's career in Ottawa, the reader may be referred to the following papers: Douglas Cole, "The Origins of Canadian Anthropology, 1850-1910", *Journal of Canadian Studies* 8.33-45 (1973), esp. pp.42-44; Stephen O. Murray, "The Canadian 'Winter' of Edward Sapir", *Historiographia Linguistica* 8.63-68 (1981), and the revised version of a 1976 paper by Hélène Bernier, "Edward Sapir et la recherche anthropologique au Musée National du Canada", published in the same journal (11.397-412, 1984). – *Ed.*]

This paper will, then, explore some important areas of Sapir's work at the Victoria Memorial Museum (predecessor of the National Museum of Man), stressing the state of the discipline, Sapir's goals for future development, constraints under which the government program operated, and Sapir's personal decision to leave Ottawa for a teaching position in the United States. It will, of course, frequently be necessary to refer to events in the history of anthropology in the United States, but I would argue that this does not detract from the Canadian-ness of what Sapir created — and left behind. Sapir maintained close contacts with Boas and many of his other former students. Moreover, because Canadian government interest in anthropology came somewhat later than that in the United States, Sapir was able to draw on the experience of that country, particularly in the Bureau of American Ethnology (hereafter: B.A.E.), where parallel institutional constraints operated to a marked degree.

Sapir was full of enthusiasm for the potentials of his new position when he left for Ottawa in 1910, at the age of twenty-six. The newly-established Division of Anthropology was part of the Geological Survey of Canada, Department of Mines. Comparably, the B.A.E., although administratively affiliated to the Smithsonian Institution, grew out of the geological survey work of John Wesley Powell (1834-1902). Sapir explicitly hoped that the Division would develop a role similar to that of the B.A.E. (Sapir 1911:789). As in the case of the B.A.E., founded in 1879, Sapir could draw on existing ethnological materials, particularly those assembled under the direction of the British Association for the Advancement of Science (hereafter: B.A.A.S.), which included a good deal of Boas' own field material. Sapir's summary report for *Science* (1911: 282) recorded his aspirations:

> The plan of the anthropological division of the Geological Survey includes fieldwork among the native tribes of Canada for the purpose of gathering extensive and reliable information on their ethnology and linguistics; archaeological fieldwork; publications of results obtained. All of these lines of work are important, but none perhaps is so pressing as that first mentioned. It is planned to make an ethnological and linguistic survey of several of the tribes of Canada.

Reginald Walter Brock (1874-1935), acting Deputy Minister of Mines and Director of the Geological Survey, wrote to Sapir (10 June 1910):*

---

* Documents are cited from Sapir's administrative files at the Canadian Ethnology Service, National Museum of Man, Ottawa, with their permission and that of the Sapir family.

The main object is, of course, to establish a thorough and scientific investigation of the native races of Canada, their distribution, languages, cultures, etc., etc., and to collect and preserve records of the same. . [to] organize, encourage, stimulate and direct individual effort throughout the country . . .

Brock continued, assuring Sapir that he could count on the support of the B.A.A.S., the Royal Society of Canada, and "Canadians, generally interested in the subject, who have organized provisionally as a Canadian Department of the Archaeological Institute of America." Clearly, the intention was to establish a major, professional research organization with Sapir as its scientific head. The crux of the work was seen to be the mapping of the languages and cultures of Canadian native peoples, a concern which was also crucial to the establishment of the B.A.E. (cf. Darnell 1969). Sapir immediately set a tone that the scientific personnel of the Division were to be involved with other anthropological scholars on an international basis. For example, in 1911, he pushed hard for approval for conference travel, then unusual in the Geological Survey (Sapir to Barbeau, 7 and 25 November 1911). That is, Sapir emphasized the scientific aims of the Division, not solely its practical service to the government.

By 1919, Sapir was writing to Boas (11 August) that administrative reorganization was necessary to facilitate the particular researches in which the Division was already engaged: "A more independent status" was crucial to further growth of the research. A year later, the separation of the Geological Survey of Canada and the Victoria Memorial Museum was confirmed (Sapir to Francis H. S. Knowles [1868-1952], Professor at Oxford, 24 December 1920), with the Anthropological Division remaining under the Museum. (All remained under Department of Mines jurisdiction.) Unfortunately, the effects of reorganization were not as dramatic as Sapir had hoped. However, by 1920, he had built up a substantial program "which takes up more ethnology proper"; the scope included ethnology and linguistics of native peoples of Canada, archaeological remains of the native peoples of Canada, and physical anthropology of the aboriginal types of man in Canada (Sapir to J. Adams, a public inquiry, 3 November 1920).

The staff in the Division in 1920 included Sapir as Chief, Charles-Marius Barbeau (1883-1969) and Diamond Jenness (1886-1969), both holding anthropological degrees from Oxford in 1910, as Associate Ethnologists, Frederick Wilkerson Waugh (1872-1924) as Assistant Ethnologist, Harlan Ingersoll Smith (1872-1940) as Archaeologist, William John Wintemberg (1876-1941) as Assistant Archaeologist, and Olivier A. Prud'homme as artist (Charles Camsell [1876-1958], then Director of the Geological Survey, to Sapir, 26

November 1920). The scope of anthropology in the Division, then, reflected the developing North American structure of four subdisciplines, which is associated with the name of Boas but was made international by Sapir's implementation in Canada.

Sapir believed in principle that the work of the Division should not be restricted to aboriginal peoples. Questions like immigration were potentially important and would involve the Division with "problems of national interest" (Sapir to Knowles, 20 November 1911). Knowles was a physical anthropologist and Sapir here followed the precedent of Boas' American work on immigrant head-form. In practice, however, anything other than aboriginal research was a threat to the core programs of the Division. The issue arose repeatedly in relation to Barbeau's work on French Canadian folklore (in addition to his Northwest coast Indian research). Sapir apparently approved of the Quebec work, but was unable to support it as strongly as he wished. He wrote to Barbeau (7 October 1918):

> I consider your work on French Canadian folklore to be perhaps the most thoroughgoing and systematically carried out investigation of European folklore that I am acquainted with. The whole of the material gathered will, when published, constitute an invaluable archive, and I am sure that some permanent Canadian organization, such as might well be found in the Province of Quebec, would be the logical development of the work that you have inaugurated and to so large an extent developed.

Barbeau, of course, wanted scientific recognition for the French Canadian work within the Anthropology Division where he was employed. Sapir, while approving the work itself, found it expedient to propose alternative institutional support. Tensions over this portion of Barbeau's research were recurrent: Sapir wrote to Boas in 1921 (12 March) that Barbeau was complaining that the *Journal of American Folklore* had credited the Quebec government for work actually done by Barbeau under Geological Survey auspices, with minimal cooperation from the Quebec branch of the American Folklore Society. The matter was corrected but was, in fact, an accurate representation of the scope of the problem. Moreover, Sapir was reluctant to purchase French Canadian material for the museum because it ". . may interfere with our purchase of aboriginal material" (Sapir to Barbeau, 24 September 1920).

Obtaining professionally trained staff was a constant problem for the Division. Throughout his administrative correspondence, Sapir wrote to colleagues, particularly in the United States, inquiring about potential researchers. A number of Boas-trained people worked for the Division during Sapir's tenure as Chief. At the same time, there were always problems of how to pay people and how to justify additional staff. Promotions for existing staff or formalization to existing status were consistently difficult to obtain (e.g., Sapir to William McInness [1858-1925], then Deputy Director of the Geological Survey, 10 November 1916; Sapir to Arthur Meighan [1874-1960], Minister of Mines and briefly Prime Minister of Canada, 3 May 1920).

Frederick Waugh had written to Sapir (20 February 1912) pointing out that his previous work for the B.A.E. had been unpaid at first so that he could acquire professional experience. Sapir also found it difficult to obtain museum personnel who were qualified to look after collections (Sapir to Charles Camsell, then Deputy Minister of Mines, 11 April 1923). During the Sapir administration, few Canadian applicants had any professional credentials at all. Virtually unique was the application of Thomas Forsyth McIlwraith (1899-1964), who held the first academic position in anthropology at Toronto from 1925. McIlwraith was a Canadian who had studied in Britain and wanted to return to Canada for fieldwork (McIlwraith to Sapir, 24 June 1921). As late as 1923, Sapir was pessimistic in responding to a fieldwork application from Marion Sutherland, a Canadian who wanted to obtain a Ph.D. from Berkeley. Sapir wrote her (14 December 1923) that he could not employ anyone except his regular staff and that "anthropology is not a very lucrative subject."

One of the most repetitive staff problems of the period was the status of James Alexander Teit (1864-1922), a Canadian métis, who was a major collaborator of Franz Boas and became an ethnologist in his own right. Already in 1911, Sapir treated Teit as a colleague and was eager to obtain his services for the Division (2 December):

> It is my desire first of all to have a systematic mapping instituted of the Athabascan tribes of Canada, and I believe that you would be the very best person that could be chosen to work out the exact tribal boundaries in British Columbia and the Yukon. Hand in hand with this preliminary work should go the gathering of representative collections for our museum. At least certain tribes, Tahltan for instance, should be chosen for complete ethnological study on the scale you have adopted for your Thompson River or Shuswap Indian monographs.

That is, in spite of the continued need for survey fieldwork, Sapir was already attempting to increase the proportion of extended fieldwork, and to ensure research was done by individuals of professional quality. Teit, however, caused administrative problems because he wanted a three or four month leave each year so that he could go hunting. Homer E. Sargent of the American Museum of Natural History in New York noted that "Like many Western men who have lived long on the frontier Mr. Teit has a taste for hunting in the fall" (Sargent to Sapir, 5 December 1911). The American Museum, too, had had to adjust to Teit's seasonal activities. In 1912, Sapir and Boas arranged for Teit to work for the Division but without a normal appointment (Sapir to Boas, 13 January):

> While Teit's position will be practically permanent, it cannot be made legally so un-less he becomes a member of the inside service and takes up his residence in Ottawa.

By 1916, however, Sapir's administrative superiors were considerably less en-thusiastic about the tenuous arrangement with Teit. For Teit to work for Boas for a couple of months would jeopardize his position with the Survey (Sapir to Boas, 19 October):.

> I am rather afraid that the nature of this arrangement, in spite of my explanations, is not as clear to the present administration as it was to Mr. Brock, with whom it was made. I must tell you frankly that I do not consider the present Deputy Minister of Mines to be in the slightest degree interested in anthropology, and I am rather afraid that he might be inclined to drop Teit altogether if we gave him any leeway.

By 1918, Sapir's protestations regarding Teit's scientific reputation were ineffec-tive in obtaining renewal of his contract (Sapir to Richard George McConnell [1857-1942], then Deputy Minister of Mines, 27 May 1918. Sapir then retreated to the position that he would buy manuscripts from Teit, although a salary was impossible (Sapir to Boas, 11 August 1919). Teit did not impress the higher administration because he produced a small quantity of manuscript, regardless of Sapir's opinion of the quality of his work. Sapir was, of course, bound by constraints on and vagaries of government funding.

Publication of scientific results was a constant problem for the Division. Sapir was convinced that anthropological publications required a separate num-bering system from other Geological Survey publications (Sapir to Brock, then Director of the Survey, 16 January 1913). This was done, but Sapir continued to have problems due to the limited public appeal of the research done by his Division. He was forced to tell Wilson Dallam Wallis (1886-1970) that his mytho-logical material collected for the Survey could not yet be published, "if only for the purely external reason that we have so much mythology on hand now that the Survey authorities are likely to get rather disgusted at the apparent one-sidedness of our work" (Sapir to Wallis, 26 October 1914). During the First World War, cutbacks in research were major, and publication was virtually halted. For Sapir, therefore, publication was an integral part of the program to be rebuilt at the end of the War (Sapir to McInness, then Director of the Survey, 12 January 1920):

> Now that the war is over the museum activities may be expected to take on a new lease of life. I think it would be eminently fitting to have the summary reports of the museum divisions published as presented. . . This is to be in harmony with the present efforts of the museum staff to obtain a more explicit recognition as a separate organization than has heretofore been accorded it.

The situaton became so restrictive that the ethnological hall of the museum had to be closed to the public because it could not be cleaned regularly; moreover, there was no security guard (Sapir to Brock, then Director of the Geological Survey, 26 October 1913). Sapir was understandably discouraged.

Fieldwork by the Division was usually a problem, reflecting the fluctuating professional standards of the period. In 1912, Sapir argued at length that more than one person should study the same tribe because 'point of view' might play a large part in the description of a single investigator (Sapir to Brock, 18 May 1912). Sapir stressed that, although aspects of a culture were related, different investigators were better at different things, chiding Alexander Goldenweiser (1880-1940), a Boas student who did fieldwork for the Division for several years, for not being glad to avoid work on material culture: "In general, I think there is altogether too much one-man ethnology in America nowadays" (Sapir to Goldenweiser, 28 March 1912).

In a period when survey fieldwork was the norm, Sapir tried to stress more intensive studies wherever possible. He wrote to Barbeau (23 October 1911) that he was not surprised to learn that Barbeau's current field trip would not exhaust the available material: Sapir hoped he would be able to return. At the same time, he was concerned to obtain a researcher for Athabascan fieldwork in the McKenzie Valley. Sapir wrote to Boas (23 September 1912) that "Of course, the important point would be to get someone who would be willing to stay quite a long time with the Indians, in other words, winter in the country." The normal field season was the summer only.

One of Sapir's methods for stretching the field time of his staff was to encourage them to train superior interpreters to record ethnographic material on their own (Sapir to Barbeau, 1 February 1915). This could effectively supplement the limited resources of the Division, and would make possible a much more long range commitment of researcher to particular group.

Another important fieldwork concern was to avoid duplication, both within the Division and in relation to other anthropological instutitions. Diamond Jenness, Sapir's successor as Chief of the Division, wrote to Arleš Hrdlička (1869-1943), the major physical anthropologist at the United States National Museum in Washington, D.C., describing Sapir's strategies (19 October 1926):

> When Sapir was in charge here, he divided up Canada into three spheres. He and Barbeau were to work on the West Coast, Waugh, an Assistant Archaeologist, among the Algonquian tribes, and I among the Eskimos and Athabascans.

Because of Boas' Northwest coast work, Barbeau was instructed to avoid the subject of mythology, to minimize duplication, as Sapir carefully reassured Boas (8 January 1915). Samuel Alfred Barrett (1879-1965) of the Milwaukee Public Museum, himself a second-generation Boasian trained at Berkeley, approached Sapir (21 March 1914) before beginning Northwest Coast fieldwork and assured him that he had "no intention of in any way encroaching upon the field of your survey in the way of research." Finally, as an official of the Canadian government, Sapir was sometimes able to intervene to facilitate the fieldwork of other researchers working in Canada. For example, when Boas had difficulties with a local post office clerk, Sapir wrote to the Postmaster General (Sapir to Pierre Edouard Blondin [1874-1943], 26 July 1918) regarding Boas' great scientific status and harmlessness of his correspondence with his interpreter George Hunt:

> Professor Boas is the leading anthropologist in America, and has devoted the greater part of his life to the careful study of the natives of British Columbia. Mr. Hunt has been his chief interpreter since 1893.

Sapir stressed that he would take personal responsibility for Boas, and that the work his former teacher was doing reflected the same interests as that of his own Division.

Much of Sapir's conviction that intensive fieldwork was necessary came from his own theoretical specialization in linguistics. The ultimate goals of description were simply not yet attainable (Sapir to Robert Harry [1883-1957] a fellow Boas student, then at the American Museum in New York, 1 October 1912):

> I assume, of course that one has the better part of a working scientific lifetime to devote to this. Perhaps it would be practicable if one could spend two years or so at a continuous stretch among a tribe instead of devoting small driblets of months, as is generally done.

In spite of his own reliance on linguistic material, Sapir was, however, inclined to underestimate the linguistic interests and/or skills of his associates. He wrote to Jenness (7 May 1913):

> I had not written to you in regard to linguistic matters, as I had imagined perhaps mistakenly that your training and interests had not been along those lines. . . Of course, the best sort of ethnological material that you could get would be texts obtained from dictation.

Sapir expressed the same position more philosophically in a letter to Wallis (10 June 1913):

> It is highly useful, I think, for one making sociological studies among primitive peoples, to know enough about linguistic matters to take down Indian words and even texts with reasonable accuracy. . . I have always been struck by a certain externality about all such studies that were not based on linguistic knowledge. I always have an uneasy feeling that misunderstandings bristle in such writings. . . And then, to look at it somewhat more broadly, what we are after in studying primitive peoples is, to a large extent, to get their scheme of classification. This scheme must be more or less reflected in their own language.

Because of such views, the work Sapir encouraged in the Division was much more significant in terms of native categories than most other work of the period.

In the case of Barbeau, however, Sapir tended to discourage detailed linguistic material, stressing only enough "to enable you to understand your text material for ethnological purposes" (Sapir to Barbeau, 7 May 1912). In fact, Sapir thought that Barbeau's literal phonetic recording was unduly laboured and un-abstract (Sapir to Barbeau, 19 January 1915). On the other hand, Barbeau provided Sapir with a source of information on languages which he had not himself studied directly. For example, in his work on the Na-Dene linguistic stock, Sapir wrote to Barbeau in the field (20 December 1920) asking about pitch and tone in Carrier. Sapir noted that his junior colleague had taken the inquiry more seriously than intended and had praised Barbeau's acumen in linguistic analysis.

In fact, Sapir also learned much about Carrier from the descriptive work of Father Adrien Gabriel Morice, O.M.I. (1859-1938). Sapir had great respect for Morice's linguistic work and tried to get it published through Boas (Sapir to Boas, 25 February 1919). Sapir's ulterior motives are clear here, since this descriptive material would lend weight to his own comparative hypotheses which resulted in his 1921 classification of the languages of native North America into only six major stocks (Sapir 1921; cf. Darnell 1971). The interaction between the work of the Division and Sapir's own theoretical concerns was always prominent and was crucial in keeping it from becoming another mere fact-finding bureau among many others.

As a government-sponsored institution, the Division was frequently involved in public defense of the native peoples of Canada, as a spokesman for them and scientific expert on Indian questions. The Northwest Coast potlatch ceremony was a constant issue. As early as 1913, Sapir was corresponding with Teit about the hoped-for repeal of the (largely unenforced) anti-potlacth law (Teit to Sapir, 18 December). Teit was uncertain what strategy would be effective, but glad to have scientific support for the local chiefs. A year later, Sapir raised the issue with Frank Williams (1858-1929), a major Nootka informant in Alberni, B.C. where he was doing fieldwork (20 October 1914). At that time, the Indian agent wanted the potlatches underplayed so that the ultimate fate of the native institution would be more secure. Sapir made clear his own support of the pot-latch system. At that time, he wrote a statement for the people at Alberni, and even offered to speak personally to the Commissioner of the Department of Indian Affairs (Sapir to Alex Thomas [d. ca. 1975], his primary Nootka informant, 14 December 1914). Early in 1915, the Commissioner, Duncan Campbell Scott (1862-1947), who, like Sapir himself, was a part-time poet, requested formal advice from Sapir on this subject. Sapir wrote to Barbeau (10 February 1915) summarizing his plan of action:

> As a first step in trying to do what I can to see justice done the West Coast Indians,
> I want to get a number of letters on the potlatch from anthropological experts that
> have had first-hand acquaintance with the institution.

Sapir had written to Boas, John Reed Swanton (1873-1958) of the Bureau of American Ethnology, Charles Frederick Newcombe (1851-1930), an ethno-grapher of British Columbia Indians, and Charles Hill-Tout (1858-1944), a former missionary turned to the ethnology of the Northwest Coast. Sapir wanted Barbeau's opinion of the current situation. Barbeau had also been asked in-formally for his opinion by Commissioner Scott (Barbeau to Sapir, 7 July 1920): "He asked me to enquire informally and report to him, but not to attract the attention of the Indians as to that, it being his intention not to alter the present law." Barbeau noted that the law was not obeyed, which he considered good. At the same time, Barbeau's ethnographic data became involved in public debate over the potlach question. Sapir (to Barbeau, 16 July 1920) decided not to create a public issue, but noted:

... I wish once more to make it perfectly clear that there are to be no communications on Indian affairs to be sent to the Department of Indian Affairs without the consent of the proper authorities within the Geological Survey, nor is any money to be accepted from the Department of Indian Affairs for incidental work except with the express permission of these same authorities. I have to make this rule so explicit, but I am afraid that if we do not follow it very literally, we will find ourselves drifting into the position of genteel spies for the Department of Indian Affairs. We cannot afford to be misunderstood by any Indians in Canada.

The questions were ethical ones, and it was the commitment of the anthropologist to support the perceived interests of the native people. By the end of 1920, Sapir was urging Barbeau (10 December) to prepare a brief pamphlet on the potlatch, using his existing knowledge, so that the Division could really have an input to decisions by the Department of Indian Affairs. That Department, of course, was composed of civil servants rather than of scientists, and the Division had a responsibility to provide accurate and professionally competent information for their use.

In the winter of 1917-18, Sapir became involved in a scheme of Commissioner Scott to introduce a basket industry among the Northwest Coast tribes and to have Indian elders teach native crafts in the schools. Sapir wrote to Scott (20 December 1917) that he considered the project far more than 'mere sentimentality' and noted:

I see no reason why distinctively Indian handicrafts and art work should not be rescued from the category of mere tourists' curios and raised to that of industrially and aesthetically desirable objects.

Sapir even urged Teit (18 April 1918) to devote some of his time to fostering this project and, in another letter written on the same day, he strongly encouraged Commissioner Scott to rely on Teit in the matter:

His acquaintance, however, with Indian handicrafts is so detailed and accurate, his popularity with the Indians so great, and his sympathy for them so cordial, that I am sure he would very soon develop the necessary business technique for the handling of industrial work.

Again, Sapir kept the Division practically involved in details of native life in Canada, where scientific expertise could aid Indian causes.

Sapir also took the initiative with Commissioner Scott in trying to have eleven treaty belts of wampum which had been lost from Six Nations Reserve in Ontario returned to their rightful owners (Sapir to Scott, 16 May 1914).

These had been located in the Heye Collection being exhibited at the University of Pennsylvania Museum and identified by Sapir's friend and colleague Frank Gouldsmith Speck (1881-1950). George Heye (1874-1957), who was a private collector without professional training in anthropology, ignored the implications of Scott's correspondence and attempted to stall (Sapir to Speck, 11 November 1914). Again, Sapir felt that the responsibility of the Division as a national body for anthropological research was to act on behalf of Canadian native peoples. In this particular case, Scott agreed.

At various times during his years in Ottawa, Sapir complained about lack of intellectual stimulation. In fact, however, many of his problems were personal ones, and he was active in Ottawa intellectual life, being a popular public speaker on a range of poetic and anthropological topics. In 1920, Sapir attempted to counter the lack of feedback by establishing an Anthropological Club of Ottawa (presumably on the analogy of the Anthropological Society of Washington, associated with the B.A.E.). Sapir was to be the President, and his colleague Harlan I. Smith the Secretary. Members were informed of their election and were permitted to attend meetings of the Ottawa branch of the American Folklore Society. Sapir reported to Rudolph Martin Anderson (1876-1961), Chief of the Division of Biology in the National Museum of Canada (16 February 1920):

> It was decided. . . to include a number of individuals in Ottawa and other parts of Canada, who have either carried on researches among the aborigines of Canada or have manifested considerable interest in Canadian anthropology.

Anderson responded (16 February 1920) that "although I am not at all an anthropologist, I suppose the qualifying phrase is in 'manifesting considerable interest'". On that basis, he accepted with pleasure. The invited members did not constitute a professional body, but the Club was intended to encourage increasing professionalization of the discipline. William Lighthall (1857-1954), Montreal writer, poet and historian, suggested to Sapir (18 February 1920) that the name ought to be Anthropological Club of Canada, and that its function as such would be significant. There was, of course, no national anthropological organization in Canada, although the American Anthropological Association had been founded in 1903. This abortive effort provides an interesting commentary on the lack of professionalization in Canadian anthropology at the time. The Club has left no record of independent activities, other than assembling a membership list.

Scientific professionalism was an issue throughout Sapir's tenure in Ottawa.

As late as 1925, Sapir expressed pessimism regarding the quality of linguistic publications which might be expected to come to the newly-established journal *Language*, founded by the Linguistic Society of America in December 1924. He wrote to George Melville Bolling (1871-1963) of Ohio State University, the first editor of *Language* (21 March 1925), that the ideal calibre of publications could not be expected: "However, we must not pick and choose too critically just now, but be glad to get material pretty much as it comes." Sapir noted that the question of publication outlets had been of concern to his Division for many years. He explained to Bolling that he was personally critical of a number of the publications of the Geological Survey but that he had been largely unsuccessful in upgrading the quality of government publications.

When Sapir first arrived in Ottawa in 1910, his initial statements about the planned work of his Division took little account of existing Canadian ethnological work. One of the people who felt slighted was Charles Hill-Tout (1858-1944) who implicitly spoke of his own ethnological work on the Northwest Coast when he wrote to Sapir (26 February 1912):

> I look forward to seeing the dreams some of us have indulged in during the last twenty years accomplished by yourself and colleagues. I feel only one thing to regret and that is that your survey of the anthropological problems in your paper in *Science* [Sapir 1911] and that tone there adopted by you may alienate the sympathies of some of the earlier students and associations devoted to the study of the aborigines of the Dominion [. . .]. I cannot think you are aware of the amount of pioneer work which had been done in this country and Canadians are very touchy [. . .]. You will see it is indiscrete to start your work by arousing feelings of antagonism to yourself.

Sapir's perception of the underlying meaning is expressed in his letter to Teit (15 March 1912), in which he notes that:

> He [Hill-Tout] claims that I adopted a "superior" and "patronizing" attitude and that I have aroused dissatisfaction among several Canadian anthropologists. I presume he means himself. I had the bad taste to omit any reference to Hill-Tout in the paper.

Sapir's relationship to Hill-Tout, or at least his estimation of that gentleman's ethnological abilities, did not improve over time. In 1916, Sapir was asked by President Frank Fairchild Wesbrook (1868-1918) of the University of British Columbia to evaluate Hill-Tout as a possible head for a new department of anthropology (Wesbrook to Sapir, 23 June 1916):

I was afraid that perhaps being self-trained and having undertaken work in a relatively new field of his subject that it would be taking a risk to place him at the head of
a department in our University, which, although new, has set itself high standards.

Sapir's reply to Wesbrook (29 June 1916) stressed with enthusiasm the long-
range goal of academic anthropology at the University of British Columbia,
but urged attention to professional standards:

> As to the first incumbent of the new position, should it be established, I should
> strongly advise that a man be selected who had received thorough training in the
> science at a University of standing, and who was imbued with the university spirit.
> Many men who have done eminently useful work in anthropology are not thereby
> necessarily ideally fitted to the charge of an anthropological department in a new and
> rapidly growing university... To be perfectly frank, I do not think Mr. Hill-Tout
> would altogether answer the needs of a university.

Sapir preferred to see the academic program wait a few years, rather than see it
begin without fully professional standards.

Indeed, university teaching was one of the things most important to Sapir,
and he attempted unsuccessfully over a period of years to involve his Division
in the field of professional training (finally leaving Canada in favour of a
teaching position at the University of Chicago). Already on 4 June 1914, he
wrote to Brock, then Director of the Geological Survey:

> I have been thinking for some time past of whether it might not be possible to put
> anthropological interest in Canada on a somewhat more solid basis by trying to get
> the subject represented in at least one of the more important of the Canadian univer-
> sities. The most likely institution at which courses in anthropology might be institu-
> ted would doubtless be McGill University, if only because of its nearness to Ottawa,
> the home of the Division of Anthropology.

Sapir suggested that he would be willing to teach in Montreal one day per week.
Apparently this proposal was received with little entusiasm, since Sapir's next
negotiations were with the University of Toronto, as indicated by a letter from
President [Sir] Robert Alexander Falconer (1867-1943) to Sapir (10 July 1914):

> The proposal interests me greatly and I have no doubt that the University of Toronto
> will be glad to avail itself of the kindness of the Geological Survey in putting at its
> disposal the services of its experts in the department of anthropology and will pay
> the travelling expenses of the lecturers. We have for some years had a few lectures in
> anthropology given to students of the third year in Arts which are also open
> to the public, but only last spring we were considering whether we could have this
> subject treated more fully.

Sapir proposed to Falconer (2 Ocotober 1914) a course of lectures by himself and various members of his staff (Barbeau, Knowles and Smith). Topics would include: What is anthropology? Early man, primitive industries, primitive society, primitive religion, languages of primitive peoples, and archaeology of Canada. Unfortunately, the course could not be offered because travel funds were not available. In spite of the abortive nature of this effort, it underscores Sapir's concern with the university as an appropriate, indeed necessary, institutional framework for anthropology. Indeed, many of the major North American academic departments did grow out of museum or government research (cf. Darnell 1969). Sapir was following established precedents within the Boasian tradition, as well as pursuing his personal desire to teach. He intended to develop a series of lectures which would stress the scope of the discipline rather than reporting facts about particular tribes (Sapir to Barbeau, 25 September 1914). This theoretical concern motivated much of his discontent in the government-museum context.

Sapir was also involved in other developments that promoted professionalism in the study of Canadian aborigines. In 1925, he was approached by Leonard Bloomfield (1887-1949), who, along with Sapir, dominated the emerging professional discipline of linguistics, in a letter of 10 February, regarding a project of the American Association for the Advancement of Science to prepare a list of American Indian languages still spoken, a catalogue of published and unpublished information about them, and a list of scientific organizations which might cooperate in studying such languages. Bloomfield agreed with Sapir that intensive study of particular languages was crucial, and urged that salvage linguistics be given priority because of the number of native languages that were dying out (Bloomfield to Sapir, 19 February 1925).

In terms of his own research, however, Bloomfield, who was originally trained in Indo-European linguistics, sought Sapir's aid in arranging fieldwork on Cree which would aid him in his comparative Algonquian studies (Bloomfield to Sapir, 26 April 1925). Bloomfield was willing to work with a different Algonquian group if funding proved difficult, but felt that Cree most clearly related to his theoretical interests (Bloomfield to Sapir, 27 May 1925). Sapir was successful in persuading Lancelot Lawrence Bolton (1881-1963), then Assistant Deputy Minister of the Department of Mines, that Bloomfield's work was worthy of support (Sapir to Bolton, 29 May 1925):

[It] will aim to throw eventual light on the comparative study of all the Algonquian languages [. . .]. The Cree speak one of the most archaic languages of the group and should, therefore, be studied afresh in the field by a technically trained specialist like professor Bloomfield [. . .]. Highly trained linguistic specialists are exceedingly difficult to find, and I can think of no one in Canada who is in the least qualified to take up this work in the way that we desire.

In linguistics, as earlier in anthropology, Sapir's concern was with professionalization and training. Indeed, Bloomfield wrote to Sapir (3 June 1925), in response to a suggestion that he increase his field budget, regarding the difficulties of a linguist:

> Our pay ought to be that of the successful business-man or lawyer. As long as we get officeboy salaries, scientific work will mostly remain undone, and teaching will be carried on as it now is, in miserable fashion by cheap labour, and preyed upon by quack "educationalists." Perhaps because my view is rather extreme, I suppressed it entirely and put in what I thought the best bid for help, but shall revise this, stating the figures as "apart from salary".

This is a remarkable statement for the year in which the Linguistic Society of America (hereafter L.S.A.) was established and began plans for the first issue of its journal *Language*. The parallel status of Sapir and Bloomfield as the leading figures of the new discipline is indicated by the care with which Bolling, as editor, planned to have a theoretical treatment from Bloomfield ("Postulates"), which eventually appeared in 1926, and a descriptive paper from Sapir ("Sound Patterns in Language") in which he defined the concept of the phoneme (Sapir to Bolling, 9 March 1925). Both the L.S.A. and its journal were perceived by their founders as milestones toward professionalization (Bolling to the Committee on Publication, 21 April 1925):

> I think we should argue to the committee that conditions for the past generation have been such as to turn students from linguistics to philology, that even those who have held on to linguistic work must have felt that the planning of any language work was a very dubious undertaking [. . .]. I should argue to the committee that if it will help the society, to assure the publication of all linguistic research, the work in that field may confidently be expected to flow more freely.

In this context, it becomes clear that Sapir's position in Ottawa was one of the most secure bases anywhere in North America for the pursuit of professional linguistic research and its consequent publication. At the time he accepted the position, Sapir, Boas' outstanding linguistic student, received enthusiastic congratulations from many colleagues. Samuel Barrett wrote (27 December 1911): "I trust you will meet with the support and success your enterprise merits and be able to build up a good big bureau." From Mexico, Boas wrote to Sapir (31 December 1910):

> I almost envy you and many other of the younger men the possibility of concen-
> trating your energies on research work, on which you start with thorough prepara-
> tion or, at least, with a good basis to work on, and without the necessity of always
> stealing the time for research from other work – as I have had to do all my life
> long; and of the fact that I had to acquire so much of the method of work in philolo-
> gy, physical anthropology, and ethnology myself. I always feel that this unavoidable
> scattering of energy in different fields in our generation must stop, if we are to make
> headway.

Boas went on to praise Sapir for his sense of purpose and dedication to "the aims for which we are working", those being Boasian and professional.

Fairly soon, however, Sapir was complaining about the administrative burdens of his position. He wrote to Thomas Talbot Waterman (1885-1936), a Boasian colleague trained primarily at Berkeley (11 January 1912):

> My work is sailing along smoothly and slowly. I am finding that there is altogether
> too much administrative and miscellaneous work to attend to, and that energy which
> might perhaps better be spent on working up field results is taken up with things of
> very slight interest, but I presume it can't be helped.

Somewhat later, Alfred Louis Kroeber (1876-1960), Boas' first Ph.D. from Columbia and founder of the Department of Anthropology at Berkeley, felt it necessary to chide Sapir (4 November 1917): "The decadence of linguistics is largely your own fault. You're an individualist and haven't built up a school. Do something general in character and you may get appeal." Sapir, of course, was forced to concern himself with the whole scope of anthropology within the Division program and had less time to devote to his own linguistic work. It is to his credit and to the advantage of Canadian anthropology that he conscien-tiously carried out his duties as Chief in their broadest possible interpretation.

In 1914, when Sapir was considering returning to the United States to take a curator's position at the American Museum of Natural History in New York or at the University of Pennsylvania Museum in Philadelphia, Boas wrote him a long philosophical letter (2 January 1914) in which he outlined his own view of the importance of Sapir's Canadian position. Major portions deserve quotation here as characterizations of the state of professionalization:

> I believe that any step of this kind would be the mistake of your life. I do not know
> whether you have a clear impression of the character of museum work in the United

States; but I feel quite certain that I judge it correctly, partly from my own experience, partly from what I see people doing who are employed by museums. The fundamental difficulty that you would find everywhere is that all purely scientic work, particularly the work in which you are interested, would have to be done as a side issue, and that the central interest of the museum is not exploration, but the exhibit, and ordinarily the popular exhibit... I understand from your previous remarks that the administrative work that you have to do in Canada worries you and is not particularly sympathetic to you; but please do not believe that in any position that you may take, you will be relieved of this kind of work in one form or another, least of all in a museum position. At present you are to a very great extent your own master. You have succeeded in establishing a great many lines of most important research; and, as I am inclined to look at it, your success in establishing this work brings with it the responsibility of its further development. A change in your administration is very likely to break up the continuity of your work, and I am inclined to think might very easily lead to a lowering of the standard that ought to be avoided. I have been happy to think that during all these years while you were in Ottawa, you have gone straight ahead according to what seemed to me sane and safe scientific principles, without yielding unduly to the clamor for premature popularization, which is the bane of our science. For this reason, I should consider it a misfortune for anthropology if you were to give up, because the organization of your work entails a certain amount of work that is irksome to you... I envy all you younger men the opportunity for work, which I have never enjoyed; and it seems to my mind that you particularly are in the best position that could be desired for any young man, with ample opportunities for original research, with the possibility of stimulating the research work in many different lines, and with a moderate amount of administrative duties. I can of course feel with you that you might like to devote all of your time to research work; but there is no position in existence in which this end could possibly be obtained, at least I do not know of any. You might think that the people in the Bureau of Ethnology [B.A.E.] are in a position of this kind, but they are not, because a great many popular demands are made upon them, and the past work of the Bureau pins them down to certain definite lines of work. In short, unless you are in a financial position to free yourself entirely from the conditions of remunerative positions, you cannot get rid of a certain amount of the kind of work that you dislike; and I do not know of any place where you would be freer in this respect than where you are now.

Boas himself had had unfortunate relations with the American Museum of Natural History and had not been able to develop the dual academic and museum context for anthropolgy at Columbia. Although Sapir lacked university outlets, Boas stressed that his research opportunities in Ottawa provided important support for the developing institutional structure of North American anthropology. Of course, Boas was also concerned that museum and government institutions be directed by people like Sapir who had adequate (defined as Boasian) professional training.

Throughout the rest of his time in Ottawa, Sapir's correspondence contains inquiries about academic positions in most of the major American universities. He finally resigned, as of 23 September 1925, to accept a position as Associate Professor of Sociology and Anthropology at the University of Chicago. The irony stressed by Commissioner Scott in a letter to Sapir (16 July 1925) was that Sapir would have to resign from the Royal Society of Canada, to which he had been elected in 1922.

Although Sapir never returned to Canada in terms of institutional affiliation (he moved from Chicago to Yale in 1931 and died in New Haven in 1939), he continued to work on field material collected for the Division and to concern himself with research developments in Canada. Sapir assured Bolton, then Assistant Deputy Minister of Mines, (3 September 1925) that fifteen items of manuscript material still in his possession would not be lost to Canadian science:

> I should like to emphasize the fact that the work that I shall be doing at the University of Chicago is very similar to researches that I have been carrying on in Ottawa, and that there is every reason to believe that the greater part of my time will be taken up with the continuation of my researches begun in this institution. Along certain lines, there is every reason to believe that the work will progress more rapidly than before, partly because I shall be relieved from administrative routine, and partly because I shall probably have the assistance of graduate students in carrying on some of the researches . . .

Sapir's assessment was fairly accurate. He quickly amassed a cadre of students and many of them did research in Canada, using Sapir's continuing ties to the Division.

In fact, however, the Division, headed by Diamond Jenness after Sapir's resignation, never again attained the prominence it had previously held. Staff, research funds, and publication were all curtailed. The developing institutional framework of anthropology in universities made the Division increasingly anachronistic. Its major importance, then, coincides with the Sapir years. At that time, Canadian anthropology desperately needed the non-parochial and professional emphasis which Sapir provided.

REFERENCES*

Bloomfield, Leonard. 1926. "A Set of Postulates for the Science of Language". *Language* 2.153-64.

Darnell, Regna. 1969. The Development of American Anthropology 1880-1920: From the Bureau of American Ethnology to Franz Boas. Unpublished Ph.D. dissertation. University of Pennsylvania.

—————. 1971. "The Revision of the Powell Classification". *Papers in Linguistics* 4.379-88.

Sapir, Edward. 1911. "An Anthropological Survey of Canada". *Science* 34.789-793.

—————. 1921. "A Bird's Eye View of American Languages North of Mexico". *Science* 54.408.

—————. 1925. "Sound Patterns in Language". *Language* 1.37-51.

---

* There are various secondary sources which deal in one way or another with Sapir and the National Museum. Many of these were written after the original of this paper and draw on it. I have chosen not to modify the original focus on the administrative career of Sapir in Ottawa. I have further devoted little attention to Sapir's considerably better known scientific works. Many complicated historiographic issues are referred to briefly in passing, only as they relate to the argument made here. My biography of Edward Sapir (in preparation) will deal with these in greater detail.

REFLECTIONS ON SAPIR'S ANTHROPOLOGY IN CANADA*

RICHARD J. PRESTON

This paper focuses on the period of Edward Sapir's residence in Ottawa from 1910 to 1925.* I have tried to show something of the relationship of his personal experience during this period to his contributions to the discipline of anthropology, and most specifically to his goal of developing a very broad, synthesizing science of man. My primary thesis is that during the Ottawa years the single most fundamental shift in Sapir's thinking occurred, the turning (Mandelbaum 1973:181-95) from a primary interest in applying methodologically elegant analysis to linguistic and ethnological problems (which we may call his Boasian orientation) to a primary interest in formulating goals and synthesizing a rigorous methodology for his 'psychiatric science' (Sapir 1949[1939]:579).

He was twenty-six years old and had recently received his Ph.D. when he obtained, apparently to his surprise, an offer from the director of the Geological Survey, on Boas' recommendation (Sapir 1910). Evidently Boas got him the job as a research position from which Sapir could get to the task of collecting 'salvage' data on the Indians of Canada. Boas had by that time three other students located in museum research positions — Kroeber at Berkeley, Speck in Philadelphia, and Lowie at the American Museum in New York. Perhaps Ottawa was the next opening to which Boas could recommend one of his students. It has been speculated that Ottawa was also in part a kind of exile; Sapir was such an intensely brilliant colleague that Boas found comfort for himself by keeping Sapir at a distance. In any event, Ottawa did become an exile, a place where intellectual isolation and personal difficulties threw Sapir very much on his own personal resources. The result was a period of great productivity, followed by a period marked more by profound rethinking than by research activity.

---

* [This paper is a slightly revised version of an article originally published in the *Revue canadienne de Sociologie et d'Anthropologie / Canadian Review of Sociology and Anthropology* 17:4.367-74 (1980). It is reprinted here with the permission of both the author and the Canadian Sociology & Anthropology Association.   *– Ed.*]

Several different kinds of experience coalesced in the development of his conception of a truly humanistic science of man. Following earlier fieldwork with four other Amerindian peoples (Wishram, Takelma, Yana and Paiute), he began field work with the Nootka Indians in September-December in 1910[1] The relation of his fieldwork experience to his intellectual development is difficult to assess, but seems to be unexceptional at this early point of his career. After his return to Ottawa he made only brief visits to closer places (e.g., Maniwaki, Pointe Bleue) to collect specimens for the museum and brief linguistic notes, until his return to the Nootka in the winter of 1913-14. During this three-year period he married, published eight articles and many notes and reviews, worked over extensive linguistic data, and began building the museum's research program. One of his early research contracts was with Paul Radin, and a friendship began that was soon quite intense and important to the development of both men as individuals and as ethnologists.

The nature of some of Sapir's friendships are very important to an understanding of him as a person, and to the development of his ideas. Sapir is described by his friends as somewhat shy with people he did not know, and according to Kroeber, he was an individualist and a genius. In a retrospective seminar held twenty years after Sapir's death Kroeber, at the age of eighty-two, said that Sapir "... is the only man that I have known at all well in my lifetime that I would unreservedly class as a genius." And in part from his own experience, he commented on Sapir's personal style, his "intense interest ... in individuals, in personalities ... He was likely to take a close friend and watch him, dissect him, try to draw him out in conversation, just from sheer interest ... And people would talk with him and reveal themselves and Sapir would be fascinated" (Kroeber 1959 = this volume, p.136).

Evidently Sapir was in agreement on this point, for he says much the same thing in one of his poems:

> You sit before me and we talk
> Calmly and unafraid.
> Calmly and unafraid
> I sink my net into your soul,
> That flows before me like a limpid stream.

1) That this fieldwork appealed to Sapir's aesthetic side is made evident by Alcock's statement that "The work of recording primitive music was begun by Sapir who, in 1910, took down 100 Nootka songs..." (1954:100).

> I draw forth many lovely things
> That you had thought were hid;
> I draw forth many ugly things
> That you had thought were pure,
> That you had never thought to hide.
>   (Sapir 1917:50)

This characteristic probing intimacy of his friendships was integral to his genius for perceiving subtle patterns and for finding, in seemingly trivial and superfluous phenomena, unsuspected significance. In personal relationships his penetrating analysis might prove to be a strain for both parties. If the same qualities characterized his fieldwork, one can better understand how he could develop the primary ethnographic insights that urged upon him a series of attempts to achieve aesthetic success in depicting a Nootka individual-in-culture (Sapir 1922, and cf. Nyce 1977); one can understand how he could base a future goal of anthropology on a broadly conceived psychiatric or personalistic approach. Psychology in the anthropological literature of that time, and as an intellectual discipline, he regarded as grossly lacking in theory and in method, and he was very critical of 'psychologizing.' It is ironic that he has been typically criticized for the same fault (e.g. Aberle 1957; Meggers 1946), and I find such criticism lacking adequate understanding of his actual contributions. But the purpose of this paper is not to defend his intentions or the value of his writings; I have done that elsewhere (Preston 1966).

During the winter of 1913-14, Sapir returned to the northwest coast for a more intense period of fieldwork with the Nootka; this was cut short by the severe digestive problems of his wife which were the beginning of a series of physical and mental breakdowns ending in death a decade later. At the time that Sapir was extending his participation in Nootka life, he received an extraordinary letter from Paul Radin, sparkling with ideas that constituted the frontier of anthropological thought of that period. Many of the ideas were subsequently given expression in Sapir's own style and context in his publications on culture and personality. Radin's letter is of considerable historical interest, characteristically dissatisfied with the state of ethnology, and particularly frustrated with Boas' cautious, objective data collection and conservatism regarding interpretations. In fairness to all concerned we must view the criticisms of Boas as exaggerated so that Radin's urgent, vitally humanist approach could be developed against the tide of mainstream ethnology (see also Radin 1933). Still, if the opposition is depicted harshly, Radin's principal points are cogent and deserve to be read in their original form:

After careful reflection, during the last year I have come to the conclusion that it is not legitimate to regard Boas' faults of commisssion and omission as little foibles. On the contrary, they are basic characteristics and affect and have affected his work, at all times. If in this letter, I dwell almost exclusively on Boas' faults, you will of course not forget that I appreciate keenly his achievements and that we all have given him his mede [sic] of praise, even hero worship. I sincerely believe that Boas' work is done. He was at his best in opening up vistas and applying a commonsense method to ethnology. The originality of his method has, it is true, been over-estimated, as anyone trained in modern history can see, but considering the conditions in which he found ethnology in the 80s and 90s – really then an apparent adjunct of biology – his work was both opportune and effective. He touched on every phase of ethnology and achieved wonders in suggesting problems, working one out here and there – but there he stopped. I maintain that he stopped not because one man could not do more, but emphatically because he does not possess the genius required for that kind of work. What is needed now, is a historian, a man with a sense of historical growth, and a man with constructive imagination. Boas has neither of these talents, as is manifest by his attitude toward languages and the fact that in ethnology he has not once insisted on the dynamic aspect of the subject. He is an anatomist, but not a physiologist. Indeed I have never heard him in his lectures express the slightest desire 'to see the wheels go round'.

Another defect is that he lays too much stress on establishing the truth of certain general factors, like dissemination, convergent evolution, independent origin, etc. No real historian ever worries much about these things in the rough. What he wants to obtain is an intimate picture of how a people lived, worked, ate – for my part urinated – but it should be intimate. To imagine for one minute, that a real historian is – or should be – interested merely in the development of a culture is lopsided. Many of course, do think so; Boas shares this trait with them. But unfortunately that is the one thing in which ethnology differs from history. It may be deplored, but it is – nevertheless a fact that chronology is and will always be impossible in primitive culture and any attempts to reconstruct one will be artificial, or what is worse, vague. It is essential to recognize this fact and the corollary it entails that corollary being – turn to the other aspect of ethnology – that of complete, comprehensive and sympathetic interpretation. From this point of view ethnology can be made a real human science instead of one of bones and dust. It is only from this angle likewise, that she can stimulate history, for naturally with the small number of individuals to be dealt with, as a rule – *a picture can be obtained of individual forces*, that is wholly impossible in the history of the past, but that will unquestionably play a great role in the new history of the present and the future.

To all these things Boas has been indifferent. He has insisted on analytical examinations, warned us against taking our analysis as historical demonstrations, yet he has not once told us to study the Indians as individuals. Thus all the real points of social organization, religion, mythology as a literary product, have escaped him. Methodology is excellent – his insistence upon the fairly correct one that he formulated will constitute one of his achievements – but it is only the beginning. Goldie [i.e.,

A.A. Goldenweiser], if he doesn't look out, will follow in his footsteps without
having Boas' justification.

There is also one other thing about Boas and for that matter about Goldie and
Lowie – they are afraid to be wrong. Being afraid to be wrong they will not hazard
interpretations. If they do not put this out of their constitutions, they will fall short
of ever, even remotely understanding primitive people. You must have the ability
to put yourself in another man's place – knowing nevertheless that you are not the
other man – and try to feel like him. Your data must of course, be kept separate
from your interpretation – but you must have the guts to interpret. I'm going to do
it with the Winnebago and shall consider myself engaging in a legitimate enterprise,
if I get as near the truth as [Jacob] Burckhardt did in his 'Cultur der Renaissance'
(Radin 1914; emphasis mine: RJP)

Radin attempted to develop his perspective on or approach to individual
forces in his Winnebago Trickster monograph and in the Winnebago life history.
But Sapir was sharply critical of Radin's lack of adequate method, as he was of
Radin's linguistic interpretations. In the matter of goals, however, of giving
primacy in their investigations to actual individuals, Sapir and Radin were
very close.

Sapir sought for a beginning of method and for some solutions to more
personal problems, in the psychoanalytic literature. After the Nootka fieldwork,
he had brought his father to live with his family in Ottawa, but his father's
emotional distress proved too much of a strain on the family. Mrs Sapir's mental
illness subsequently became a problem of serious proportion, and Sapir looked
for help. He was doubtful of psychoanalysts; one that he wrote to had responded with a diagnosis without having met the patient! Mrs Sapir was in and
out of hospital and asylum and sanitarium until her death in 1924. Her physical
illness (an abscess of the lung) which was the eventual cause of her death was
thought to be somehow associated with her mental illness, *dementia praecox*,
or schizophrenia. Her medical expenses as well as the costs of maintaining his
father in New York kept Sapir in chronic personal anxiety and financial trouble.
His distress and loneliness were made all the more intense by the lack of means
to assist in his wife's recovery; psychiatry was not adequate to the task required
of it.

It is during this period that Sapir probed more deeply into humanist pursuits,
composing music and writing a great deal of poetry. But he also found solace, or
at least serene detachment, in linguistic work. His contact with friends was
maintained, and his scholarly output was quite substantial, if below what it
might have been. He evaluates his disposition in a letter to Lowie, stating "I do
not really believe that my temperament is so very unscientific either, for I am

surely critical and almost unreasonably analytical. A scientific spirit but an aesthetic will or craving! A sort of at-cross-purposes-with-oneself type of temperament that entails frequent inhibitions, frustration, anything but a smooth flow of selfsatisfied and harmonious effort" (Sapir 1916).

His poetry and literary criticism also allowed him to examine the relationship of anthropology to larger, more cosmopolitan domains — the World War, social philosophy, and the relationship of history and science, and he argued the latter in an exchange of letters with Kroeber on the superorganic approach. To Lowie he reflected that, "Problems interest me less and less; impressions and temperaments, more and more. Actually I am poetically getting ready for something" (Sapir 1918). He does not, however, indicate what the something will be. More and more he hopes for a return 'home' to New York and a linguistics position, where the intellectual stimulus will somehow resolve his temperamental cross-purposes. But no position was available. Between the summer of 1920 and April 1921 he wrote his only book, *Language*. It was not dictated in a month, as rumour had it. He had developed an outline years before, and over the ten months of the actual writing, he commented that it was slow work. One of its effects was his deeper realization "... that language, broadly considered, touches large problems at an astonishing number of points" (Lowie 1965:46f). His notion of the dynamics of drift interested him a great deal, as a process quite different from evolution, but with similar generality of reference — not only to language but also "in the history of art, religion, [and] social forces" (cf. Preston 1981).

The development of Sapir's integrative or synthesizing humanist views seems to be both an emotional and intellectual response to his wife's illnesses, the war, and a decline in the bureaucratic support of the museum. Whether in his thinking about language or ethnology or the arts, his own personal 'drift' was to attempt to grasp the whole of human experience (and most immediately, his own experience) with his whole personality. This is ambitious stuff, and has led others to be branded mystics for their wild use of inadequate intuitions. Kroeber diagnosed Sapir's efforts as "wish fulfillment against the backdrop of a partially regretted career" (Kroeber 1952:148), although in later years he was not sure whether he would still maintain that or not (Kroeber 1959; cf. this volume, p. 137). As a source of motive, perhaps Kroeber's description fits Sapir well enough. But his efforts were not an undisciplined expression of motives; Sapir knew perhaps better than any of his fellow anthropologists the importance of adequate and appropriate method. If his "Culture, Genuine and Spurious" (written in 1918 or 1919) was more an expression of goals than method, his "The Unconscious Patterning of Behaviour in Society" (1927) was very much an approach to method. One finds in his correspondence that he is over and over having to point out defects of method to his colleagues, most noticeably in regard to the genetic relationships of languages (to Boas, Radin, Kroeber, and many others), but also in ethnology, literature, and psychiatry (the latter to Kroeber, who had taken up a part-time psychiatric practice).

Finding a method for a psychiatric science was involved in his attempt to make a satisfactory represenation of the data collected during his Nootka fieldwork. His experience with the Nootka had made a profound impression that motivated several forms of written expression. Similarly, poetry, literature, literary criticism, social criticism, and musical composition all had their place alongside his linguistics and ethnology. By the early 1920s he had become more and more interested in combining these styles of communication, first combining ethnography with poetry and literature (Nyce 1977), then adding linguistics and psychology, as he did in "Sound Patterns in Language" (1925), which he characterizes as "a special illustration of the necessity of getting behind the sense data of any type of expression in order to grasp *the intuitively felt and communicated forms* which alone give significance to such expression" (1949 [1925]:45; emphasis mine:RJP)

Two years later he published the article that presents his argument for the importance of intuition in the functioning of the human personality. The paper is titled "The Unconscious Patterning of Behavior in Society" (1927), and it deserves our close attention. Sapir begins with a conception of the human individual as

> not simply a biologically defined organism maintaining itself through physical impacts and symbolic substitutes of such impacts, but that total world of form, meaning, and implication of symbolic behavior which a given individual partly knows and directs, partly intuits and yields to, partly is ignorant of and is swayed by. (1949 [1932]:518)

He proceeds with the premise that individual behaviour and social (cultural) behaviour are "contrastive only in a limited sense", since each is, at base, individual (1949[1927]:544). That is, behaviour and its interpretation are acts of and by individuals; they may be studied with the purpose of understanding individuals per se, or from a point of view which selects those aspects that correspond to *norms of* conduct and to *modes of* interpretation — in other words, to social patterns and to cultural patterns, respectively.

To say that social behaviour (or cultural interpretation) is unconsciously patterned, and not so much known by an individual as intuited by him, does not thereby imply any kind of collective unconscious, or any variety of superorganic. Rather, the study of unconscious patterning directly acknowledges the locus of ideas and action in individuals, while deliberately selecting typical or nomothetic data from the raw phenomena of actual individuals interacting with each other. A pattern so derived, cannot be expected to be homogeneous and stable, since "[e]very typical human reaction has a certain range of variation" (Sapir 1949[1925]:34). For Sapir the variation is of central importance in understanding unconscious patterning. Variation requires understanding at the level of single individuals, illustrated by Sapir in the now classic case of Two Crows. But variation in the relations between different types of pattern or between large domains of patterning, as between the domain of symbols and the domain of action, is no less crucial.

A challenging comparison may now be drawn to the patterning of language. Just as the precise understanding of the relation of any social or cultural pattern to the phenomenal world from which it is abstracted must involve statements of its variance, so the precise understanding of the relation of language to culture, and of both to the phenomenal world, requires cognizance of the "... failure of a given universe of speech symbols, a language, to correspond to the universe of phenomena, physical and mental" (Sapir 1923:572). The variance of language elegantly evidences the psychology of forms, and the subtle distortions that time and usage and habit bring, since language froms "are, for the most part, indirect in their functional significance" (1949[1927]:549). This makes language a good place to start in the study of "the general tendency of cultural behavior to work out all sorts of formal elaborations that have only a secondary, and, as it were, 'after the event' relevance to functional needs" (pp.549-50). And language forms, for all their abstractness of patterning, are usefully compared with other cultural forms in that a similar principle is demonstrated: the variance and relational complexity of patterned behaviour (or patterned thought) points to the discontinuities between form and function, between norms (or codes) and actual behaviour, between ideas and actions, between words and events. In sum, Sapir's view allows for, *indeed directs us to find, the complex and dynamic nature of social and cultural patterns.*

This complexity and dynamism is all the more difficult to perceive and explain because

> ... the relations between elements of experience which serve to give them their form and significance are more powerfully "felt" or "intuited" than consciously perceived. It is a matter of common knowledge that it is relatively easy to fix the attention on some arbitrarily selected element of experience, such as a sensation or emotion, but that it is far from easy to become conscious of the exact place which such an element holds in the total constellations of behavior. It is easy ... to say by

what kinship term ... [one] ... calls so and so or whether or not ... [one] may undertake such and such relations with a given individual. It is exceedingly difficult ... to give a general rule of which these examples of behavior are but illustrations, though all the while ... [one] ... act as though the rule were perfectly well known ... *In a sense it is well known* [to the normal individual]. But this knowledge is not capable of conscious manipulation in terms of word symbols. It is, rather, a very delicately nuanced feeling of subtle relations, both experienced and possible. To this kind of knowledge may be applied the term "intuition," which, when so defined, need have no mystic connotations whatever. It is strange how frequently one has the illusion of free knowledge, in the light of which one may manipulate conduct at will, only to discover in the test that one is being impelled by strict loyalty to forms of behavior that one can feel with the utmost nicety but can state only in the vaguest and most approximate fashion. It would seem that we act all the more securely for our unawareness of the patterns that control us. (Sapir 1949[1927]:548-49)

And so, as persons and as scientists, we seek a greater awareness of the patterning of behaviour that affects us and others, and Sapir urges us to proceed by being explicit about the nonmystical, *indeed commonplace,* role of the unconscious and of intuition. This can be done, if one has method.

The problem of developing a method adequate to the task was, and is, more challenge than it is accomplished fact. But if the task is a very difficult one, and if Sapir's psychiatric science is still largely a future condition, it is no less a worthwhile effort. We have now a relatively mature methodology for social anthropology as an empirical science, a procedure which is far simpler and more efficient in producing, on the whole, rather atheoretical results (Murphy 1971: 36ff). But the fact that empiricism is easier does not necessarily mean that it is capable of better explanations or is more productive of fundamental knowledge. It means primarily that the domain of inquiry that has been selected is more accessible, and has an apparently greater simplicity of structure and function. But there is clearly room for other methods and other goals.

When Sapir moved to Chicago in 1925, he was only beginning to address the problem of method. He recognized that neither linguistic nor ethnological method was adequate, though these and other human-oriented disciplines might well provide the initial, tentative first steps. In his 1927 article, he prefers to indicate some possibilities for method by giving a number of examples of unconsciously patterned behaviour. His first example is linguistic, the patterning of the plural form in English. He thus begins with an illustration of patterning's autonomy relative to the functional behavioural needs of effective communication, and thereby to show that "Whatever may be true of other types of cultural behavior ... of the forms of speech developed in the different parts of the world are at once free and necessary" (1949[1927]:550). The forms are free in the sense that they are not constrained by their particular function; the speech forms that function to express plurality in different languages are quite dissimilar. Yet each form serves, within any particular language, as the necessary mode for the expression of plurality.

Sapir's second example is also linguistic, but is chosen to show greated variety of elaboration and generality of reference than the example of plurality. The domain is the basic element of spoken communication — the work — and he chooses a specific sample case from Yana, a polysynthetic language ". . . in which . . . the word is a sentence microcosm full of delicate formal elaborations of the most specialized type" (p.551). He details nine formal elements which are drawn from a much larger range of possible elements, and shows their necessary relationships of sequence and cohesion that define the structure of the word and, at the same time, give it its significance as a communicative act: "Every element falls into its proper place in accordance with definitively formulable rules which can be discovered by the investigator but of which the speakers themselves have no . . . conscious knowledge" (553).

The third and last linguistic example is a summary statement of the psychological reality of the phoneme as an aesthetically correct point in a phonetic pattern; it anticipates his 1933 article on "The Psychological Reality of Phonemes" (see Sapir 1949:46-60). In this account he makes an interesting comparison of the intuitively correct phonetic sounds (the functionally significant units of speech) to intuitively correct musical tones (the functionally significant units of musical scales) and indicates that both are the products of their particular traditions. He concludes:

> In the simple facts of language we have an excellent example of an important network of patterns of behavior, each of them with exceedingly complex and, to a large extent, only vaguely definable functions, which is preserved and transmitted with a minimum of consciousness. (Sapir 1949[1927]:555)

Sapir now turns to the rest of culture for his further examples. He begins by acknowledging that different forms of cultural behaviour will vary in the degree to which they illustrate the processes of unconscious patterning. He makes the transition from linguistics to ethnology with the topic of gestures, which he presents briefly and in a nontechnical fashion. Then he gets to a standard ethnological domain, that of economic organization. He says:

In the economic life of a people, too, we are constantly forced to recognize the pervasive influence of patterns which stand in no immediate relation to the needs of the organism and which are by no means to be taken for granted in a general philosophy of economic conduct but which must be fitted into the framework of social forms characteristic of a given society. There is not only an unconscious patterning of the types of endeavor that are classed as economic, there is even such a thing as a characteristic patterning of economic motive. (Sapir 1949[1927]:557)

Drawing on his Nootka fieldwork (and probably on the literature on other cultures of the Northwest Coast), he builds a contrast of economic motives with the norm of the Western individualist (pp.557-58):

Even when there is a definite feeling that wealth should be accumulated, the motives which are responsible for the practice and which give definite form to the methods of acquiring wealth are often signally different from such as we can readily understand. ...No West Coast Indian, so far as we know, ever amassed wealth as an individual pure and simple, with the expectation of disposing of it in the fullness of time at his own sweet will . . . The concepts of wealth and the display of honorific priviliges such as crests and dances and songs and names, which have been inherited from legendary ancestors, are inseparable . . . One cannot publicly exhibit such a privilege without expending wealth in connection with it. Nor is there much object in accumulating wealth except to reaffirm privileges already possessed, or . . . to imply the possession of privileges none too clearly recognized as legitimate by one's fellow tribesmen. In other words, wealth, beyond a certain point, is with these people much more a token of status than it is a tool for the fulfillment of personal desires. We may go so far as to say that among the West Coast Indians it is not the individual at all who possesses wealth. It is primarily the ceremonial patrimony of which he is the temporary custodian that demands the symbolism of wealth . . . I should not like to go so far as to say that the concepts of wealth among ourselves and among the West Coast Indians are utterly different things. Obviously they are nothing of the kind, but they are measurable distinct and the nature of the difference must be sought in the total patterning of life in the two communities from which the particular pattern of wealth and its acquirement has been extracted.

Sapir lets this example suffice to illustrate the unconscious patterning of the types of behaviour that correspond to the standard ethnological topics. One wishes for more detail and discussion of method and for more examples. But perhaps this was all that he was sure he saw at that point in his career.

His study of 'total patterning of life' of the Nootka was never written, and his notes are still waiting in the archives of the Museum of Man in Ottawa. While he devoted much of his career to seeking a satisfactory method, the progress was difficult. We can, however, look for implications for method in his examples. It is particularly striking to compare his linguistic method with that used in his depiction of the pattern of Nootka wealth just cited. In the linguistic examples his superb skill in finely analysing minute technicalities with a synthesizing holism of reference was (and still is) exemplary (cf. Newman 1951). But in dealing with the intuited rules of economic behaviour and motive, where form appears far less elegantly arranged, Sapir seems to show a similar adaptation, relying on his own less elegantly arranged but sensitive and perceptive intuitions regarding personal motives and their relation to behaviour.

This, I believe, is where Sapir stood in the mid-1920s, already cutting across the disciplinary boundaries of psychiatry, psychology, sociology, history, linguistics, and ethnology with a perspective and nascent method based on the dynamic process of individual personalities-in-culture. The study of the psychology of culture has not stood still in the intervening fifty years (Bock 1980), but most of the hard problems of method and conceptualization remain today more in the domain of promise than that of science. For many of us, the processes of intuition have been relegated back into the closet of mysticism, and most of the more recent methods have proven rather specialized in their application, though they remain holistic in their stated goals (Sturtevant 1964:123-24; Scholte 1973:687-704). Unconscious patterning as Sapir conceived it is *not* a given of structural method. This is not simply because the context of structuralism is more restricted, but more particularly because the norm ('transform'), rather than the dynamics of variance, is the focus of structural analysis.

It was Sapir's genius to combine the scholar's precision *of analysis* with an intensely self-aware, aesthetic humanness — a precision *in perceiving* the whole of the human significance of his experience — that, in the retrospect of half a century, gives us a sense that we are still only beginning to understand the vistas he intuitively knew, and urged us to pursue.

It is my impression that the period from the early 1920s until his death was spent in trying to work out for his 'psychiatric science' a statement of method that would do for that intellectual domain what his *Time Perspective* monograph did for historical reconstruction, i.e., provide a sound and systematic basis for a whole field of inquiry. Part of Sapir's wish to move from Ottawa sprang from the desire to get into the intellectual mainstream of work on these problems, to find intense first-hand contact with people who were working in related areas.

But there were many reasons for leaving Ottawa. His first wife's terminal lung condition was aggravated by the climate, and her psychological problems were aggravated by a sense of social isolation. As Sapir increasingly became committed to his psychiatric science, at the same time he wished for a more senene and contemplative career, not in anthropology or psychiatry, but in linguistics. He was still at odds with himself, on the one hand forced into a personal recognition of the importance of the individual and his psychiatric and cultural pitfalls, on the other hand, finding serenity in linguistics. Yet he had already been urged by Kroeber: "The decadence of linguistics is largely your own fault. You're an individualist and haven't built up a school" (Kroeber 1917).

Another aspect of Sapir's desire to move from Ottawa was his frustration with superiors who failed to support anthropology. He saw his research contracts program diminished by the shrinking budget allowed him. This was not simply a matter of impersonal forces in the economic climate of that period. But involved bureaucratic competition as well. Internal friction also increased when Sapir made the decision to move Diamond Jenness ahead of Marius Barbeau in his internal hierarchy, as the better ethnologist of the two. In subsequent budget cuts, the museum suffered badly, and did not build back up to the equivalent level of research contract support for nearly forty years (Darnell 1976:101-104, 119; McFeat 1976:150-51, 160-61; MacNeish, personal communication). Sapir, and thus Canadian ethnology, lost financial support. But when Sapir left for Chicago, he did succeed in getting Jenness into his vacated position. And if Jenness was not agile and manipulative enough to master the intrigues that plagued the museum, he nevertheless justified Sapir's support with solid ethnological work.

Sapir's wish to move into a purely linguistic position did not materialize. He went to Chicago in 1925 and found larger satisfactions than he may have thought possible. His Psychology of Culture seminars were very well received and stimulated his students and himself. He remarried and had a happy and supportive family life (Mandelbaum 1949:ix). Professional recognition also came more quickly. When he finally did receive an offer for a linguistics position at Columbia, he declined it in favour of a prior offer from Yale for a combined anthropology and linguistics position.

His intended contributions to his envisaged discipline, with culture and society and language understood in a context of psychiatry or personality psychology, remained largely an unresolved problem. He was very much concerned to make progress and develop method, and he established friendships with psychiatrists whose interests were similar (Sullivan 1953; Lasswell 1948). But the problem did not yield, and, as his widow has said,

Edward died with the feeling that he had an important point to make that he hadn't managed to get across. His last years were marked, of course, by failing energy, long before his illness was recognized for what it was. In any case, he gave up even hoping to get it written, even before he accepted the fact that he was ill. His work on languages was such a pleasure to him that he was able to remain "busy" in that manner, but he did deeply feel that he died without saying his full say! (J.V. Sapir 1967).

REFERENCES

Aberle, David F. 1957. "The Influence of Linguistics on Early Culture and Personality Theory". *Essays in the Science of Culture* ed. by Gertrude Dole and Robert Carniero, 1-29. New York: Thomas Y. Crowell Co.

Alcock, Floyd J. 1954. "Folklore Studies at the National Museum of Canada". *Journal of American Folklore* 67.99-101.

Bock, Philip K. 1980. *Continuities in Psychological Anthropology*. San Francisco: W. H. Freeman.

Darnell, Regna. 1976. "The Sapir Years at the National Museum, Ottawa". *The History of Canadian Anthropology* ed. by James Freedman, 98-121. Hamilton: The Canadian Ethnology Society. (Rev. version pp.159-78 above.)

Kroeber, Alfred L. 1917. Letter from Kroeber to Sapir, 4 November 1917. Ottawa: The National Museum of Man Archives.

—————. 1952. *The Nature of Culture*. Chicago: Univ. of Chicago Press.

—————. 1959. Transcript of a tape-recorded seminar by Kroeber on Sapir, 11 May 1959. Files of the author. (Rev. version published in this volume, pp.131-39.)

Laswell, Harold D. 1948. *Power and Personality*. New York: W. W. Norton.

Lowie, Robert H., ed. 1965. *Edward Sapir's Letters to Robert H. Lowie*. [Berkeley, Calif.: privately printed].

McFeat, Tom F. S. 1976. "The National Museum and Canadian Anthropology". *The History of Canadian Anthropology* ed. by James Freedman, 148-74. Hamilton: The Canadian Ethnology Society.

Mandelbaum, David G. 1949. "Introduction". *Selected Writings of Edward Sapir*, v-xii. Berkeley & Los Angeles: Univ. of California Press.

—————. 1973. "The Study of Life History: Gandhi". *Current Anthropology* 14.177-206.

Meggers, Betty J. 1946. "Recent Trends in American Ethnology". *American Anthropologist* 48.176-214.

Murphy, Robert F. 1971. *The Dialectics of Social Life: Alarms and excursions in anthropological theory.* New York: Basic Books.

Newman, Stanley. 1951. Review of *Selected Writings of Edward Sapir in Language, Culture and Personality,* ed. by David G. Mandelbaum (Univ. of California Press, 1949). *IJAL* 17.180-86. (Repr. in this volume, pp.59-65.)

Nyce, James M. 1977. The Relationship between Literature and Ethnography: The example of Edward Sapir, 1917-1922. Paper read at the 4th Congress of the Canadian Ethnology Society, Halifax. Unpublished manuscript.

Preston, Richard J. 1966. "Edward Sapir's Anthropology: Style, structure and method. *American Anthropologist* 68.1105-27.

—————. 1981. "Sapir's Conception of Drift as a Cultural Process". *Papers from the Sixth Annual Congress, 1978, Canadian Ethnology Society,* ed. by Marie-Françoise Guedon & Doyle Hatt, 213-19. Ottawa: National Museum of Man.

Radin, Paul. 1914. Letter from Radin to Sapir, 27 January 1914. Ottawa: The National Museum of Man Archives.

—————. 1933. *The Method and Theory of Ethnology.* New York: McGraw-Hill. (Repr., New York: Basic Books, 1965.)

Sapir, Edward. 1910. Letter from Sapir to Boas, 6 June 1910. Ottawa: The National Museum of Man Archives.

—————. 1916. Letter from Sapir to Lowie, 29 September 1916. *Edward Sapir's Letters to Robert H. Lowie,* ed. by R. H. Lowie, 20-21. [Berkeley: privately printed], 1965.

—————. 1917. "A Conversation". *Dreams and Gibes* by E. Sapir, p. 50. Boston: The Poet Lore Company, The Gorham Press.

—————. 1918. Letter from Sapir to Lowie, 31 Ocotober 1918. *Edward Sapir's Letters to Robert H. Lowie* ed. by R. H. Lowie, 31-32. [Berkeley: privately printed], 1965.

—————. 1921. Letters from Sapir to Lowie, 8 April and 23 May 1921. *Ibid.*, 46-47 and 48-49.

—————. 1922. " 'Sayach'apis, a Nootka Trader' ". *American Indian Life* ed. by Elsie C. Parsons, 247-323. New York: B. W. Huebsch. (Re-issue by Bison Books, Lincoln, Nebraska, 1967.)

—————. 1923. "An Approach to Symbolism (Review of Ogden & Richards, *The Meaning of Meaning)*". *The Freeman* (22 August 1923), 572-73.

—————. 1925. "Sound Patterns in Language". *Language* 1.37-51. (Repr. in Sapir 1949.33-45.)

—————. 1927. "The Unconscious Patterning of Behavior in Society". *The Unconscious: A symposium* ed. by Ethel S. Dummer, 114-42. New York: A. A. Knopf. (Repr. in Sapir 1949.544-59.)

—————. 1932. "Cultural Anthropology and Psychiatry". *Journal of Abnormal and Social Psychology* 27.229-42. (Repr. in Sapir 1949.509-521.)

—————. 1949. *Selected Writings of Edward Sapir.* Edited by David G. Mandelbaum. Berkeley & Los Angeles: Univ. of California Press.

Sapir, Jean V. 1967. Letter from Jean V. Sapir to R. J. Preston, 4 December 1967. Files of the author.

Scholte, Bob. 1973. "The Structural Anthropology of Claude Lévi-Strauss". *Handbook of Social and Cultural Anthropology* ed. by John Joseph Honigman, 637-716. Chicago: Rand McNally.

Sturtevant, William C. 1964. "Studies in Ethnoscience". *Transcultural Studies in Cognition* ed. by A. Kimball Romney & Roy Goodwin D'Andrade, 99-131. Menasha, Wisconsin: American Anthropological Association. (Special issue of *American Anthropologist* 66:3, part 2.)

Sullivan, Harry S. 1953. *The Interpersonal Theory of Psychiatry.* New York: W. W. Norton.

PART IV

Bibliography of Edward Sapir's Publications
in Linguistics, Anthropology, and other Behavioral
and Social Sciences

E. サ ピ ア 著

音 声 構 造 の 型
音 素 の 心 理 的 実 在

愛知女子大学教授

黒 川 新 一 訳 注

SOUND PATTERNS IN LANGUAGE

by Edward Sapir (1925)

THE PSYCHOLOGICAL REALITY OF PHONEMES

by Edward Sapir (1933)

音 声 構 造 の 型

音 素 の 心 理 的 実 在

黒 川 新 一 訳 注

大 修 館 書 店 ©

1 9 5 8

Facsimile of title and copyright statement of Shin-ichi Kurokawa's Japanese translation of two well-known papers of Edward Sapir for an 'English Teaching Series' (Tokyo: Taishukan, 1958).

SCIENTIFIC PAPERS AND PROSE WRITINGS*
of
EDWARD SAPIR

1906

"The Rival Chiefs, a Kwakiutl Story Recorded by George Hunt" [edited, with synopsis, pp. 108–110, by Edward Sapir], in *Boas Anniversary Volume* (New York), pp. 108–136.

1907

"Religious Ideas of the Takelma Indians of Southwestern Oregon," *Journal of American Folk-Lore*, 20: 33–49.

"Notes on the Takelma Indians of Southwestern Oregon," *American Anthropologist*, n.s., 9: 251–275.

"Preliminary Report on the Language and Mythology of the Upper Chinook," *American Anthropologist*, n.s., 9: 533–544.

"Herder's *Ursprung der Sprache*," *Modern Philology*, 5: 109–142.

1908

"Luck-Stones among the Yana," *Journal of American Folk-Lore*, 21: 42.

"On the Etymology of Sanskrit áśru, Avestan asru, Greek dákru," in *Spiegel Memorial Volume*, J. J. Modi, ed. (Bombay), pp. 156–159.

1909

"Characteristic Features of Yana" [abstract], *Science*, n.s., 29: 613; *American Anthropologist*, n.s., 11: 110.

Review of Frank G. Speck, *Ethnology of the Yuchi Indians*, in *Old Penn Weekly Review* (Philadelphia), December 18, p. 183.

Wishram Texts, together with Wasco Tales and Myths, collected by Jeremiah Curtin and edited by Edward Sapir, American Ethnological Society Publications, Vol. II (Leyden). 314 pp.

Takelma Texts, University of Pennsylvania, Anthropological Publications, 2 (no. 1): 1–263.

1910

"An Apache Basket Jar," *University of Pennsylvania Museum Journal*, 1 (no. 1): 13–15.

"Some Fundamental Characteristics of the Ute Language" [abstract], *Science*, n.s., 31: 350–352; *American Anthropologist*, n.s., 12: 66–69.

"Two Paiute Myths," *University of Pennsylvania Museum Journal*, 1 (no. 1): 15–18.

"Takelma," in *Handbook of American Indians North of Mexico*, Bureau of American Ethnology, Bulletin 30, Pt. II, pp. 673–674.

"Wasco," in *Handbook of American Indians North of Mexico*, Bureau of American Ethnology, Bulletin 30, Pt. II, pp. 917–918.

Review of C. Hart Merriam, *The Dawn of the World*, in *Science*, n.s., 32: 557–558.

Yana Texts (together with *Yana Myths*, collected by Roland B. Dixon), University of California Publications in American Archaeology and Ethnology, 9: 1–235.
"Song Recitative in Paiute Mythology," *Journal of American Folk-Lore*, 23: 455–472.

1911

"Some Aspects of Nootka Language and Culture," *American Anthropologist*, n.s., 13: 15–28.
Review of R. B. Dixon, *The Chimariko Indians and Language*, in *American Anthropologist*, n.s., 13: 141–143.
"The Problem of Noun Incorporation in American Languages," *American Anthropologist*, n.s., 13: 250–282.
"An Anthropological Survey of Canada," *Science*, n.s., 34: 789–793.
"Chinook" (incorporated in Franz Boas, "Chinook"), in *Handbook of American Indian Languages*, Bureau of American Ethnology, Bulletin 40, Pt. I, pp. 578, 579, 625–627, 638–645, 650–654, 673–677.
"The History and Varieties of Human Speech," *Popular Science Monthly*, 79: 45–67; reprinted in *Annual Report*, Smithsonian Institution (1912), pp. 573–595; also in *Selected Readings in Anthropology*, University of California Syllabus Series, No. 101, pp. 202–224.

1912

"The Mourning Ceremony of the Southern Paiutes" [abstract], *Science*, n.s., 35: 673; *American Anthropologist*, n.s., 14: 168–169.
Review of A. A. Goldenweiser, *Totemism: An Analytical Study*, in *Psychological Bulletin*, 9: 454–461.
"The Work of the Division of Anthropology of the Dominion Government," *Queen's Quarterly*, 20: 60–69.
Summary Report, Geological Survey of Canada, for 1910 (Ottawa), pp. 3–4.
Summary Report, Geological Survey of Canada, for 1911 (Ottawa), pp. 5–7, 15–16.
Review of Franz Boas, *Kwakiutl Tales*, in *Current Anthropological Literature*, 1: 193–198.
"Language and Environment," *American Anthropologist*, n.s., 14: 226–242.
"The Indians of the Province" [of British Columbia], in *British Columbia: Its History, People, Commerce, Industries, and Resources* (London), pp. 135–140.
"The Indians of Alberta, Saskatchewan, and Manitoba," in *The Prairie Provinces* (London).
Review of Carl Stumpf, *Die Anfänge der Musik*, in *Current Anthropological Literature*, 1: 275–282.

1913

"A Note on Reciprocal Terms of Relationship in America," *American Anthropologist*, n.s., 15: 132–138.
"A Tutelo Vocabulary," *American Anthropologist*, n.s., 15: 295–297.
Review of Carl Meinhof, *Die Sprachen der Hamiten*, in *Current Anthropological Literature*, 2: 21–27.
"Southern Paiute and Nahuatl, a Study in Uto-Aztekan," Pt. I, *Journal, Société des Américanistes de Paris*, n.s., 10: 379–425.
"Algonkin *p* and *s* in Cheyenne," *American Anthropologist*, n.s., 15: 538–539.

"A Girls' Puberty Ceremony among the Nootka Indians," *Transactions, Royal Society of Canada*, 3d series, 7: 67-80.

Summary Report, Geological Survey of Canada, for 1912 (Ottawa), pp. 448-453, 505-506.

"Methods and Principles," review of Erich von Hornbostel, "Ueber ein akustisches Kriterium für Kulturzusammenhänge," in *Current Anthropological Literature*, 2: 69-72.

"Wiyot and Yurok, Algonkin Languages of California," *American Anthropologist*, n.s., 15: 617-646.

1914

"Indian Tribes of the Coast" [of British Columbia], in A. Shortt and A. G. Doughty, eds., *Canada and Its Provinces* (Toronto), 21: 313-346.

Notes on Chasta Costa Phonology and Morphology, University of Pennsylvania, Anthropological Publications, 2 (no. 2): 271-340.

Summary Report, Geological Survey of Canada, for 1913 (Ottawa), pp. 355-363, 389.

1915

Abnormal Types of Speech in Nootka, Canada Department of Mines, Geological Survey, Memoir 62, Anthropological Series, No. 5. 21 pp.

Noun Reduplication in Comox, a Salish Language of Vancouver Island, Canada Department of Mines, Geological Survey, Memoir 63, Anthropological Series, No. 6. 53 pp.

"The Social Organization of the West Coast Tribes," *Transactions, Royal Society of Canada*, 2d series, 9: 355-374.

Summary Report, Geological Survey of Canada, for 1914, (Ottawa), pp. 168-177.

A Sketch of the Social Organization of the Nass River Indians, Canada Department of Mines, Geological Survey, Museum Bulletin 19, Anthropological Series, No. 7. 30 pp.

"Notes on Judeo-German Phonology," *The Jewish Quarterly Review*, n.s., 6: 231-266.

"Algonkin Languages of California: a Reply," *American Anthropologist*, n.s., 17: 188-194.

"Southern Paiute and Nahuatl, a Study in Uto-Aztekan," Pt. II, *American Anthropologist*, n.s., 17: 98-120, 306-328; *Journal, Société des Américanistes de Paris*, n.s., 11(1914): 443-488.

"The Na-dene Languages, a Preliminary Report," *American Anthropologist*, n.s., 17: 534-558.

"Corrigenda to Father Morice's *Chasta Costa and the Dene Languages of the North*," *American Anthropologist*, n.s., 17: 765-773.

1916

Summary Report, Geological Survey of Canada, for 1915 (Ottawa), pp. 265-274.

Review of Paul Abelson, ed., *English-Yiddish Encyclopedic Dictionary*, in *The Jewish Quarterly Review*, 7: 140-143.

"Phonetic Orthography and Notes to 'Nootka,' " in "Vocabularies from the Northwest Coast of America," Franz Boas, ed., *Proceedings, American Antiquarian Society*, 26: 4-18.

"Phonetic Orthography and Notes to 'Nootka,' " in *Phonetic Transcriptions of Indian Languages*, Smithsonian Miscellaneous Collections, 66: 1–15.

"Terms of Relationship and the Levirate," *American Anthropologist*, n.s., 18: 327–337.

"Percy Grainger and Primitive Music," *American Anthropologist*, n.s., 18: 592–597.

Time Perspective in Aboriginal American Culture: A Study in Method, Canada Department of Mines, Geological Survey, Memoir 90, Anthropological Series, No. 13. 87 pp.

"Culture in the Melting Pot," comments on John Dewey's article, "American Education and Culture." In *The Nation Supplement* (December 21), pp. 1–2.

1917

The Position of Yana in the Hokan Stock, University of California Publications in American Archaeology and Ethnology, 13: 1–34.

Summary Report, Geological Survey of Canada, for 1916, Anthropological Division, Part I, Ethnology and Linguistics, pp. 387–392, 394, 395.

"Do We Need a 'Superorganic'?" *American Anthropologist*, n.s., 19: 441–447.

"The Status of Washo," *American Anthropologist*, n.s., 19: 449–450.

"Linguistic Publications of the Bureau of American Ethnology, a General Review," *International Journal of American Linguistics*, 1: 76–81.

Review of C. C. Uhlenbeck, "Het Passieve Karakter van het Verbum Transitivum of van het Verbum Actionis in Talen van Noord-Amerika," in *International Journal of American Linguistics*, 1: 82–86.

Review of C. C. Uhlenbeck, "Het Identificeerend Karakter der Possessieve Flexie in Talen van Noord-Amerika," in *International Journal of American Linguistics*, 1: 86–90.

"A Freudian Half-Holiday," review of Sigmund Freud, *Delusion and Dream*, in *The Dial*, 63: 635–637.

" 'Jean-Christophe': An Epic of Humanity," review of Romain Rolland, *Jean-Christophe*, in *The Dial*, 62: 423–426.

"Realism in Prose Fiction," *The Dial*, 62: 503–506.

"A Frigid Introduction to Strauss," review of Henry T. Finck, *Richard Strauss, the Man and His Works*, in *The Dial*, 62: 584–586.

"The Twilight of Rhyme," *The Dial*, 63: 98–100.

Psychoanalysis as a Pathfinder," review of Oskar Pfister, *The Psychoanalytic Method*, in *The Dial*, 63: 267–269.

1918

Yana Terms of Relationship, University of California Publications in American Archaeology and Ethnology, 13: 153–173.

Review of Benigno Bibolotti, *Moseteno Vocabulary and Treatises*, in *International Journal of American Linguistics*, 1: 183–184.

"Representative Music," *The Musical Quarterly*, 4: 161–167.

"An Ethnological Note on the 'Whiskey-Jack'," *The Ottawa Naturalist*, 32: 116–117.

"Kinship Terms of the Kootenay Indians," *American Anthropologist*, n.s., 20: 414–418.

"Sancho Panza on His Island," review of G. K. Chesterton, *Utopias of Usurers and Other Essays*, in *The Dial*, 64: 25–27.

"God as Visible Personality," review of Samuel Butler, *God the Known and God the Unknown*, in *The Dial*, 64: 192–194.

"A University Survey of Religions," review of James A. Montgomery, ed., *Religions of the Past and Present* (Faculty Lectures, University of Pennsylvania), in *The Dial*, 65: 14–16.

"Tom," *Canadian Courier* (Dec. 7), p. 7.

1919

"Data on Washo and Hokan," in R. B. Dixon and A. L. Kroeber, *Linguistic Families of California*, University of California Publications in American Archaeology and Ethnology, 16: 108–112.

"A Flood Legend of the Nootka Indians of Vancouver Island," *Journal of American Folk-Lore*, 32: 351–355.

"Corrigenda and Addenda to W. D. Wallis' *Indogermanic Relationship Terms as Historical Evidence*," *American Anthropologist*, n.s., 21: 318–328.

"Corrigenda to 'Kinship Terms of the Kootenay Indians,' " *American Anthropologist*, n.s., 21: 98.

"Civilization and Culture," *The Dial*, 67: 233–236, Pt. 2 of "Culture, Genuine and Spurious," 1924, *q.v.*

Review (unsigned) of Cary F. Jacob, *The Foundations and Nature of Verse*, in *The Dial*, 66: 98, 100.

"The American Indian," review of C. Wissler, *The American Indian*, in *The New Republic*, 19: 189–191.

"The Poet Seer of Bengal," review of Tagore's *Lover's Gift, Crossing, Mashi and Other Stories*, in *The Canadian Magazine*, 54: 137–140.

1920

"A Note on French Canadian Folk-Songs," *Poetry*, 16: 210–213.

"The Hokan and Coahuiltecan Languages," *International Journal of American Linguistics*, 1: 280–290.

"A Note on the First Person Plural in Chimariko," *International Journal of American Linguistics*, 1: 291–294.

Review of J. Alden Mason, *The Language of the Salinan Indians*, in *International Journal of American Linguistics*, 1: 305–309.

"Nass River Terms of Relationship," *American Anthropologist*, n.s., 22: 261–271.

"The Heuristic Value of Rhyme," *Queen's Quarterly*, 27: 309–312.

"Primitive Society," review of R. H. Lowie, *Primitive Society*, in *The Nation*, 111: 46–47.

"Primitive Humanity and Anthropology," review of R. H. Lowie, *Primitive Society*, in *The Dial*, 69: 528–533.

"Primitive Society," review of R. H. Lowie, *Primitive Society*, in *The Freeman*, 1: 377–379.

"The Poetry Prize Contest," *The Canadian Magazine*, 54: 349–352.

1921

Language: An Introduction to the Study of Speech (New York, Harcourt, Brace. 258 pp.

Summary Report for Anthropological Division, Victoria Memorial Museum: Ethnology and Linguistics, 1920 (Ottawa), pp. 18–20.

"A Bird's-eye View of American Languages North of Mexico," *Science*, n.s., 54: 408.

"A Characteristic Penutian Form of Stem," *International Journal of American Linguistics*, 2: 58–67.

"A Supplementary Note on Salinan and Washo," *International Journal of American Linguistics*, 2: 68–72.

"A Haida Kinship Term among the Tsimshian," *American Anthropologist*, n.s., 23: 233–234.

"The Musical Foundations of Verse," *Journal of English and Germanic Philology*, 20: 213–228.

"The Life of a Nootka Indian," *Queen's Quarterly*, 28: 232–243, 351–367; reprinted under title of "Sayach'apis, a Nootka Trader," 1922, *q.v.*

"The Mythology of All Races," review of *The Mythology of All Races*, Vols. 3, 11, 12, in *The Dial*, 71: 107–111.

"Gerard Hopkins," review of Robert Bridges, ed., *Poems of Gerard Manley Hopkins*, in *Poetry*, 18: 330–336.

"Writing as History and as Style," review of W. A. Mason, *A History of the Art of Writing*, in *The Freeman*, 4: 68–69.

"Myth, Historian, and Psychologist," review of H. B. Alexander, *Latin-American* (Vol. XI, *The Mythology of All Races*), in *The Nation*, 112: 889–890.

"The Ends of Man," review of J. M. Tyler, *The New Stone Age in Northern Europe*; Stewart Paton, *Human Behavior*; E. G. Conklin, *The Direction of Human Evolution*. In *The Nation*, 113: 237–238.

"Maupassant and Anatole France," *The Canadian Magazine*, 57: 199–202.

"A Touchstone to Freud," review of W. H. R. Rivers, *Instinct and the Unconscious*, in *The Freeman*, 5: 357–358.

1922

"Culture, Genuine and Spurious," [Pt. 2], *The Dalhousie Review*, 2: 165–178; 358–368. Pts. 1 and 2 reprinted in *American Journal of Sociology* (1924), *q.v.*

The Fundamental Elements of Northern Yana, University of California Publications in American Archaeology and Ethnology, 13: 215–234.

"Athabaskan Tone," *American Anthropologist*, n.s., 24: 390–391.

"The Takelma Language of Southwestern Oregon," in *Handbook of American Indian Languages*, Bureau of American Ethnology, Bulletin 40, Part II, pp. 1–296.

"Vancouver Island Indians," in James Hastings, ed., *Encyclopaedia of Religion and Ethics* (New York), 12: 591–595.

"Sayach'apis, a Nootka Trader," in E. C. Parsons, ed., *American Indian Life* (New York), pp. 297–323.

"Language and Literature" (chap. 11 of *Language*, 1921), *The Canadian Magazine*, 59: 457–462.

"Practical Psychology," review of Frederick Pierce, *Our Unconscious Mind and How to Use It*, in *The Literary Review, New York Evening Post* (July 1), p. 772.

Review (unsigned) of Arthur Davison Ficke, *Mr. Faust*, in *The Dial*, 73: 235.

Review (unsigned) of George Saintsbury, *A Letter Book*, in *The Dial*, 73: 235.

Review (unsig.) of Gilbert Murray, *Tradition and Progress,* in *The Dial,* 73:255.
Review (unsigned) of Selma Lagerlöf, *The Outcast,* in *The Dial,* 73: 354.
Review of Edgar Lee Masters, *Children of the Market Place,* in *The Dial,* 73: 457.
"A Symposium of the Exotic," review of E. C. Parsons, ed., *American Indian Life,* in *The Dial,* 73: 568–571.
"The Manner of Mr. Masefield," review of John Masefield, *King Cole,* in *The Freeman,* 5: 548–549.
"Mr. Masters's Later Work," review of Edgar Lee Masters, *The Open Sea,* in *The Freeman,* 5: 333–334.
"A Peep at the Hindu Spirit," review of *More Jataka Tales,* retold by Ellen C. Babbitt, in *The Freeman,* 5: 404.
Review of John Masefield, *Esther and Berenice,* in *The Freeman,* 5: 526.
"An Orthodox Psychology," review of R. S. Woodworth, *Psychology: A Study of Mental Life,* in *The Freeman,* 5: 619.
"Heavens," review of Louis Untermeyer, *Heavens,* in *The New Republic,* 30: 351.
"Introducing Irony," review of Maxwell Bodenheim, *Introducing Irony,* in *The New Republic,* 31: 341.
"Maxwell Bodenheim," review of Maxwell Bodenheim, *Introducing Irony,* in *The Nation,* 114: 751.
"Poems of Experience," review of Edwin Arlington Robinson, *Collected Poems,* in *The Freeman,* 5: 141–142; published also (under title, "Edwin Arlington Robinson") in *The Canadian Bookman* (August), pp. 210–211.
"Spoon River Muddies," review of Edgar Lee Masters, *The Open Sea,* in *The Canadian Bookman* (April), pp. 132, 140.
Review of Edward Thomas, *Collected Poems,* in *The New Republic,* 32: 226.
Summary Report for Anthropological Division, Vicotria Memorial Museum: Ethnology and Linguistics, fiscal year ending March 31, 1922 (Ottawa), pp. 22–25.

1923

Text Analyses of Three Yana Dialects, University of California Publications in American Archaeology and Ethnology, 20: 263–294.
"The Algonkin Affinity of Yurok and Wiyot Kinship Terms," *Journal, Société des Américanistes de Paris,* n.s., 15: 36–74.
"A Note on Sarcee Pottery," *American Anthropologist,* n.s., 25: 247–253.
"A Type of Athabaskan Relative," *International Journal of American Linguistics,* 2: 136–142.
"The Phonetics of Haida," *International Journal of American Linguistics,* 2: 143–159.
Review of Truman Michelson, "The Owl Sacred Pack of the Fox Indians," in *International Journal of American Linguistics,* 2:182-184.
[With Hsü Tsan Hwa] "Two Chinese Folk-Tales," *Journal of American Folk-Lore,* 36: 23–30.
[With Hsü Tsan Hwa] "Humor of the Chinese Folk," *Journal of American Folk-Lore,* 36: 31–35.
"Archaeology and Ethnology" [bibliography], *Canadian Historical Review,* 4: 374–378.
Summary Report for Anthropological Division, Victoria Memorial Museum: Ethnology and Linguistics, fiscal year ending March 31, 1923 (Ottawa), pp. 28–31.

"The Two Kinds of Human Beings," review of C. G. Jung, *Psychological Types, or the Psychology of Individuation*, in *The Freeman*, 8: 211–212.

Review of Edwin Björkman, *The Soul of a Child*, in *The Double Dealer*, 51: 78–80.

"An Approach to Symbolism," review of C. K. Ogden and I. A. Richards, *The Meaning of Meaning*, in *The Freeman*, 7: 572–573.

"The Epos of Man," review of Johannes V. Jensen, *The Long Journey*, in *The World Tomorrow*, 6: 221.

"Mr. Housman's Last Poems," review of A. E. Housman, *Last Poems*, in *The Dial*, 75: 188–191.

1924

"Culture, Genuine and Spurious," *American Journal of Sociology*, 29: 401–429; Pt. 2, *The Dalhousie Review* (1922), *q.v.*; Pt. 1, (under title "Civilization and Culture") *The Dial* (1919), *q.v.*

"The Grammarian and His Language," *American Mercury*, 1: 149–155.

"Anthropology at the Toronto Meeting of the British Association for the Advancement of Science, 1924," *American Anthropologist*, n.s., 26: 563–565.

"Personal Names among the Sarcee Indians," *American Anthropologist*, n.s., 26: 108–119.

"The Rival Whalers, a Nitanat Story (Nootka Text with Translation and Grammatical Analysis)," *International Journal of American Linguistics*, 3: 76–102.

"Racial Superiority," *The Menorah Journal*, 10: 200–212.

"Twelve Novelists in Search of a Reason," review of *The Novel of Tomorrow and the Scope of Fiction*, by Twelve American Novelists. In *The Stratford Monthly* (May).

1925

"Memorandum on the Problem of an International Auxiliary Language," *The Romanic Review*, 16: 244–256.

"The Hokan Affinity of Subtiaba in Nicarague," *American Anthropologist*, n.s., 27: 402–435, 491–527.

"Pitch Accent in Sarcee, an Athabaskan Language," *Journal, Société des Américanistes de Paris*, n.s., 17: 185–205.

"Indian Legends from Vancouver Island," *Transactions, Women's Canadian Historical Society of Ottawa*, 9: 142–143.

"Sound Patterns in Language," *Language*, 1: 37–51.

"The Heuristic Value of Rhyme," *Queen's Quarterly*, 27: 309–312.

Summary Report for the Fiscal Year Ending March 31, 1924, Anthropological Division: Ethnology and Linguistics (Ottawa), pp. 36–40.

"Is Monotheism Jewish?" review of Paul Radin, *Monotheism among Primitive Peoples*, in *The Menorah Journal*, 11: 524–527.

"Are the Nordics a Superior Race?" *The Canadian Forum* (June), pp. 265–266.

Report of the Department of Mines, Dominion of Canada, for the Fiscal Year Ending March 31, 1925: Anthropological Division, Ethnology and Linguistics (Ottawa), pp. 37–41.

Review of A. Meillet and Marcel Cohen, eds., *Les Langues du monde*, in *Modern Language Notes*, 40: 373–375.

"Undesirables—Klanned or Banned," *The American Hebrew*, 116: 286.

"Let Race Alone," *The Nation*, 120: 211–213.

"The Race Problem," review of: F. G. Crookshank, *The Mongol in Our Midst;* H. W. Siemens, *Race Hygiene and Heredity;* Jean Finot, *Race Prejudice;* J. H. Oldham, *Christianity and the Race Problem.* In *The Nation,* 121: 40–42.

"An American Poet," review of H.D., *Collected Poems,* in *The Nation,* 121: 211.

"Emily Dickinson, a Primitive," review of *The Complete Poems of Emily Dickinson,* and M. D. Bianchi, *The Life and Letters of Emily Dickinson,* in *Poetry,* 26: 97–105.

"The Tragic Chuckle," review of Edwin Arlington Robinson, *Dionysus in Doubt,* in *Voices* (November), pp. 64–65.

1926

"Philology," in *The Encyclopaedia Britannica* (*Supplementary Volumes,* 13th, ed.), 3: 112–115.

"Speech as a Personality Trait," abstract of a paper delivered before the Illinois Society for Mental Hygiene (Oct. 19) in *Health Bulletin,* Illinois Society for Mental Hygiene, December; also published in *American Journal of Sociology* (May, 1927), *q.v.*

"A Chinookan Phonetic Law," *International Journal of American Linguistics,* 4: 105–110.

Review of Knight Dunlap, *Old and New Viewpoints in Psychology,* in *American Journal of Sociology,* 31: 698–699.

Review of George A. Dorsey, *Why We Behave Like Human Beings,* in *American Journal of Sociology,* 32: 140.

Review of Otto Jespersen, *Mankind, Nation and Individual from a Linguistic Point of View,* in *American Journal of Sociology,* 32: 498–499.

Review of Father Berard Haile, *A Manual of Navaho Grammar,* in *American Journal of Sociology,* 32: 511.

"Leonie Adams," review of Leonie Adams, *Those Not Elect,* in *Poetry,* 27: 275–279.

Review of Ludwig Lewisohn, *Israel,* in *The Menorah Journal,* 12: 214–218.

1927

"Anthropology and Sociology," in W. F. Ogburn and A. Goldenweiser, eds., *The Social Sciences and Their Interrelations* (Boston), chap. 9, pp. 97–113.

"Language as a Form of Human Behavior," *The English Journal,* 16: 421–433.

"The Unconscious Patterning of Behavior in Society," in E. S. Dummer, ed., *The Unconscious: A Symposium* (New York), pp. 114–142.

"Speech as a Personality Trait," *American Journal of Sociology,* 32: 892–905; published also in *Health Bulletin,* (Illinois Society for Mental Hygiene, 1926), *q.v.*

"A Reasonable Eugenist," review of F. H. Hankins, *The Racial Basis of Civilization,* in *The New Republic,* 53: 146.

"Speech and Verbal Thought in Childhood," review of Jean Piaget, *The Language and Thought of the Child,* in *The New Republic,* 50: 350–351.

Review of Paul Radin, *Crashing Thunder: The Autobiograpyy of an American Indian,* in *American Journal of Sociology,* 33: 303–304.

Review of A. Hyatt Verrill, *The American Indian: North, South, and Central America,* in *American Journal of Sociology,* 33: 295–296.

"An Expedition to Ancient America: A Professor and a Chinese Student Rescue the Vanishing Language and Culture of the Hupas in Northern California," *The University of Chicago Magazine*, 20: 10–12.

1928

"A Summary Report of Field Work among the Hupa, Summer of 1927," *American Anthropologist*, n.s., 30: 359–361.

Review of James Weldon Johnson, ed., *The Book of American Negro Spirituals*, in *Journal of American Folk-Lore*, 41: 172–174.

"The Meaning of Religion," *The American Mercury*, 15: 72–79; published also under title "Religions and Religious Phenomena," (1929), *q.v.*

Review of Roland G. Kent, *Language and Philology*, in *The Classical Weekly*, 21: 85–86.

"When Words Are Not Enough," review of Clarence Day, *Thoughts without Words*, in *New York Herald Tribune Books*, 4: xii.

Proceedings, First Colloquium on Personality Investigation; Held under the Auspices of the American Psychiatric Association, Committee on Relations with the Social Sciences (New York), pp. 77–80.

"Observations on the Sex Problem in America," *American Journal of Psychiatry*, 8: 519–534.

Review of Knut Hamsun, *The Women at the Pump*, in *The New Republic*, 56: 335.

"Psychoanalysis as Prophet," review of Sigmund Freud, *The Future of an Illusion*, in *The New Republic*, 56: 356–357.

1929

"Central and North American Languages," *Encyclopaedia Britannica* (14th ed.), 5: 138–141.

"The Status of Linguistics as a Science," *Language*, 5: 207–214.

"Male and Female Forms of Speech in Yana," in St. W. J. Teeuwen, ed., *Donum Natalicium Schrijnen* (Nijmegan-Utrecht), pp. 79–85.

"Nootka Baby Words," *International Journal of American Linguistics*, 5: 118, 119.

[With Charles G. Blooah] "Some Gweabo Proverbs," *Africa*, 2: 183–185.

"Religions and Religious Phenomena," in Baker Brownell, ed., *Religious Life* (Man and His World, Vol. 11) (New York), pp. 11–33; printed also in *The American Mercury* (1928), *q.v.*

"A Study in Phonetic Symbolism," *Journal of Experimental Psychology*, 12: 225–239.

"The Discipline of Sex," *The American Mercury*, 16: 413–420; printed also in *Child Study* (1930), *q.v.*

"A Linguistic Trip among the Navaho Indians," *The Gallup Independent* (Ceremonial Ed., Aug. 23, 1929, Gallup, N.M.), pp. 1–2.

"What Is the Family Still Good For?" *Winnetka Conference on the Family* (Oct. 28), pp. 31–34; also published in *The American Mercury* (1930), *q.v.*

Review of M. E. DeWitt, *Our Oral Word as Social and Economic Factor*, in *American Journal of Sociology*, 34: 926–927.

Review of Waldo Frank, *The Rediscovery of America*, in *American Journal of Sociology*, 35: 335–336.

"The Skepticism of Bertrand Russell," review of Bertrand Russell, *Sceptical Essays*, in *The New Republic*, 57: 196.

"Franz Boas," review of Franz Boas, *Anthropology and Modern Life*, in *The New Republic*, 57: 278–279.

"Design in Pueblo Pottery," review of R. L. Bunzel, *The Pueblo Potter*, in *The New Republic*, 61: 115.

1930

[With Leslie Spier] *Wishram Ethnography*, University of Washington Publications in Anthropology, 3: 151–300.

Totality, Linguistic Society of America, Language Monographs, No. 6. 28 pp.

The Southern Paiute Language: Southern Paiute, a Shoshonean Language; Texts of the Kaibab Paiutes and Uintah Utes; Southern Paiute Dictionary, Proceedings, American Academy of Arts and Sciences, 65: (no. 1), pp. 1–296; (no. 2), pp. 297–536; (no. 3) (1931), pp. 537–730.

Proceedings, Second Colloquium on Personality Investigation; Held under the Joint Auspices of the American Psychiatric Association and of the Social Science Research Council (Baltimore, Md.), pp. 37–41, 122–125.

[With Albert G. Sandoval] "A Note on Navaho Pottery," *American Anthropologist*, n.s., 32: 575–576.

"Our Business Civilization," review of James Truslow Adams, *Our Business Civilization: Some Aspects of American Culture*, in *Current History*, 32: 426–428.

"The Discipline of Sex," *Child Study* (March), pp. 170–173, 187–188; printed also in *The American Mercury* (1929), q.v.

"What Is the Family Still Good For?" *American Mercury*, 19: 145–151; printed also in *Winnetka Conference on the Family* (1929), q.v.

1931

"Communication," *Encyclopaedia of the Social Sciences* (New York), 4: 78–81.

"Dialect," *Encyclopaedia of the Social Sciences* (New York), 5: 123–126.

"Fashion," *Encyclopaedia of the Social Sciences* (New York), 6: 139–144.

"Custom," *Encyclopaedia of the Social Sciences* (New York), 4: 658–662.

"Language, Race, and Culture," (chap. 10 of *Language*, New York, 1921, q.v.) in V. F. Calverton, ed., *The Making of Man* (New York), pp. 142–156.

Review of Ray Hoffman, *Nuer-English Dictionary*, in *American Anthropologist*, n.s., 33: 114–115.

"The Concept of Phonetic Law as Tested in Primitive Languages by Leonard Bloomfield," in Stuart A. Rice, ed., *Methods in Social Science: A Case Book* (Chicago), pp. 297–306.

"Notes on the Gweabo Language of Liberia," *Language*, 7: 30–41.

"The Case for a Constructed International Language" *Propositions, Deuxième Congrès International de Linguistes* (Geneva, Aug. 25–29), pp. 42–44.

"The Function of an International Auxiliary Language," *Psyche*, 11: 4–15; also published in *International Communication: A Symposium on the Language Problem*, by H. N. Shenton, E. Sapir, O. Jespersen (London, 1931), pp. 65–94.

"Wanted, a World Language," *The American Mercury*, 22: 202–209.

1932

"Group," *Encyclopaedia of the Social Sciences* (New York), 7: 178–182.

[With Morris Swadesh] *The Expression of the Ending-Point Relation in English, French, and German* (Alice V. Morris, ed.), Linguistic Society of America, Language Monographs, No. 10. 125 pp.

"Two Navaho Puns." *Language*, 8:217-219.
"Cultural Anthropology and Psychiatry," *Journal of Abnormal and Social Psychology*, 27: 229-242.
Review of James G. Leyburn, *Handbook of Ethnography*, in *American Journal of Science*, 5th series, 23: 186-189.

1933

"Language," *Encyclopaedia of the Social Sciences* (New York), 9: 155-169.
"La Réalité Psychologique des Phonèmes," *Journal de Psychologie Normale et Pathologique* (Paris), 30: 247-265.

1934

"Personality," *Encyclopaedia of the Social Sciences* (New York), 12: 85-87.
"Symbolism," *Encyclopaedia of the Social Sciences* (New York), 14: 492-495.
"The Emergence of the Concept of Personality in a Study of Cultures," *Journal of Social Psychology*, 5: 408-415.
"Hittite *hepatis* "Vassal" and Greek ὁ παδός," *Language*, 10: 274-279.
[With others] "Some Orthographic Recommendations," *American Anthropologist*, n.s., 36: 629-631.
"The Bush Negro of Dutch Guiana," review of Melville J. Herskovits and Frances S. Herskovits, *Rebel Destiny: Among the Bush Negroes of Dutch Guiana*, in *The Nation*, 139: 135.

1935

Review of A. G. Morice, *The Carrier Language (Déné Family): A Grammar and Dictionary Combined*, in *American Anthropologist*, n.s., 37: 500-501.
"A Navaho Sand Painting Blanket," *American Anthropologist*, n.s., 37: 609-616.

1936

"Kutchin Relationship Terms," in Cornelius Osgood, *Contributions to the Ethnography of the Kutchin*, Yale University Publications in Anthropology, No. 14, pp. 136-137.
"Hupa Tattooing," in R. H. Lowie, ed., *Essays in Anthropology Presented to Alfred Louis Kroeber* (Berkeley), pp. 273-277.
"Greek ἀτύζομαι, a Hittite Loanword, and Its Relatives," *Language*, 12: 175-180.
"Tibetan Influences on Tocharian. I," *Language*, 12: 259-271.
Review of D. Westermann and Ida C. Ward, *Practical Phonetics for Students of African Languages*, in *American Anthropologist*, n.s., 38: 121-122.
"Internal Linguistic Evidence Suggestive of the Northern Origin of the Navaho," *American Anthropologist*, n.s., 38: 224-235.
"Hebrew 'argáz, a Philistine Word," *Journal of the American Oriental Society*, 56: 272-281.
"κύβδα, a Karian Gloss," *Journal of the American Oriental Society*, 56: 85.

1937

"The Contribution of Psychiatry to an Understanding of Behavior in Society," *American Journal of Sociology*, 42: 862-870.
"Hebrew 'Helmet,' a Loanword, and Its Bearing on Indo-Europear Phonology," *Journal of the American Oriental Society*, 57: 73-77.

"The Negroes of Haiti," review of Melville J. Herskovits, *Life in a Haitian Valley*, in *The Yale Review*, 26: 853–854.

Review of James A. Montgomery and Zellig S. Harris, *The Ras Shamra Mythological Texts*, in *Language*, 13: 326–331.

1938

"Hittite *siyanta* and Gen. 14: 3," *American Journal of Semitic Languages and Literatures*, 55: 86–88.

"Glottalized Continuants in Navaho, Nootka, and Kwakiutl (with a Note on Indo-European)," *Language*, 14: 248–274.

Foreword to Walter Dyk, *Son of Old Man Hat* (New York), pp. v–x.

"Why Cultural Anthropology Needs the Psychiatrist," *Psychiatry*, 1: 7–12.

Review of Thurman W. Arnold, *The Folklore of Capitalism*, in *Psychiatry*, 1: 145–147.

"Psychiatric and Cultural Pitfalls in the Business of Getting a Living," (advance contribution to Symposium on Mental Health, Section on Medical Sciences, American Association for the Advancement of Science, Winter Meeting, Richmond, Va.: Session IV, Physical and Cultural Environment, Thursday afternoon, December 29, 1938). Mimeographed. Published also in *Mental Health* (1939), *q.v.*

1939

[With Morris Swadesh] *Nootka Texts: Tales and Ethnological Narratives with Grammatical Notes and Lexical Materials*, William Dwight Whitney Linguistic Series, Linguistic Society of America (Philadelphia). 334 pp.

"Indo-European Prevocalic *s* in Macedonian," *American Journal of Philology*, 40: 463–465; published also in "From Sapir's Desk . . ." (1939), *q.v.*

"Songs for a Comox Dancing Mask" (edited by Leslie Spier), *Ethnos* (Stockholm), 4: 49–55.

Review of Zellig S. Harris, *A Grammar of the Phoenician Language*, in *Language*, 15: 60–65.

"From Sapir's Desk: Indo-European Prevocalic *s* in Macedonian; The Indo-European Words for 'Tear'" (edited by H. S. Sturtevant), *Language*, 13: 178–187.

"Psychiatric and Cultural Pitfalls in the Business of Getting a Living," *Mental Health*, Publication of the American Association for the Advancement of Science, No. 9, pp. 237–244; also mimeographed (1938).

1942

Navaho Texts, with Supplementary Texts by Harry Hoijer, edited by Harry Hoijer, Linguistic Society of America (Philadelphia). 543 pp.

1943

[With Leslie Spier] *Notes on the Culture of the Yana*, University of California Publications: Anthropological Records, 3: 239–298.

1944

"Grading, a Study in Semantics," *Philosophy of Science*, 11: 93–116.

エドワード・サピア著

言語・文化・パーソナリティ
——サピア言語文化論集——

平林幹郎訳

北星堂書店

Facsimile of title page of the Japanese translation by Mikio Hirabayashi of major portions from 'Selected Writings by Edward Sapir' (Tokyo: Hokuseido, 1983).

ADDENDA TO EDWARD SAPIR'S SCIENTIFIC BIBLIOGRAPHY
1916-1984

Introductory note: This listing makes no claim to completeness; however, an attempt has been made to include all publications in English in the field of linguistics and/or anthropology that have either been missed in the preceding bibliography or (re)published since then. With the exception of Sapir's famous 1933 paper, "La réalité psychologique des phonèmes", only translations of his 1921 book *Language* and of selections from the 1949 *Selected Writings* (if published in book form) have been included.* For a full bibliography of the translations into Japanese, for instance, see the one compiled by Tetsuro Hayashi in *Historiographia Linguistica* 11:3.461-66 (1984).

1916

"Phonetic Transcription of Indian Languages". *Smithsonian Miscellaneous Collections* 66:6. [Report of the Committee of the American Anthropological Association, Washington, D.C., chaired by Franz Boas, with Pliny Earle Goddard and Alfred Louis Kroeber as members, and Sapir as secretary.]

1917

"Ireland's Debt to Foreign Scholars". *The Dial* 62:7.513 (July). [Letter to the editor of 5 Juni 1917.]

1925

"The Similarity of Chinese and Indian Languages". *Science* 62, No.1607 – Supplement of 16 Oct. 1925, p.xii [Report from an interview (?) with "the Canadian anthropologist now on the faculty of the University of Chicago" on Sapir's speculations about the relationship between Chinese, Tibetan and Siamese with American Indian languages.]

* As a result, translations of individual articles, such as "Položenie lingvistiki kak nauki [The Status of Linguistics as Science (1929)]" and "Jazyk [Language (1933)]" in *Istorija jazykoznanija XIX i XX vekov v očerkax i izvlečenijax* by V[ladimir] A[ndreevič] Zvegincev, vol.II (Moscow: Izd. Prosveščenie, 1960; 2nd ed., 1964), pp.175-81 and 182-96, are not included in the present bibliography.

1931

"Conceptual Categories in Primitive Languages". *Science* 74.578 [Introduced by Clark Wissler]. (Repr. in *Language in Culture and Society* ed. by Dell H[athaway] Hymes, p.128. New York: Harper & Row, 1964.)

1934

Jazyk: Vvedenie v izučenie reči. Transl. into Russian by A.M. Suxotin.† Preface by S.L. Belevickij. Moscow & Leningrad: Socekgiz, 223 pp. [Transl. of *Language.*]

1943

Gengo: Kotoba no kenkyu josetsu [Language: An introduction to the study of speech]. Transl., with biobibliographical notes and indices, by Chiaki Kisaka, and a preface by Izuru Shinmura. Tokyo: Toko Shoin, xiii, 319 pp. [First Japanese transl. of *Language* for a 2nd transl., see under 1957.]

1946

[With Morris Swadesh.] "American Indian Grammatical Categories". *Word* 2.103-112. (Repr. in *Language in Culture and Society* ed. by Dell H. Hymes, 100-107. New York: Harper & Row, 1964.)

"Sapir on Arapaho". Ed. by Charles F[rancis] Hockett from a MS turned over to him for possible publication by Morris Swadesh in 1939. *International Journal of American Linguistics* 12.243-45.

1947

"The Relation of American Indian Linguistics to General Linguistics". *Southwestern Journal of Anthropology* 3.1-4.

1949

Selected Writings of Edward Sapir in Language, Culture and Personality. Ed. by David G[oodman] Mandelbaum. Berkeley & Los Angels: Univ. of California Press, xv, 617 pp. (6th printing, 1970)

Wat is taal? Inleiding tot de taalkunde. Voor Nederland bewerkt door A[ugust] L[ammert] Sötemann. Amsterdam: Noord-Hollandsche Uitg. Mij., 272 pp. [Dutch transl. of *Language.*]

† In 1933 Suxotin translated Saussure's *Cours* into Russian, but whereas Saussure's text was republished in 1977, no such action was taken with regard to Sapir's book.

1953

Le Langage: Introduction à l'étude de la parole. Traduction par S[olange] M[arie] Guillemin. Paris: Payot, 222 pp. [First French transl. of *Language*; rev. ed., 1967.]

[With Morris Swadesh.] "Coos-Takelma-Penutian Comparisons". *IJAL* 19.132-37.

1954

A linguagem: Introdução ao estudo da fala. Traduzido por J[oaquim] Mattoso Câmara. Rio de Janeiro: Instituto Nacional do Livro, Ministerio de Educação y Cultura, 229 pp. [Portuguese transl. of *Language.*]

El lenguaje: Introducción al estudio del habla. Traducción de Margit [Frenk] y Antonio Alatorre. México: Fondo de Cultura Económica, 280 pp. [Spanish transl. of *Language*; Repr. in 1962, 1966, 1971, 1974.]

1955

[With Morris Swadesh.] *Native Accounts of Nootka Ethnography.* (= *International Journal of American Linguistics* 21:4.) Bloomington: Indiana Univ. Research Center in Anthropology, Folklore and Linguistics, 457 pp. [Appreciation, p.5, dated 1950.] (Repr., New York: AMS Press, 1978.)

[Helen Heffron Roberts & Morris Swadesh, *Songs of the Nootka Indians of Western Vancouver Island.* Based on phonographic records, linguistic and other field notes made by Edward Sapir. Philadelphia: American Philosophical Society.]

1956

Culture, Language and Personality: Selected essays. Ed. by David G[oodman] Mandelbaum. Berkeley & Los Angeles: Univ. of California Press, ix, 207 pp. (8th printing, 1966.) [Reprint of 8 papers first published in 1933, 1931, 1929, 1924, 1928, 1932, 1939, and 1934 (in that order) and also included in *Selected Writings* (1949).]

1957

Gengo: Kotoba no kenkyu [Language: The study of speech]. Transl. into Japanese by Hisanosuke Izui. Tokyo: Kinokuniya, xv, 254 pp. [2nd transl., though largely based on the first by Kisaka (1943).]

"Sound Patterns in Language". *Readings in Linguistics: The development of descriptive linguistics in America, 1925-56* ed. by Martin Joos, 19-25. New York: American Council of Learned Societies. (4th ed., Chicago: Univ. of Chicago Press, 1966.) [Repr. of paper first published in 1925.]

1960

[With Morris Swadesh.] *Yana Dictionary.* Ed. by Mary R[osamond] Haas. (= *Univ. of California Publications in Linguistics,* 22.) Berkeley: Univ. of California Press, xi, 267 pp.

1961

Die Sprache: Eine Einführung in das Wesen der Sprache. Aus dem Englischen übersetzt und für den deutschen Leser bearbeitet von Conrad P[aul] Homberger. Einführung von William G[amwell] Moulton. München: Max Hueber Verlag, 206 pp. [German transl. of *Language*; chap.XI of the original, "Language and literature", was not translated.]

Linguística como ciência: Ensaios. Seleção, tradução y notas de J[oaquim] Mattoso Câmara. Rio de Janeiro: Livraria Acadêmica, 203 pp. [A selection of papers, translated into Portuguese, with notes.]

1963

Language: An introduction to the study of speech. London: Rupert Hart-Davis, ix, 242 pp. (2nd impression, 1970; 3rd impression, 1971.) [Repr. of 1921 original; copyright held by Harcourt, Brace & World, New York, and renewed in 1949, 1963, and 1970.]

1964

"Conceptual Categories in Primitive Languages". *Language and Culture in Society* ed. by Dell H[athaway] Hymes, p.128. New York: Harper & Row. [Repr. of 1931 note (see above), with a reference note by the editor.]

1965

"Yana Terms of Relationship". New York: Kraus, 21 pp. [Repr. of 1918 paper, published in *Univ. of California Publications in American Archaeology and Ethnology* 13:4. 153-73.]

"The Fundamental Elements of Northern Yana". Ibid., 20 pp. [Repr. of 1922 paper, published in the same periodical as preceding item, No.6. 215-34.]

1966

[With Morris Swadesh.] *The Expression of the Ending-Point Relation in English, French, and German.* Ed. by Alice V[anderbilt] Morris. New

York: Kraus, 125 pp. [Repr. of 1932 'Language Monographs' No.10, published with the support of the International Auxiliary Language Association, and for the Linguistic Society of America, by Waverly Press, Baltimore, Md.]

Totality. Ibid., 28 pp. [Repr. of 'Language Monographs' No.6, published in 1930, with the support of the same agency and at the same place as preceding item.]

1967

[With Harry Hoijer.] *The Phonology and Morphology of the Navaho Language.* (= *Univ. of California Publications in Linguistics*, 50.) Berkeley: Univ. of California Press, 124 pp.

Le Langage: Introduction à l'étude de la parole. Traduit de l'anglais par Solange-Marie Guillemin. (= *Petite Bibliothèque Payot*, 104.) Paris: Payot, 231 pp. (Repr., 1970.) [Revised version of 1953 French translation (see above).]

Anthropologie. 1. Culture et personnalité. Traduction de Christian Baudelot et Pierre Clinquart; introduction, index et notes de Christian Baudelot. Paris: Les Editions de Minuit, 209 pp. (Repr., together with the 2nd volume, 1971.)

Anthropologie. 2. Culture. Traduction de Christian Baudelot ... [as above]. Ibid., 225 pp. [This and the preceding volume contain French translations of 24 items published in *Selected Writings* (1949), and in the following order – date of the original publication precedes the page reference in the Mandelbaum edition: 1927 (544-59), 1934 (564-68), 1927 (533-44), 1934 (560-63), 1934 (590-97), 1932 (509-521), 1938 (569-77), 1934 (578-84), 1917 (522-25), 1922 (528-29), 1923 (529-32), 1921 (525-28), 1927 (332-45), 1931 (373-81), 1931 (365-72), 1932 (357-64), 1928 (346-56), and in volume II: 1916 [i.e., Sapir's *Time Perspective*, 389-462], 1915 (468-87), 1924 (308-331). – Volume I contains a detailed 'Avant-propos' (9-34); volume II carries explanatory notes (167-88), an index of tribes and languages (189-92), a brief biography (193) and a full bibliography (195-213) of Sapir, and a full index of names and subjects (217-224). – For specifically linguistic selections in French transl., see under 1968.]

1968

Linguistique. Traduction de Jean-Élie Boltanski et Nicole Soulé-Susbielles.

Présentation den Jean-Élie Boltanski. Paris: Les Editions de Minuit, 289 pp. (New impression, 1976.) [This volume unites the following papers not included in the 2-volume *Anthropologie* (1967) edition of selections, in French translation, from *Selected Writings* (to which the page referencen ces given here refer): 1933 (7-32), 1931 (83-88), 1912 (89-103), 1931 (104-109), 1931 (110-21), 1924 (150-59), 1925 (3345), 1933 (46-60), 1929 (61-72), 1944 (122-49), 1915 (1979-96), and 1929 (206-212), in that order.]

Time Perspective in Aboriginal American Culture: A study in method. New York: Johnson Reprint Co., 87 pp. [Repr. of 1916 monograph.]

1969

Il linguaggio: Introduzione alla linguistica. Traduzione a cura di Paolo Valesio. Turin: Giulio Einaudi, xxiv, 227 pp. (2nd ed., 1971.) [Italian transl. of *Language.*]

"La réalité psychologique des phonèmes". *Essais sur le langage* présentés par Jean-Claude Pariente, 167-88. Paris: Les Editions de Minuit. [Republication of 1933 article; for another translation, see *Linguistique* (1968) above (pp.165-86).]

1970

Language: An introduction to the study of speech. New York: Harcourt, Brace & World, ix, 242 pp. [Unchanged reprint of 1921 edition; see also under 1963.]

1971

Anthropologie. Traduit de l'américain par Christian Baudelot et Pierre Clinquart. Introduction et notes de Christian Baudelot. Paris: Les Editions de Minuit, 388 pp. [Combination of the 2 1967 volumes, but without the biobibliographical information on Sapir and the indices.]

1972

"Sound Patterns in Language". *Phonological Theory: Evolution and current practice* ed. by Valerie Becker Makkai, 13-21. New York: Holt, Rinehart & Winston. (2nd printing, Lake Bluff, Ill.: Jupiter Press, 1978.) [Repr. of 1925 article.]

"The Psychological Reality of Phonemes". *Ibid.*, 22-31. [Repr. of 1933 article, first published in English in 1949.]

1973

[With Leslie Sper.] *Notes on the Culture of the Yana.* Berkeley & Los Angeles: Univ. of California Press, 59 pp. [Repr. of 1943 publication.]

1974

Wishram Texts: Together with Wasco Tales and Myths, collected by Jeremiah Curtin [(1860-1906)], ed. by Edward Sapir. New York: AMS Press, xv, 314 pp. [Repr. of 1909 Leiden (E.J. Brill) edition.]

1975

[With Harry Hoijer.] *Navaho Texts.* With supplementary texts by Harry Hoijer, ed. by H.H. New York: AMS Press, 543 pp. [Repr. of 1942 (Iowa City: Univ. of Iowa for Linguistic Society of America) edition.]

1978

[With Morris Swadesh.] *Native Accounts of Nootka Ethnography.* New York: AMS Press, 457 pp. [Repr. of 1955 edition.]

[With Morris Swadesh.] *Nootka Texts: Tales and ethnological narratives.* With grammatical notes and lexical materials. Ibid., 334 pp. [Repr. of 1939 vol.]

A linguagem: Introduçao ao estudo da fala. Traduçao e apendice de J[oaquim] Mattoso Câmara Jr. Sao Paulo: Editora Perspectiva. [New ed. of 1954 Brazilian Portuguese transl. of *Language.*]

1983

Gengo - Bunka - Personality: Sapir Gengo Bunka Ronshu [Language, culture and personality: Selected writings of Edward Sapir in language and cul-ture]. Transl. and ed. by Mikio Hirabayashi. Tokyo: Hokuseido Shoten, [iv], 352 pp. [Japanese transl. of altogether 14 papers from *Selected Writings*; see T. Hayashi's survey in *Historiographia Linguistica* 11:3,464-465 [1984] for details.]

1984

"Herder's 'Ursprung der Sprache'". *Historiographia Linguistica* 11:3.355-88. [Repr. of Sapir's 1905 M.A. thesis first published in 1907.]

Postscript:

In his letter of 4 August 1984, Mr Philip Sapir, commenting on the preceding addenda to Sapir's scientific bibliography, draws my attention to the existence of various excerpts from *Language* in recent textbooks. As well, he mentions a translation of the same book into Marathi, a copy of which has, however, not yet been seen, and also a translation into Esperanto (Helsinki and Stockholm, 1927) of Sapir's 1925 "Memorandum on the Problem of an International Auxiliary Language". All these and other items should, I feel, be included in a full bibliography of Edward Sapir, but need not appear in the present volume.   KK.

INDEX OF NAMES*

---

* References to individual contributions are given in italics; mentions in (foot)notes are simply marked by an 'n' added to the page,
  without the actual footnote number.

ADDENDA:

Burstynsky, E.: xxv
Grant, P. H.: 122
Lippmann, W.: 122

Chafe, W. L.: xxiv
Teeuwen, St. W. J.: 206
Thomas, E.: 203

Postscriptum:

For those not familiar with the story of Ishi (cf. the picture on page 120 above), the Southern Yana (Yahi) Indian, who was discovered on 29 August 1911 near Oroville, Butte County, California, and who turned out to be the last survivor of his tribe, Theodora Kroeber's moving account, *Ishi in Two Worlds: A biography of the last wild Indian in North America* (Berkeley & Los Angeles: Univ. of California Press, 1960; frequently reprinted), of some 260 pages and many pictures is highly recommended.

More recently, the essential material on Ishi (who died of tuberculosis in Berkeley on 25 March 1916) has been made available in a book by Robert F. Heizer, Director of the Archaeological Survey of the University of California, together with the late Theodora Kroeber (d.1979), under the title of *Ishi, the Last Yahi: A documental history* (Berkeley & Los Angeles: Univ. of California Press, 1979), viii, 242 pp.

Edward Sapir studied Ishi's language in summer 1915 in Berkeley, at the home of Thomas T. Waterman, where Ishi stayed for some time, Waterman having been the first anthropologist to gain Ishi's confidence. Sapir had already studied the language family on previous fieldwork in California, publishing a collection of Yana texts as early as 1910 (cf. the bibliography of Sapir's writings in this volume, p. 198). Following his work with Ishi, Sapir published several papers on Yana in 1917, 1918, 1922, 1923, and 1929; a *Yana Dictionary*, compiled together with Morris Swadesh, appeared in 1960 (cf. below, pp. 200, 202, 203, 206, and 214).

STUDIES IN THE HISTORY OF THE LANGUAGE SCIENCES (SiHoLS)
General Editor: E.F. Konrad Koerner.   ISSN 0304-0720
Vols. 1-36. (Series in progress; further volumes are in preparation; *standing orders are invited*).

The companion series to *Historiographia Linguistica, International Journal for the History of Linguistics,* (which is now in its 11th year of publication), established to meet the revival of interest in the field and to provide an organized reservoir of information concerning the heritage of linguistic ideas of more than two millennia.

The following titles have been published and will be published during 1984/85:

13. DRAKE, Glendon F.: *The Role of Prescriptivism in American Linguistics 1820-1970.* Amsterdam, 1977. Hfl. 52,--/$ 21.00

14. SIGERUS DE CORTRACO: *Summa modorum significandi; Sophismata.* New edition, on the basis of G. Wallerand's *editio prima,* with additions, critical notes, an index of terms, and an introd. by Jan Pinborg. Amsterdam, 1977.
Hfl. 58,--/$ 23.00

15. PSEUDO-ALBERTUS MAGNUS: *Quaestiones Alberti de Modis significandi.* A critical edition, translation and commentary of the British Museum Inc. C.21.C.52 and the Cambridge Inc.5.J.3.7, by L.G. Kelly. Amsterdam, 1977.
Hfl. 82,--/$ 33.00

16. PANCONCELLI-CALZIA, Giulio (1878-1966): *Geschichtszahlen der Phonetik* (1941), together with *Quellenatlas der Phonetik* (1940). New ed., with an introd. article and a bio-bibliographical account of Panconcelli-Calzia by Jens-Peter Köster. Amsterdam, 1984. n.y.p. ca. Hfl. 90,--/$ 36.00

17. SALMON, Vivian: *The Study of Language in 17th-Century England.* Amsterdam, 1979. Hfl. 82,--/$ 33.00

18. HAYASHI, Tetsuro: *The Theory of English Lexicography 1530-1791.* Amsterdam, 1978. Hfl. 58,--/$ 23.00

19. KOERNER, E.F. Konrad: *Toward a Historiography of Linguistics. Selected Essays.* Foreword by R.H. Robins. Amsterdam, 1978. Hfl. 70,--/$ 28.00

20. KOERNER, E.F. Konrad (ed.): *PROGRESS IN LINGUISTIC HISTORIOGRA-PHY: Papers from the International Conference on the History of the Language Sciences, Ottawa, 28-31 August 1978.* Amsterdam, 1980. Hfl. 110,--/$ 44.00

21. DAVIS, Boyd H. & Raymond K. O'CAIN (eds.): *FIRST PERSON SINGULAR. Papers from the Conference on an Oral Archive for the History of American Linguistics. (Charlotte, N.C., 9-10 March 1979).* Amsterdam, 1980. Hfl. 82,--/$ 33.00

22. McDERMOTT, A. Charlene Senape: *Godfrey of Fontaine's Abridgement of Boethius the Dane's MODI SIGNIFICANDI SIVE QUAESTIONES SUPER PRISCIANUM MAIOREM.* A text edition with English transl. and introd. Amsterdam, 1980.
Hfl. 82,--/$ 33.00

23. APOLLONIUS DYSCOLUS: *The Syntax of Apollonius Dyscolus.* Translated, and with commentary by Fred W. Householder. Amsterdam, 1981.
Hfl. 82,--/$ 33.00

24. CARTER, M.. (ed.): *ARAB LINGUISTICS, an introductory classical text with translation and notes.* Amsterdam, 1981. Hfl. 126,--/$ 50.00

25. HYMES, Dell H.: *Essays in the History of Linguistic Anthropology.* Amsterdam, 1983. Hfl. 110,--/$ 44.00

26. KOERNER, Konrad, Hans-J. NIEDEREHE & R.H. ROBINS (eds.): *STUDIES IN MEDIEVAL LINGUISTIC THOUGHT,* dedicated to Geoffrey L. Bursill-Hall on the occassion of his 60th birthday on 15 May 1980. Amsterdam, 1980.
Hfl. 110,--/$ 44.00

27. BREVA-CLARAMONTE, Manuel: *Santius' Theory of Language: A contribution to the history of Renaissance linguistics.* Amsterdam, 1983. Hfl. 90,--/$ 36.00

28. VERSTEEGH, Cornelis H.M., Konrad KOERNER & Hans-J. NIEDEREHE (eds.): *THE HISTORY OF LINGUISTICS IN THE NEAR EAST*. Amsterdam, 1983.　　　　　　　　　　　　　　　　　　　Hfl.　100,--/$　40.00

29. ARENS, Hans: *Aristotle's Theory of Language and its Tradition*. Amsterdam, 1984.　　　　　　　　　　　　　　　　　　　Hfl.　150,--/$　60.00

30. GORDON, W. Terrence: *A History of Semantics*. Amsterdam, 1982.　　　　　　　　　　　　　　　　　　　Hfl.　82,--/$　33.00

31. CHRISTY, Craig: *Uniformitarianism in Linguistics*. Amsterdam, 1983.　　　　　　　　　　　　　　　　　　　Hfl.　50,--/$　20.00

32. MANCHESTER, M.L.: *The Philosophical Foundations of Humboldt's Linguistic Doctrines*. Amsterdam, 1985. n.y.p.　　　　　ca. Hfl.　77,--/$　31.00

33. RAMAT, Paolo, Hans-Josef NIEDEREHE & E.F. Konrad KOERNER (eds.): *STUDIES IN THE HISTORY OF LINGUISTICS IN ITALY*. Amsterdam, 1985.　　　　　　　　　　　　　　　　　ca. Hfl.　113,--/$　45.00

34. QUILIS, Antonio & Hans J. NIEDEREHE (eds.): *THE HISTORY OF LINGUISTICS IN SPAIN*. Amsterdam, 1985. n.y.p.　　　ca. Hfl.　113,--/$　45.00

35. SALMON, Vivian (ed.): *A READER ON THE LANGUAGE OF SHAKESPEARE*. Amsterdam, 1985. n.y.p. Bound.　　　　　　Hfl.　85,--/$　34.00

36. KOERNER, Konrad (ed): *EDWARD SAPIR: APPRAISALS OF HIS LIFE AND WORK*. Amsterdam, 1984.　　　　Hardbd.　Hfl.　75,--/$　30.00
　　　　　　　　　　　　　　　　　Paperbd.　Hfl.　45,--/$　18.00